/10 ang

G000057103

Paths are Made by Walking

– JENNIFER & IAN HARTLEY –

A small part of our lives you may find interesting!!

With love from,

Jennifer & Ian
X

An environmentally friendly book printed and bound in England by
www.printondemand-worldwide.com

Mixed Sources
Product group from well-managed
forests, and other controlled sources
www.fsc.org Cert no. TT-COC-002641
© 1996 Forest Stewardship Council
FSC

PEFC
PEFC/16-33-415

PEFC Certified
This product is
from sustainably
managed forests
and controlled
sources
www.pefc.org

This book is made entirely of chain-of-custody materials

www.fast-print.net/store.php

Paths are Made by Walking
Copyright © Jennifer & Ian Hartley 2013

A catalogue record for this book is available from the British Library

ISBN 978-178035-552-8

First published 2013 by
FASTPRINT PUBLISHING
Peterborough, England.

This book was written between 1986 and '87 and is a full account of our witness outside the proposed cruise missile base at Molesworth in Cambridgeshire.

We dedicate it to our children Debbie, Tom, Antony and Ollie and to all our grandchildren. We continue to pray for a nuclear-free world for future generations.

There is no way to peace, peace is the way.

We wish to thank the following people:

Ruth Rendell for the support and advice she gave us when writing this book and our families for their understanding. All the friends we met in the Peace Movement for their support. And all the people we had conversations with whose views differed from our own; we thank them for listening. We remember Caroline Taylor with love, she was our inspiration.

★★★

Chapter One
They Came In Darkness

We sat in silence, holding hands. It was very dark. We had parked the car broadside across the road and now we waited. There was no sound. I looked at Ian and he smiled and squeezed my hand. Our breath was steaming up the windows. I remember noticing a full moon earlier, but now it seemed very black. I could hardly see the fields that lay in front of us. The night was mild for the time of year; the snow had turned to slush.

We had driven into Cockbrook Lane. Half way down, where it narrowed, Ian had swung the car round, blocking the road. It couldn't be long now. I turned and looked out of the window and could just make out the headlights slowly coming towards us. The lights stretched back as far as I could see. The old Mini had done well. Now it stood, creaking every so often as the engine cooled.

"What do you think they will do to us?" I asked Ian.

"Goodness knows. Don't think about it," he replied.

"I wonder what's happened to Tim; I thought he'd be here by now."

Ian didn't answer.

"Do you think the message will have got round to the others by now?"

"I don't know. Lock your door!"

The first vehicle drew near. The headlights glared at us, and the jeep or truck (or was it a lorry?) ground to a halt. Doors slammed and raised, angry voices filled the night air. Men surrounded the car, one trying to open my door.

"They've locked themselves in," he called out.

We gripped each other's hand tighter.

"Right, let's get this shifted out of the way," someone else said.

We felt the car being lifted bodily into the air. It was dropped with a bump on to the verge at the side of the road. The men returned to their vehicles. We felt dazed. It was not enough; we had only stopped them for about three minutes. We could hear the engines revving up again as the convoy started to move off past us down the road.

Ian eased the handbrake off and the car rolled back into the path of the lorries.

"Please be careful, this is really dangerous," I said.

We both felt the tremendous sense of urgency, we simply had to stop what was about to happen. The lorries pulled round us and on down the road to the entrance of the base. We felt strong; our apprehension had turned to determined anger.

I wound down the car window and called out to the soldiers, crammed in the back of the canvas-topped trucks.

"Please think what you are doing, we don't need any more nuclear weapons."

My words were met with laughs and jeers.

"Think about all the people starving in the world, the money spent here could feed them all."

The soldiers responded by shouting out words of abuse. I watched as one man raised two fingers at us in defiance.

"It's not too late, turn back! We must all take responsibility for the world we live in."

My voice was lost, drowned by the roar of engines.

The last vehicle droned past. We had done what we could. Molesworth, the small village nestling in the heart of the Cambridgeshire countryside was to become the home of the second cruise missile base in Great Britain. It was the night of February 5th,

1985 and what we had feared had happened. They had come in the darkness to fence in the fields. The dream had become a nightmare.

Chapter Two
Why Us?

I can remember vividly the moment when I knew that everything had to change. Ian and I were lying in bed in the old Cistercian Abbey, home of the Community of the Arch, in France. We were attending the triennial conference of the International Fellowship of Reconciliation. IFOR is a global, multi-faith organisation, dedicated to world peace through non-violence. We are both members of the Religious Society of Friends (Quakers) and also members of the Church of England. Meeting with people from 23 countries had made quite an impact on us. Listening each day to the concerns and problems affecting people from different parts of the world had left us feeling that our own lives should have more purpose. So, here we were lying awake in the early hours of the morning, talking and going over and over our worries and fears for the future. What could we do to try to make the world a better place? We knew it would mean our lives being turned upside down, but how this would happen was not clear. All we knew was that the seed had been sown and there was no going back.

When we returned home we decided to 'be still and wait'. We felt sure in our hearts that if we were to change the whole pattern of our lives we would know when the time was right. In the August of 1984 we went with Ian's sons, Tom and Ollie, to Molesworth to spend the day at the Green Gathering. Our friend, Caroline Taylor, was one of the organisers. Caroline, who came from Ipswich, had been among the first group of women to walk to Greenham Common to protest against the deployment of cruise missiles. She had spent most of her adult life working for peace and justice and had made a big impression on us. She had those rare qualities of both total dedication and a warm and loving personality. She had recently become a mother and I can picture her at Molesworth, with her baby Lucy strapped to her chest in a papoose. Her walk reminded me of an African woman carrying a water container on her head. She moved slowly and gracefully, across the uneven fields to her tent, her hips swaying from side to side. When the Green Gathering ended Caroline had planned to go and live with a friend in Wales. On the way there she was killed in a road accident.

Not long after this, I switched on the television to watch the lunchtime news. I heard the announcer say that surveyors had been measuring the land at Molesworth in preparation for the construction of the perimeter fence. A feeling of utter disbelief ran through me, which gradually turned to anger. How dare they! This was East Anglia, our own region. We already had more bases than anywhere else in the country. At the same time, day after day, news bulletins were full of pictures showing thousands of starving children, women and men in Ethiopia. How could we contemplate spending billions of pounds creating yet another nuclear missile base?

I turned off the television. I was on my own. I knew that we had to go and live at Molesworth. I had no doubts. I wanted to put myself in the place where a great wrong was about to be perpetrated. I looked around the room, so secure and cosy. The red-brick fireplace where, in the winter, we had huge log fires; the pine ceiling that we struggled to put up one hot summer weekend. I walked over to the window and stared out at the trees. Could I really give all this up?

My thoughts were broken by a loud mewing sound at my feet. Lucky was demanding her tea. "It's far too early," I said.

How could I go away and leave her? We had bought her as a kitten from the animal welfare centre when the children were small. The children! What on earth would they say? Although they were living away from home, how would they react? I needed to speak to Ian but he was at work. I thought about phoning him, but how could I explain my idea over the telephone? Would he want to give up his job? If he did, how would we manage financially? It was all beginning to get too complicated, yet still I felt quite sure that this was what we had to do.

I don't know why I took the Bible down from the shelf. I seldom read it. I opened it at random at *Matthew, Chapter six*. It was the passage telling us that we cannot serve two masters, God and money. It seemed quite relevant. It went on to say that we do not have to worry about our

7

own security; if we are doing God's Will, He will provide for us. This was what I needed to read. I felt reassured. I watched the clock hoping that Ian wouldn't be late home. I felt excited and apprehensive, wondering what his reaction would be. I can remember thinking to myself, 'I must be calm and tell him slowly and quietly, so that he can take in what I am saying'. I heard the latch of the back gate open and listened while Ian parked his bike. He came in the back door.

Before he had time to take his coat off I found myself saying, "Ian I think I know what we should do, we have to buy a caravan, let the house and go to live at Molesworth!"

"Hang on," he said. "What about my job?"

Later, when he had got his breath back, we sat down and quietly considered all we would need to do to put our plan into action. Before we could go any further, Ian would have to speak to his employers and after that we would take things a step at a time. If we met with obstacles we would have to think again. Very slowly, things started to fall into place, though at this stage we kept our idea to ourselves. We were a couple of middle-class, fairly conventional people, and we had never really done anything vaguely adventurous in our lives.

I was 33 when I met Ian. It was like starting another life. I had been married when I was nineteen and had both my children by the time I was 23. I was glad to leave home and become independent. I think I have always been a bit of a rebel by nature and I often felt an odd one out at home. I was born in Slough during the war. My family had left their home in Leigh-on-Sea when my father's job had moved from the City to near Slough. It was thought to be too dangerous for my mother, brother and sister to stay in Leigh because of the threat of invasion and so they moved to Buckinghamshire. Meanwhile, our house in Leigh was requisitioned by the army, and we learnt afterwards that 22 soldiers were stationed there. They dug a trench in the top lawn and many years later you could still see the slight dent in the grass where it had been.

I was a bit of a surprise to my parents. They had not intended to have any more children, and my arrival was not altogether convenient with a war raging. I am told that my brother Tony and sister Angela, both several years older, thoroughly spoilt me, putting away my toys and giving me lots of attention. My father worked in a bank. He was a little man, only five feet tall. When he was young he used to do comedy turns and my mother said he was a riot, but I seldom saw him in this role. He believed in discipline and was rather Victorian in his attitudes. By the time I was born he was beginning to experience a great deal of pain in his legs, because of a muscular disease. This made him very short tempered at times. He was not a man to show emotion and it was only towards the end of his life that he seemed to soften; sometimes tears would come into his eyes when watching an old film, but one was not supposed to notice. My father, who we all called Daddy, had served in the First World War and fought at the Battle of the Somme. He celebrated his 21st birthday on the front line where he saw his best friend shot to pieces beside him. His regiment was the Lancashire Fusiliers, popularly known as the 'Bantams' as all the men were short. I never heard him speak about his experiences and the only occasion I tried to ask him about it, his voice began to quaver, and we knew we should change the subject.

My school reports always said, *'Jennifer tries hard and is conscientious. Could do better with a little more effort'*. I liked religious education, domestic science and music. I was in the school choir and went on to be in the church choir too. Looking back now, my early years were very easy. I belonged to a family who loved and cared for me and I seldom lacked for anything. We were certainly not 'well to do', but my father was a thrifty man. He spent his money carefully and used to tell me to "look after the pennies and the pounds will look after themselves". I was taught to 'never lend or borrow' and never to have conversations about politics, religion or sex! I can remember one lunchtime when I asked my father why it was that some people had so much whilst others had nothing.

"Why can't everything be shared out equally?" I queried.

I was bewildered by the response. "That's being a communist," he said in no uncertain terms.

I realised that I must have said something terribly wrong. I had no idea what a communist was, but it was clearly not very nice! The conversation went no further.

Although politics was not a subject for discussion, it played a big part in the life of our family. We were staunch Conservatives. In 1908 my grandfather had stood as a candidate for the local council elections and I am told he hired a coal cart and decorated it with flowers, ribbons and banners saying 'Vote for Medhurst'. He won and was made chairman of the Highways Committee of Malden Coombe Urban

District Council. My father always helped at the elections, leafleting and acting as a teller outside the polling stations. I do not recall ever knowing the policies of another political party and was brought up to believe that those voting Labour were 'not quite our class'. I accepted what I was told without question and when I first married I was on the committee of our local Conservative branch.

It was after I met Ian that I began to see things from a different angle. I have always had a social conscience and my views did not always tie up with my Conservative upbringing. It was a gradual change. I started to find out things for myself, by reading different newspapers. At home we had *The Daily Telegraph*, not that I was often allowed to read it. There might have been articles of an unsavoury nature in it, not suitable for children's eyes, but the main reason was that I never put the pages back tidily and this used to irritate my father intensely!

All this was in marked contrast to Ian's upbringing. My introduction to his parents stays in my mind. It was lunchtime on a Saturday. His mother greeted me at the door in her apron and I followed her into the kitchen. She was preparing a roast lunch.

"Oh, I am sorry, we've come at the wrong time," I said, being very polite.

"Well, aren't you going to stay and have some dinner with us dear?" she replied, as though she had known me for ages.

Ian just smiled, he knew his parents. It did not matter at what time anyone called they would always be made welcome, and if it was at meal times an invitation to stay would always be made. I felt completely at home. His father poured us a drink and we sat down and got to know each other. I soon discovered, to my horror, that they were socialists. How could they be? They were so nice. They were also active, long-standing members of the Methodist Church.

Ian was born in the August of 1946, almost a year to the day after the dropping of the atomic bomb on Hiroshima. He had no memory of the war and belonged to a new and different generation. The dropping of that bomb marked a watershed, afterwards the world would never be the same again.

Ian's parents, Cathy and John, were married in 1945 soon after John's demob' from the army. He had served as a sergeant in the Royal

Army Medical Corps until his unit surrendered to the Germans on the Greek island of Cos. John had then experienced a hellish journey by cattle truck through occupied Europe ending in a prisoner-of-war camp in Munich. As a child, Ian's romantic ideas of escaping POWs were shattered by his father's recollections. In some ways, John had enjoyed himself, acting and producing plays, but Cathy says that he came home emaciated. He had been infected with lice and the Germans had shaved all his hair off.

Cathy had a very different war, on Tyneside, as a nursing sister in Newcastle General Hospital. It was there that she and John met in 1940. John was stationed nearby and had contracted glandular fever. They both enjoy telling how they discovered a shared love of Gilbert and Sullivan. It was Cathy singing '*Good Morrow, Good Mother*' that alerted John's attention. They were separated by an overseas posting and only saw each other again when the war was over. All that time, their only contact was by letter. I have seen some of those carefully preserved letters from Stalag 7B written in pencil, covering every inch of space.

When they got married, they bought a house in Ipswich, where Ian was brought up and where his grandfather also lived. Willie Johnson came from the Shetlands. He was a shipwright. Ian was kept entertained for hours as a child, hearing about his exploits, he was a great story teller. While working in the shipyard on Tyneside in the First World War, he talked about being given a white feather because he didn't wear uniform. He lived through the Depression in the North East and the Jarrow March, selling off his furniture to buy food for his wife and four daughters.

After he left school, Ian went to Goldsmiths' College to study drama and it was there that he met his first wife. Through Diana, Ian joined the Religious Society of Friends and became a Quaker. They were married at the old Quaker Meeting House at Jordans in Buckinghamshire. After their two sons were born, Ian went back to college on a Teacher Education course at a college in Norwich. This time he specialised in religious studies. His involvement with the Quakers had rekindled his deep interest in Christianity and he enjoyed studying theology, but he found himself unable to complete the course. It was not long after this that his marriage failed and he had a nervous breakdown.

One good thing happened to Ian when he left college. He had agreed to do some research on apartheid for a friend, a clergyman who lived in London. Ian asked Lydia Vulliamy and Eric Walker, a couple who were members of the Quaker Meeting in Ipswich, whether their film library had any documentaries on South Africa. They said they had and he arranged to go to see them. This was Ian's introduction to the Concord Films Council. Eric and Lydia talked to Ian after he had finished viewing, asking him what he was doing and what his plans were. He was surprised and pleased when they asked him if he was interested in a part-time job. He accepted and before long was involved in the film library at Nacton near Ipswich helping to choose films, writing descriptions and producing leaflets. Concord distributes television plays like *Cathy Come Home* and the powerful dramatisation of a nuclear attack called *The War Game*. There were also classic documentaries such as *Gale is Dead*, the story of a drug addict. Ian liked talking to the hundreds of people who phoned to book the films. Gradually, he was able to advise them on the choice of suitable material for their particular needs. Eventually, he was asked to share management of the company and he was made Assistant Secretary.

In the autumn of 1974 we were to meet for the first time. I had separated from my husband and was living in Ipswich with my two children. For the first time in my life I had to stand on my own feet, although my husband continued to support us financially. As Deborah and Antony were both at school, I looked for a part-time job, which allowed me to be home by the time they arrived back from school and during the school holidays. I became a school dinner lady. This was a really hard slog; one week I washed plates, knives and forks, and the other I cleaned saucepans and baking tins. The best part about the job was that our midday lunch was provided. I then decided to try to be a nursing auxiliary two nights a week. I chose a Friday and Saturday night as the children stayed with their father over the weekend. I only stuck it for a few weeks, because I found sleeping in the daytime almost impossible, and I just wasn't cut out to be a nurse, although I really loved communicating with the patients. I then became a home help. It was another boring, tiring job with no mental stimulation but I carried on for many months. I always looked in the local paper for part-time vacancies and was interested when I read one asking for a part-time clerk at an educational film library.

I applied for the job and was asked to go for an interview. I had always been told that one should look smart for an interview, so I put on a navy and white striped dress, high-heeled shoes with a matching handbag and set off in the car for Nacton. The directions had seemed a bit odd, but I followed them until I came to the top of a muddy lane by a huge oak tree. I parked the car and set off on foot. The track plunged steeply downhill and the surface was very uneven with deep ruts. I have never been much good at walking in high-heeled shoes as I have weak ankles, so I wobbled a bit. As I walked on and on, I began to wonder where on earth I would end up. A film library? What sort of films were they and why was the office in such a remote place? I finally turned a corner and saw ahead of me a small cottage. A group of chickens rushed to meet me and a dog started to bark. Surely this couldn't be the place I was looking for. I tentatively knocked on the door. Nothing happened. I knocked again. A man with a beard, long hair and glasses opened the door.

He introduced himself with, "I'm Ian, come in."

He began to ask me questions and take down details. It was all very informal and nothing like any other interview I had been to before. He seemed quite satisfied with me, and said he would show me around the general office and explain what the job would entail. I was taken into a room with a low, beamed roof and an open fireplace. There was a large round table in the middle of the room and various other tables, desks and chairs. It all looked rather cluttered and not at all like an office. Several people were working and one of the women introduced herself to me.

This was Lydia Vulliamy who, with her husband Eric, had started the film library when they lived in London. They then moved down to live in the cottage in Suffolk and set up the library there. They hired out 16mm films to schools, colleges, hospitals and other institutions. The films were all social documentaries on a range of themes. Talking to Lydia I felt dreadfully out of place. She was dressed very casually in faded blue denim jeans with the legs rolled up and a baggy sweater. She had bare feet. There could scarcely have been a greater contrast between two women. She began to tell me what I would be required to do if I decided to take the job. It would involve answering the telephone and booking films. I would also have to do some filing and accounts work. It didn't seem too difficult, and it was certainly different and more interesting than anything I had previously done. I asked how soon they would want me to start. They said as soon as possible, so we arranged a date. I looked up and glanced out of the window and I was surprised to see the river Orwell. Large ships passed to and fro from Ipswich Dock, further up the river. The cottage was surrounded by woods and it was a beautiful, if unusual, setting in which to work.

I loved working for Concord Films. In the springtime the woods would be a mass of wild daffodils and we would stop work to pick a bunch to take home with us. Later, bluebells would cover ground like a thick blue carpet. From time to time work would come to a halt when someone noticed a deer standing, motionless, under the trees outside the window. We would all down pens and look, hardly daring to breathe, lest we should frighten the animal away. The chickens were very friendly. One of them, called Henrietta, took a liking to the filing basket and would hop in, wriggle around, and when she was comfortable, lay an egg there.

Ian and I had become close friends. We had something in common as his first marriage had recently broken up. We were glad of each other's company, though any thoughts of re-marriage could not have been further from my mind. He often came for a meal and we spent the evening talking and listening to records. He was easy to get on with and it felt very effortless. The children liked him. I introduced him to some of my family at Easter 1975. In the summer of the same year he moved in with us. I was terrified of making another commitment, as I was unsure I could live with anyone again. We were both working for Concord and things just drifted along.

One day, quite out of the blue, Ian said to me, "Well, when are we going to get married then?"

"Married!" I nearly had a fit. The last thing I wanted to do was to get married again.

"But what's the difference, you love me and we are living together, so why not?" he responded.

I couldn't think of a good answer. I had been worried for some time about what effect our living together might be having on the children. I did not like the thought of them having to refer to Ian as 'the man who lives with Mummy', when friends at school asked who he was. We were married on May 29th, 1976.

Chapter Three

That Rainbow Hat Again

Being with Ian helped to change some of my views. He brought out in me beliefs I had perhaps always secretly held. We talked endlessly about the state of the world and what man was doing to the environment, and we were becoming increasingly concerned about nuclear weapons. Living in East Anglia, we were aware of the many American bases all around us. When we heard the decision to deploy new, ground-launched cruise missiles, not only at Greenham Common, but also at an East Anglian base, we felt it was time to put our energies into trying to resist this. We attended meetings, stood in the street with petitions and went on marches. We wrote letters to newspapers and prominent people. I have been writing regularly to the Queen. I don't quite know why, except that I feel she is a mother and grandmother and must have the same fears that I have. I always get a reply from an equerry, not from the Queen, but they usually say that she sees my letters. I find it hard to believe.

I was now working for the Methodist Home for the Aged near Christchurch Park in Ipswich. This was once the home of the Bishop of Ipswich and St. Edmundsbury. Sitting in the staffroom one morning having my coffee break, I was listening to a conversation that turned to the subject of an article in the paper about Greenham Common. My workmates were unable to understand the motives of the women who had gone to live there. I had been thinking for some time of visiting Greenham and I found myself impulsively saying, "I am planning to go and stay there for a week to see what's going on."

"Are you really?" one of my friends said. "When are you going?"

I had absolutely no idea and had not even made up my mind until that moment but I said, "I thought I'd go at Easter."

"Well, I certainly wouldn't fancy it!" someone else remarked.

"Why not, I think that the idea of women leaving their homes for peace, instead of men leaving home to fight in wars, is really intriguing."

I decided that if I was to take a more active role in the Peace Movement I would have to give up my job. I realised that if I took part in actions I would run the risk of being arrested. I would be irresponsible to ask my employers for time off for court appearances. I was sorry to leave, but was sure I was doing the right thing. On February 25th, 1983 I left work. One month later I was at Greenham. Green was certainly how you could describe me! It was a cold March day. I was full of enthusiasm and wanted to show my solidarity to the women living there. I had no idea what to expect.

I put up my tent near the Main Gate where huge lorries were thundering in and out non-stop. Ian and Robbie, our Sheltie dog, got into the car to return home and I waved to them until the car disappeared. Over by the campfire women were brewing up tea. I walked over and introduced myself. The women had been living at Greenham for a long time. I felt out of place and very 'new'. I had not been sure about the set-up regarding food and had not brought any with me. I was relieved when two women visitors offered to drive me to Newbury to buy some. The day seemed to pass terribly slowly, and I spent it getting used to the surroundings and trying to make conversation. I was glad when it was time to climb into my sleeping bag.

"Why," I asked myself, "do I do these stupid things?"

I hated it and wanted to go home. Lying awake inside my tent I felt lonely and miserable.

Someone called out, "Goodnight Jennifer, hope you sleep okay." It was one of the women I'd met on my arrival.

Those few words made all the difference; I no longer felt alone. I couldn't sleep as it was freezing cold. At regular intervals during the night I rummaged around in my rucksack to find something else to put on. I ended up wearing all my clothes, including my hat and gloves. I put the torch on and looked at my watch every few minutes, wrote notes in my diary and nibbled biscuits to pass the time.

At last the sky started to get light and I heard signs of life outside the tent. Having got through my first night I felt better and began to relax. I made friends with a woman from Derby called Lesley and she suggested I move my tent nearer hers.

During the following few days leading up to Easter, groups of women arrived and tents were springing up all over the common. On Good Friday there would be thousands of women coming to encircle the base. Lesley and I found plenty to do. We helped distribute litter bags to each of the gates and attended a meeting at the Friends Meeting House in Newbury, to discuss preparations for the following days.

By Friday I felt as though I had been at Greenham for weeks. I was longing for a bath and a private loo. Squatting in the woods wondering who might be watching was something I didn't find very easy. On Friday coaches full of women from all over the country arrived every few minutes. Lesley and I had been asked if we would act as a decoy for a group who were going to try and get inside the base. In the early afternoon we set off to walk around the fence. It soon became apparent that many women were already on the base as we could see a lot of activity inside. Vans and police vehicles were dashing up and down the runways. I had no intention whatsoever of going inside. This was all a new experience but I found myself getting excited about what was happening. When we came to a huge hole in the fence Lesley said, "Come on let's go in." I did not hesitate and with several other women who had joined us, we stepped through the fence and ran up a steep bank on to a runway. I did not stop to think what I was doing.

Before long, soldiers rounded us up and we were put on to a coach. We were driven over to some buildings where several other coach loads of women were parked and were told that, provided we made no attempt to get back on to the base, we would be driven to a gate and let out with no charges. On the point of agreeing, we heard shouting from the building and realised that women had been taken inside. Everyone felt that we should stand together as we had all done the same thing. In the end we were taken into the building that was like a huge gymnasium. We sat on the floor. There must have been well over a hundred women, of all ages and from all walks of life. We were cautioned, not charged, and finally dragged out to the waiting coaches. I was quite worried, as I knew I had acted on impulse.

We were let out at a gate at the opposite side to where we were camping. We hitched a lift from a passing supporter, who drove us most of the way back. In the meantime Ian had arrived with his sons, Tom and Ollie and my daughter Debbie, to take me home. He walked over to where he had seen me pitch my tent and, of course, it was not there. He then walked around looking for me and came across my tent in its new place. Some of the Derby women were sitting around a campfire and he asked them if they knew where I was.

"Oh, I think she's been arrested," one said casually.

"ARRESTED." Ian was dumbfounded. "Oh, no, she wouldn't have been arrested." At that point I arrived, hot and bothered, and breathlessly explained what had been happening. Ian said, "Have you seen yourself? You look like a lobster!"

"I'm not surprised; do you know what I've got on? Under my waterproofs I've got two thick jumpers, thermal tights, jeans and thick socks. It's been really freezing all the time I've been here." I was wearing a rainbow-striped woolly hat, which I'd bought from Fruits of the Earth in Ipswich.

The next action I took part in was in June, when eleven of our local CND group, including Ian, went to Upper Heyford in Oxfordshire. We joined in a week-long blockade. It was a protest about the building of new runways designed for the F1-11 nuclear bombers. These were the ones that in 1986 were to be used in the Libyan bombing. Groups from different regions all over Britain undertook to blockade for a day. Our group arrived at eleven at night and stayed until the afternoon of the following day. Ian and I had discussed the possibility of arrest and agreed that he would act as an observer. Nine of our group were arrested on that action. I was the first. We all sat down in front of the gate to prevent a contractor's van getting in. The police removed us all, warning us that if we obstructed the road again we would be arrested. As I sat down for the second time, the policeman who had removed me recognised me. It was that rainbow hat again! I was detained for eight hours, and gradually, one by one, my friends joined me. About seven hundred people were arrested during the week-long action.

In July I went to Greenham again with Joy, a friend from Ipswich, to join in a blockade. I had recently come out of hospital after having a minor operation, which had required a couple of stitches. In view of this, I decided this time I would not risk sitting in the road and being dragged off, but I would act as an observer. It was high summer and very hot. All the gates at Greenham had been named after colours. We camped at Green Gate. This gate is at the end of a long and winding lane, with woods on either side. The action itself was very frightening, and I watched in disbelief as hundreds of policemen charged at the mass of women sitting, singing and smiling in front of the gates. After the road was cleared, women stood about in small huddles, many weeping tears of frustration and despair. Within an hour or two they were back again, strong and determined as ever, ready for the next onslaught. It was difficult to keep a grip on one's emotions. Back at the camp, Joy and I would sit with our friends Lesley and Barbara from Derby and talk about what had taken place. Lying on the ground, gazing up at the tall silver birch trees gently swaying in the warm breeze, helped to release some of the tension inside us. It seemed a long week.

At the beginning of August I joined in the Star March from East Anglia to Greenham, arriving there on 'Hiroshima Day'. Then in October, Joy and I went again to Greenham for a big action. The idea was to try and take down the whole of the perimeter fence and reclaim the common. We had both had doubts about this action. I had already decided that I must not get arrested as I still had the Upper Heyford case outstanding. We met up with our Derby friends and walked around the fence through the woods, to Orange Gate. There we sat down among the trees and each of us tried to decide what we felt able to do. There was a great air of uncertainty about the action and everyone was edgy and nervous. At the appointed hour, four o'clock, we went up to the fence and some of the women began cutting. Soon it was clear that fencing all around the base was coming down. Suddenly it felt right. There were no barriers between us and the soldiers. We spoke to them in a warm and friendly way but they did not respond, they had been given no orders to deal with a situation like this. Policeman soon arrived from all directions and the bolt-cutters were taken away.

Our little group decided to walk back to Green Gate, where we had left our car. Jonathan, a friend from Ipswich, had come with us to share the driving and he was waiting for us.

"We just want to see how much of the fence has been taken down around here and then we will go. We'll be about five minutes." Jonathan nodded and got back into the car.

We walked around, staring at the green mesh fence trailing on the ground. A woman asked Joy if she could borrow her bolt-cutters. She took them out of her bag and the woman went off to the fence. A few moments later she gave them back and we continued to walk on. Suddenly there was a shout: "Get those two!", and out of the darkness we saw two young policemen running towards us. One of the policemen cautioned Joy saying, "You are under arrest."

I said, "Why just her? I have been here all day for the same reason as everyone else, surely you will have to arrest me too."

So he did! We were frogmarched into the base, a policeman holding each arm. I called out to Lesley and Barbara who were still walking along, quite oblivious to what had happened.

"Where are you?" shouted Lesley.

"Inside! We've been arrested," I called back.

When she saw us, she looked amazed. It had all happened so quickly.

We were kept on the base for six hours where we were searched and 'processed'. All our possessions were put into a plastic bag. We were taken to a police station at Newbury Racecourse where we were finally charged at 3:48am. We were hungry, tired and cold. It was a freezing cold night. Someone gave us a lift back to the car and we found Jonathan curled up asleep on the back seat. We woke him up and tried to start the car. It wouldn't go. We had to push it to get it going. We got back home about nine in the morning.

Early in November a 24-hour peace camp was set up at all the 102 American bases in Great Britain. It was in support of the Greenham Women's action in the USA to take President Reagan to court over the proposal to deploy cruise missiles. Several of us went to Bentwaters and slept outside in sleeping bags inside big, orange plastic bags. The next morning more people arrived and by midday there was quite a crowd. We sent a telegram to President Reagan from Ipswich CND appealing to him and the American people not to deploy cruise. It ended with the words: 'We do not inherit the world from our ancestors we borrow it from our children. Give peace a chance.'

At the end of November Joy and I had to appear in court at Newbury. We defended ourselves. I was shocked to hear the two young policemen who had arrested us, say in their evidence that they had seen both of us cutting the fence. When it was my turn to question them, I said, "But surely you remember me saying to you, if you are going to arrest my friend, you will have to arrest me too?"

Later, when the stipendiary magistrate asked me if I wanted to ask the policemen any further questions, I looked at him and said, "As the evidence they have given so far is completely untrue, I see no point in asking any further questions."

He said, "Case dismissed. No case to answer."

I sat in court and listened as Joy asked her arresting officer if he had seen her cut the fence. He said he had not. Joy's case was dismissed, too, and we received expenses for getting to the court.

In December cruise missiles were deployed at Greenham Common.

★★★

I appeared at Ipswich Magistrates' Court for the non-payment of legal costs on February 6th, 1984. Steve, Richard and I had all refused to pay our costs arising from the action at Upper Heyford where we were charged with 'wilfully obstructing the free passage of a highway leading to Gate 8, USAF Upper Heyford'. We had waited many months to appear in court and I was glad when the day finally came. Over a hundred supporters were outside the court house when we arrived. I felt calm and composed. I had a bag with me containing a few essentials to take to prison. I was the first person to be called. I walked into court and up the steps into the box. I had taken a great deal of time to prepare my statement and was looking forward to reading it out aloud.

My daughter Debbie was sitting in the public gallery with Ian, surrounded by many friends. The magistrate read out the charge and asked if I had anything to say. I launched into my statement.

"I am refusing to pay these costs because whilst I committed an offence, I believe I was justified in doing so. I realise that I have broken the law of the land, but I believe that the law of God is more important. I am quite sure that it is wrong to have, or contemplate using, nuclear weapons, knowing the effect that they will have on thousands, perhaps millions of people who are supposed to be our 'enemies'.

"I believe that the ordinary people living in Russia feel just the same way as I do, and do not see me as an enemy any more than I see them as one.

"I have no choice other than to listen to my conscience as I know from past experience that if I do not, I will have no peace of mind. How can I ignore the fact that there are children dying every minute due to hunger and lack of medical care? Not to mention the very real hardship being experienced by people here in our own country, whilst our government continues to spend millions of pounds on weapons which all sane people believe could never be used and are therefore no deterrent.

"We do not own this world it is on loan to us for our lifetime. Nuclear weapons, if used, would destroy all that is precious to us; beautiful countryside, birds, insects, flowers, not to mention buildings that have stood for centuries, and last, but most important, children, women and men who want to live their lives in peace.

"The world now has thousands and thousands of nuclear warheads, many of them, a thousand times greater than the Hiroshima bomb, and sooner or later, without doubt, one or more are going to go off either by accident or design."

The clerk of the court interrupted and tried to stop me reading it.

I said, "I have waited a long time to say this, so I would like to continue please. It will only take a few moments."

I carried on in a louder voice as the clerk continued to try and intervene. He did not succeed.

"It is up to each and every person who truly treasures this earth to stand up and say to the governments of this world STOP, we have had enough. We want to try to live together in love and trust, trying, as the Quakers say, to find that of God in every man, or to see the good in everyone. I am sure if we really want peace and security enough, we can make it happen and if we do not act soon it will be too late.

"I feel that the words of E.F. Schumacher sum all this up: "We must do what we conceive to be the right thing and not bother our heads or trouble our souls with whether we are going to be successful. Because if we don't do the right thing we'll be doing the wrong thing, and we'll just be part of the disease and not a part of the cure.'

"I hope you, the magistrates here in Ipswich will be understanding and sympathetic to my friends and myself. Like thousands of others throughout the world who are working for peace, our beliefs are sincerely and honestly held.

"Thank you."

I finished my statement and received a round of applause from the gallery. The magistrate then said that he had no alternative other than to sentence me to seven days imprisonment. As I was being led out, Debbie leapt out of her seat and pressed a bunch of jonquils into my hands, giving me a big hug. She had hidden the flowers under her coat. Holding them high I swept out of court, smiling. Later, when I was below in the cell I heard that the magistrate had refused to allow Steve or Richard to make their statements. He said that I had spoken for us all. I was furious. I only speak for myself. I know how important it is for individuals to be able to give their own reasons for steps they have taken. It would have taken no more than five minutes.

I went through all the usual procedures, filling in forms and handing over all my possessions. I had to hand over my badges and my shoelaces. The first night I spent in a police cell in Ipswich Police Station. It was small and measured seven steps by eight. It had grey walls, covered with graffiti. There was a lavatory, open to view, and a hard wooden bench seat. Ian was allowed down to see me, but we had to talk through a glass partition. A woman gave me a cup of tea and asked, "Would you like something to read?"

"Yes, please, it will help to pass the time."

She brought me a book about people in an underground train when a nuclear accident occurred. I have often wondered if she chose it especially or whether it was a coincidence. Later the same afternoon, a policeman came to the cell and gave me some Kentucky Fried Chicken and chips. I felt it would not be right to say that I didn't eat meat, so I ate it. All through the evening, policemen would look through the small opening in the door to ask me if I was all right. I felt fine, completely relaxed and sure about what I was doing. Everyone was very kind to me. Ian came again quite late in the evening and brought my son Antony with him. I was taken out of the cell into an interview room and we sat and talked for ages. He told me about all the support the three of us were getting and described the report in the local paper. There was a woman on duty all night and about 10:30 she brought me some grey blankets and a mattress.

"You don't need to worry, dear," she said, "The blankets are always sent to the laundry, so they are quite clean."

I wasn't worried. I still had one stem of my flowers, the others I had given to Ian to take home. We still have one pressed in a book. The bright yellow flower became very important to me. Sitting in my drab surroundings, I found myself looking at it over and over again, breathing in its evocative scent. It was beginning to flag a bit so every so often I dunked it in the loo to try and revive it. I didn't want it to die. I lay down and tried to sleep, but it was quite impossible as the bright light stayed on all night in the cell. Just before eleven I had two visitors, friends from Ipswich. I went to the interview room again and no one seemed in a hurry to tell them to go. Eventually I was taken back to my cell by another woman, who had just come on duty for the night. She came and sat on my bench, leaving the door open and talked to me while we had a cup of coffee. Around midnight she asked me if I would like a shower. I was so surprised, but as I had no idea when I might get the chance again, I accepted the offer.

I slept fitfully all night, waking when I heard the sound of voices stopping near my door. Whoever they were they just looked at me and didn't come in. I pretended I was asleep. At seven in the morning the shift changed again and another woman came on duty. She introduced herself as Pat, and in the course of conversation said she used to work for a firm that delivered films to Concord Films.

When she realised who I was married to she exclaimed, "Oh, the one with the beard, I used to fancy him!"

'Great,' I thought, 'just what I want to know when I am locked up for seven days!'

Pat was a great character and chatted to me whenever she got the chance. She kept saying, "Why don't you ask if your husband can come in again to see you?"

I replied, "I didn't know I could."

"I'll see what I can do," Pat said.

Not long afterwards she unlocked the door and said, "Follow me." We walked along several passages and up some stairs into a room. Several policemen were in there. A policeman sitting at a desk asked me my home telephone number and dialled it. He passed me the receiver. Ian answered. It was about 8:30 in the morning.

"Hello, it's me," I said.

"Where are you?" came the bewildered reply.

"Where do you think I am? I'm at the police station," I said. I think perhaps Ian thought I had escaped, as he could not make out what was going on any more than I could.

"They say you can come and see me again, if you want to," I told him.

"Great, I'll be down as soon as I can," he said.

On the way back to my cell I was allowed to stop and wash my face and hands. I was given a cheese roll and a cup of coffee for breakfast. Ian arrived and we spoke through the glass partition again, before saying yet another goodbye. At 2:30, a policewoman looked in and said I would be leaving for Holloway in the next half hour.

Pat arrived and said, "Shall I ring your husband and see if he can come down?"

"No," I almost pleaded. I could not go through another goodbye session.

She did ring him, though, and came back to say, "Ian sends you his love and says he will be thinking of you." This was the only time I felt near to tears. I just wanted to get on with it. I drove to Holloway in a white police car, unmarked, with a plain-clothes policewoman and a uniformed driver. We talked about why I was going to prison and I showed her my statement. She thought it was good. I really liked the policewoman, she seemed concerned about me and how I would cope in Holloway. I have met her in Ipswich several times since and we always stop and have a chat.

We drove up to the large steel gates of Holloway and stopped. The driver spoke to the man on the gate, which opened to allow us through them. "This is it," I quietly said to myself. The policewoman handed over my possessions to the girl on the reception desk, and after wishing me good luck we said cheerio to each other. I was given a royal blue towelling dressing gown with no tie-up and told to go into a cubicle and put it on. It was 3:30 in the afternoon. I was shown into a room full of other women all wearing dressing gowns. I recognised two women I had seen at Greenham so went over to talk to them. We were brought some tea, flan, potato, bread and shortbread. I like my food and am not usually fussy, but this food was inedible. Every few minutes the door would open and a few names would be called. When my turn came, I was taken to see a doctor who asked me all sorts of questions. I was weighed and my height recorded. I told the doctor that I was on a low dose of blood pressure pills, which I had brought with me along with a letter from my own doctor. He said I could not have my own pills in Holloway, they would provide them. He gave me a brief examination and then I was shown back into the room.

I stayed in the crowded room until 12:30 at night. By then many of the women had found it difficult to cope. One woman screamed and threatened to throw a plastic cup of water over the warder when she came in. Another young woman, a drug addict, was in the lavatory vomiting and moaning. She needed an injection. Every time the warder came in the room someone would ask for help for her, but she was told she would have to wait her turn. I thought that many of the women should have been in a hospital, not a prison. Every hour about three women left the room. I was beginning to feel very tired and fed up. I had been in there for nine hours.

At last my turn came to leave. I was taken into a small room. There were three warders, one of whom sat at a desk. I was asked to take off the dressing gown and turn round slowly while one warder looked me up and down. It was a humiliating experience. Then they went through my bag of belongings making a list of all the contents. The warder called out each item, one at a time and someone else wrote it down. She made a great point of saying, "Six pairs of knickers, BLACK," giving me a disdainful look as she did so. I was allowed to keep my toothbrush, paperback books, a pen and a comb. I also kept my clothes and handkerchiefs. I asked if I could have the photos of Ian, Debbie and Antony but this was refused. I was given a flannel, towel, shampoo, soap, deodorant and another toothbrush and comb, and told to pick up a bed roll and a pillowcase. Clutching all my things under my arm I was taken along endless corridors to a dormitory. On the door it said: B3 Room 20. There were four double bunk beds inside and most of them had people asleep in them. I was so glad when a voice from over the other side of the room called out to me.

"Is it all right if I sleep here?" I asked, indicating the bottom bunk of the bed nearest to the door.

"Yes, that's okay but you will have to make it up. Did they give you some sheets?"

I threw the sheets and blankets on and climbed in. "Good night, thanks for your help," I whispered to the shadow in the bunk opposite. I already felt quite at home! I slept well.

When it was still dark I was vaguely aware of someone calling out names. I heard "Hartley" and replied with a sleepy, "Yes". Everyone else made some sort of comment when their name was called. I went back to sleep again. The next thing I heard was the clanking of keys and the door being unlocked. A voice shouted, "They're all in bed. Right, you lot you can stay there."

'Good,' I thought, 'suits me.'

A girl opposite me jumped out of her bunk and said in a Belfast accent, "We'd better get up, else we'll have no breakfast."

Apparently we were usually allowed up the corridor to fetch our food but because we were in disgrace, it was pushed through the hatch. Two slices of white sliced bread, a white bread roll, marge and jam, all very stodgy. And a cup of tea. The room was furnished with lockers, a table and chairs. It had a wash basin, and I noticed that my roommates washed out their pants and tights and hung them on the radiators rather than send them to the laundry. In one corner of the room there was a cubicle containing a lavatory. Inside there was a peephole to the corridor so that those on the outside could look in. Someone had stuck a piece of tape over the hole.

The room was warm and comfortable and I soon got to know the other women. They seemed to accept me and were interested to know why I was there. Everyone shared things with one another. One of the women received a food parcel. She immediately shared out the contents, biscuits, sweets and chocolate, equally. The chaplain came in and said that the Reverend Cliff Read, the Unitarian Minister from Ipswich and a member of the Christian CND group I belonged to, was coming to see me. I really enjoyed his visit. He brought me a prayer written by Dietrich Bonhoeffer while he was in prison. It felt as though I had been there ages when in fact it was only a couple of days. I tried to read but found it hard to concentrate. Someone gave me a piece of paper so I could keep some notes. I put it inside my shoe as I knew I was not supposed to keep a diary. One of the women gave me some toothpaste, as I had not been allowed to keep my own and had not been issued with any. My request for vegetarian food seemed to cause a problem and it was some time before it was put into effect. Even then it just seemed to be the same food as everyone else, but without the meat. I was asked if I took sugar and as I didn't I gave my teaspoonful away each meal time. It was always in great demand. The food was tasteless. We had no fresh fruit and the only vegetable was cabbage, which had been boiled for so long that it was no longer recognisable.

I was allowed to write one letter. The paper and stamp were provided. I could receive post and was quite unprepared for the amount that I got. The messages of love and support were overwhelming. I felt very embarrassed when the post came, though. I seemed to get dozens while the women I was with had none. But they were all so nice to me about it.

"How many have you got today, Jennifer?" Flo would ask.

Each day we had one half hour of exercise. We were taken into a yard, where we walked around and around in circles. Warders stood watching us. They searched us going out and coming in. It was lovely to be in the fresh air. The atmosphere inside was so stuffy and my mind was becoming fuddled. One night we stayed awake for hours while someone told jokes. They started off quite mildly, but later some of them became crude and racist.

Bev said, "I hope you're not offended, Jennifer, you'll have to put your fingers in your ears if you don't want to hear."

It did help to pass the time though and it was good to hear everyone laughing. We did crossword puzzles and would call across to one another the clues and answers. I took my turn in scrubbing the floor on my hands and knees, as we had an inspection of the room each day. Each evening we had a cup of tea and once a plate of golden-brown scones was handed in. They looked delicious. In fact they were so hard it was impossible to bite them. One of the women opened the window and threw them out onto the flat roof below, for the birds. It came as no surprise the next morning to see that the birds had also rejected them.

I found it hard to believe that the women I was living with were supposed to have committed crimes such as grievous bodily harm, smuggling heroin, burglary, shoplifting and deception, soliciting and receiving stolen goods. I liked and got along well with them all. Several of the women were on remand and had been in prison for many months. The woman I felt most sorry for was from Bolivia. She spoke very little English. Her visa had expired and she had been brought to

Holloway while things were sorted out. She did not understand why she was being kept locked up and no one had explained anything to her. After a day or two she was sent to another floor to be with other people waiting to be deported. Her face still haunts me. She had a look of terror in her eyes.

The night before my release I was allowed to have a bath. What a luxury! I wallowed in the hot water. Sharon lent me her talcum powder and Flo gave me a bath cube. I felt no excitement about leaving, although I was looking forward to being home again. At seven in the morning I said goodbye to my room-mates and gathered up my bedding and belongings from the top shelf of the locker I was using. I was taken to a room downstairs where other women waiting to be released were standing around in groups. We had some breakfast but I couldn't face any more white sliced bread. I was called into an office and given a travel warrant. I was leaning over the desk to read what it said when the warder standing nearby suddenly shouted at me, "Stand up straight!"

I was amazed and told her I did not have my glasses on and could not see very well without them. I was given my possessions and I asked if I might check them. This was refused. After some considerable time we were escorted to the gate. The man on gate duty was asking everyone's number. I had purposely not learnt my number. I have a perfectly good name and saw no reason why I should not be called by it. The woman in front of me refused to give her number and was told to go back inside until she was ready to. I said I could not remember mine and was told it was on the piece of paper I was holding. I did not want to have to stay any longer so pointedly read it out and then I was free to go. One of the women from Greenham who was released at the same time had been given some flowers. She gave me a red carnation.

On the train back to Ipswich I found myself looking at my travelling companions and wondering if they could tell that I had just come out of prison. I felt just the same but I knew the experience had changed me. I was secretly dreading arriving at Ipswich, as I knew that there would be a group of people there to greet me. I did not want any attention. I had done what I had to do and now I wanted to get on with my life. I kept thinking about the women back in Holloway who would be there for years and years. I know I would have gone mad if I had been there for very long. I got out of the train and saw Ian, Debbie and friends waiting for me. I felt a rush of pleasure at seeing them all again. Steve and

Richard were there. They had been released a few hours earlier from Norwich Prison. They gave me a wonderful homecoming.

A few weeks after my release from prison I went to Greenham again, with Joy and Sue, another friend from Ipswich. We decided to take some food and do a night watch. The women were being evicted many times each day and were getting exhausted. We drove up on the Thursday morning and drove around to the different gates to see where we could be of most use. More women were needed at Blue Gate, so we parked the car there. For some reason I felt very despondent and depressed. The atmosphere seemed tense. The women at Blue Gate had been evicted twice that day already. They were exhausted. Joy, Sue and I walked from Blue Gate around the fence to Green Gate and sat around the campfire with other women. Nobody talked much. Numbers were low and the conditions were bad. It had been a hard winter, living out in the open. Back at Blue Gate we shared the food we had brought with us.

When it got dark, women began to set up the tents again. They needed a night's sleep. A small group of us huddled around the campfire drinking tea and quietly talking. Suddenly, just after one o'clock, we heard the noise of traffic approaching. Out of the darkness we could see a line of white police vans. They screeched to a halt. Policemen leapt out and surrounded the whole camp. We didn't know what was going on. My only thought was that it was because the camp had been set up again after constant evictions.

A policeman called out, "Stand still! Don't move, and nothing will happen to you…"

Women were climbing out of sleeping bags and tents half asleep. The police stood silently in a circle. We stood still too. The realisation of what was going to happen slowly hit us. Bright lights shone from inside the base.

"Oh, my God they are going to bring the cruise convoy out," I called to Joy and Sue.

It was all over in a flash. The gates opened and one by one the long grey vehicles roared out and away down the road, led by police outriders on motorbikes. We stared in disbelief. It had happened so quickly. It was the first time that the cruise convoy had been taken out of the base and driven on British roads.

There was nothing we could have done to stop it. Women were crying and clinging on to one another. I was shaking. The police returned to their vans. We rushed to Sue's car and drove to Newbury to alert the telephone tree, the network of people who had agreed to pass on news of any urgent happening at the base. A few hours later the convoy returned through the same gate. By this time the media had arrived and during the coming day the world would witness the scenes on their television screens.

Chapter Four

39 Widgeon

Only a few miles away from the base at Molesworth lies Little Gidding, of which T.S. Eliot wrote in the *'Four Quartets'*:

'There are other places
Which also are the world's end, some at the sea jaws,
Or over a dark lake, in a desert or a city -
But this is the nearest, in place and time,
Now and in England.'

On December 28th 1981, Holy Innocents' Day, a few caravans were towed through snowy Cambridgeshire roads and deposited on the almost non-existent entrance to RAF Molesworth. The people who came called it Peace Corner. The Peace Campers weathered the winter and began to make a garden and grow vegetables. Eventually the local council, on whose land the camp stood, evicted them and dumped rubble on the spot to prevent their return. The rubble was conveniently close to hand; it was the torn-up runway from the Second World War. The Peace Camp found another site for their caravans on the other side of the base in Faye Way. In the spring of 1984 peacemakers returned to Peace Corner and removed the rubble from the gardens, rescued the rose bushes and made walled flower beds with the rubble. The building of a Peace Chapel was begun on the edge of the airfield. They called it Eirene.

Opposition to peace camp activity at Molesworth was sporadic. In the spring of 1984 wheat was sown for the hungry in Ethiopia, making the links between the cost of the arms race and the plight of the starving. A cruise missile base was being turned into wheat fields. At first, small areas of the airfield were dug by hand and then a hand plough was used. Finally, tractors were used to plough larger areas of military land. The Ministry of Defence ignored all these activities.

Side by side with the building of Eirene and the cultivation of the land, came an influx of women, men and children attracted by the idea of living in a new kind of way. Black leather-clad motorcyclists met corduroy-jacketed ecologists; anarchists met respectable, middle-aged social workers; pagans met Christians. Buses converted into homes drove onto quiet corners sheltered by trees. Tepees went up, while strange, personalised structures of bent wood, polythene and canvas began to grow. Wood fires crackled, children played, and dogs, goats and the occasional horse wandered around. The inhabitants called their new community Rainbow Village. Winter came and the solstice was celebrated alongside the nativity. The weather grew bleak and wood-burning stoves were constructed from old gas cylinders and bits of galvanised pipe. The pungent smell of wood smoke was everywhere. Inside it was warm and snug; outside it was icy, or a quagmire of mud. The year turned and a feeling of optimism prevailed.

We arrived to live at Molesworth in mid-January. In trying to define the attraction of the place, it seems on reflection that there were three distinct and separate elements. First, it was a way of linking disarmament with the concern for global development. Second, the witness attempted to provide a holistic approach to peacemaking. Third, it placed emphasis on spirituality as a motivating factor. The first element is exemplified by the series of projects linking the proposed use of the land for war with its potential as a provider of bread for the world. In a very real sense, people were trying to turn swords into ploughshares.

The second component was the holistic approach, in other words seeing the problem in its entirety. In terms of nuclear weapons, this approach means recognising that cruise missiles are a sickness in one of the parts, but they are also a symptom of a disease that affects the whole body politic. The world is out of joint. Therefore, remedies have to work not with isolated symptoms but with the whole system. Using another metaphor, biologists looking at the breakdown of stable patterns in nature, talk about 'ecosystems'. They see that the destruction of one organism may have enormous effects on other parts of the system because a fine ecological balance exists, all the parts being interdependent. At Molesworth it meant recognising that there is a relationship between the way we live as individuals and the manifest evil of the arms race. In a divided world, every person's lifestyle is contributing to the sense of injustice, insecurity and fear that has lead us to the brink of catastrophe. We cannot have global peace without personal peace.

The third element that attracted us was symbolised at Molesworth by the story of the Peace Chapel called Eirene. The name is a Greek word meaning peace, the word for peace used by the writers of the books of the New Testament. As such it was the successor to the even older Hebrew word for peace, 'Shalom'. It is perhaps no coincidence that scholars tell us that the Hebrew 'Shalom' linked the concept of peace with that of wholeness. The peace referred to by Jesus and Paul was frequently an inner peace. Moving to more recent times, when the Christian pacifist organisation, the Fellowship of Reconciliation, was looking for a badge symbol, it chose the word Eirene. In May 1981, the FOR organised a Peace Pilgrimage from the abbey at Iona to the cathedral at Canterbury. They stopped at Molesworth and planted a cherry tree. Some were to return in December that year to start the Peace Camp, and were offered a specially designed wooden building to be used as a meeting place. They decided to call it Eirene.

That first Eirene was the gift of a group of architects known as Architects for Peace.

Someone who remembers it described it as being built of wood and polythene. "It seemed great because it looked permanent... it was down the bottom corner of Peace Lane."

Its look of permanence clearly bothered members of the County Council as it is described in a County Council minute as being a significant factor in the decision to remove the camp. When the Peace Camp was finally evicted by the Council in July 1983, Eirene was dismantled. To prevent the return of the camp the County Council dumped concrete rubble on the site. This rubble came from the runways from the Second World War, which had recently been removed from the base. Most of the original campers moved to a new site on the other side of the base, but some had the idea of rebuilding the garden and used the rubble to create dry-stone walls. They also decided to build a new Eirene with the concrete from the old runways.

It was agreed deliberately to build the new Peace Chapel on MOD land. Plans were drawn up and foundations dug, and on the Easter Sunday of 1984 at a special All Faiths ceremony the cornerstone was laid. Satish Kumar, a Jain and one of two followers of Gandhi who had walked around the world in the cause of peace, laid the stone. The Bishop of Huntingdon, the Right Reverend Gordon Roe said prayers and Japanese Buddhists and a Native American also took part. At the same time, 200lb of spring wheat was sown on Ministry of Defence land. The ground was prepared by those present using an assortment of spades, forks and hand trowels.

A local newspaper, the *Trader*, records on April 25th, '*Another interesting facet of the event was that, while there was a police presence, and the planters were in fact in breach of the law by attending on Ministry of Defence land, no action was taken against them. Some 250 people attended, but all went off quietly.*'

As the summer progressed, so did Eirene. The building received an added impetus from the Green Gathering in late August. People in the Green Movement came from all over Britain to set up camp on the Ministry land. MOD police were at hand but merely watched as the festival unfolded. In the late summer sunshine there was a carnival atmosphere, with tents and multi-coloured vans and buses. There was also time for intense discussions, sitting in circles on the grass or in marquees. There were also new volunteers to help with building the chapel. Many were to leave a memento cemented into the walls: a piece of bright blue pottery, glass bottles, even a car cylinder head. On September 2nd, when the Dedication Service was held, the walls were several feet high, and at either end the brick-built arched doorways were completed. The chapel was quite small, about twelve feet wide and 25 feet long. The walls were built in large, uneven chunks of stone and concrete rubble. Only the doorways and the corners were built of brick. At either end were the archways, and on one of the long sides stood a pillar, part of an incomplete doorway. People packed inside, sitting on the floor, leaning on the walls or peering in from outside. There were times of quiet meditation and prayer, songs were sung and some tried to give word to their feelings about peace and love. Bishop Gordon Roe had once more come to lend his support by blessing the building.

Our second visit to Molesworth was in mid-October 1984. A memorial service for Caroline Taylor was to be held in the Peace Chapel. It was to coincide with the sowing of the winter wheat and tree planting on the MOD fields. We travelled to Cambridgeshire with our local CND group, and during the journey sounded one or two people out about our idea to move there. They were very supportive.

It was a bright autumn day with a hard, biting wind blowing across the fields. A long ribbon of women, men and children walked forward in a line, scattering wheat over the turned earth. As well as the large group of people now living on the base, the Rainbow Villagers, there were hundreds of visitors who had come from all over the country, just for this day. Some had brought trees to plant in memory of Caroline. Lucy, Caroline's small daughter was there in the arms of her grandmother, wearing a rainbow-coloured woollen hat. Lucy had survived the accident and despite head injuries had made a complete recovery.

We wanted to meet Tim and Bridie Wallis, the Quaker couple we had heard so much about. They had both spent a considerable time living at the Peace Camp and had been instrumental in the building of the new Eirene and the attempt to grow wheat on the base.

We kept asking people, "Do you know Tim and Bridie?" and the answer was almost always yes.

But when we said, "Can you see them?" the person we were speaking to would look around, saying, "Well... they were here just a moment ago, but..."

Eventually we caught up with them. They were in great demand that day, as they were organising the shipment of wheat from Molesworth to Eritrea. We stood watching them, waiting for them to finish their conversation.

Bridie's face had a classical, natural beauty in repose. It was often transformed by a radiant smile. Her long, fair hair was blowing across her face in the gusting wind. She glanced from Tim to the other speaker, occasionally looking over to where we were standing. When she spoke, her voice was clear and well-modulated. Despite the urgency of the conversation, she exuded an air of tranquil calm. Listening to Tim speaking, we were surprised to detect an American accent. He smiled a lot. His face creased up and his eyes twinkled. His hair and beard were dark. He was wearing a bold green, white and black check jacket, and while Bridie's clothes looked neat there was no sense that Tim cared about his appearance. The conversation engrossed him and he was oblivious of our presence. They both seemed young to us and we guessed they were in their mid-twenties.

After a while we were able to speak to them. We said who we were and started to tell them of our plans. We were both disappointed at their reaction. They seemed wary of us and they were clearly very busy with the arrangements for the day.

Sensing they were in a hurry, Ian said, "So you see, we are hoping to find a caravan and come and live here. We want to join in what you're doing here."

Their response surprised us. Tim said, "Oh, but we don't live here any more. We live in a house in a village on the other side of the base."

We left them feeling bewildered. For Ian especially, Tim and Bridie's presence at the base had seemed essential. Their approach to peacemaking was one with which we identified. The building of the Peace Chapel, and the creation of positive alternatives to the arms race was the way we wanted to show our opposition. We walked away, trying not to feel despondent.

A huge container lorry stood in the bridleway. The wheat that had been sown in the spring had been harvested, although it was only a symbolic amount. This, together with donations of several tonnes from local farmers, was to begin its journey from Molesworth to Eritrea that afternoon. Later, after the container lorry of wheat, rice and clothing had left for the docks, we gathered in the chapel and remembered Caroline.

★★★

Slowly our plans began to take shape. Ian had a meeting with Eric and Lydia, his employers at Concord Films. We were relieved to find them sympathetic. They were anxious not to lose Ian and suggested that he could take a six-month sabbatical. He declined this offer as we felt uncertain about our future. We just did not know what we would want to do once we had spent a few months living at Molesworth. After a lot of discussion, involving the Council of Management, Ian accepted voluntary redundancy. It was a difficult decision to make after eleven years, but we both felt confident that this was the right way forward.

We had put off breaking the news to our families, uncertain as to how they would respond. We were surprised to find that, although they were concerned as to how we would manage living an unorthodox lifestyle, they accepted our decision and gave their loving support.

A few weeks later, we returned to Molesworth to discuss our ideas with Tim and Bridie in greater detail. There were few people about as we parked our car by the entrance. We walked a few yards down the old bridle way that ran through the base. Tim and Bridie were busy mixing cement.

Tim looked up and called out, "Hi, we have to finish what we are doing before we stop to talk, hope that's okay?"

"Can we help?"

"Sure!" Tim said.

Ian shovelled the cement into a barrow and wheeled it over to the chapel. Tim produced some tools for working the mortar into the spaces between the bricks and assorted stones that made up the walls. Neither of us had ever done any bricklaying, but we were determined to try. For an hour or so we worked and talked and then we decided it was time to eat. We walked over to the road, where a small green caravan stood. Tim opened it up and we went inside. Tim and Bridie had lived in it until a month or so before. Now they used it to brew up when they worked on the chapel, it was also a safe place to store valuable tools. The caravan was tiny and we squeezed round the table explaining our plans in more detail, while Tim prepared cheese on toast on the small gas cooker.

This was to be the first of many meals we were to share together in the coming months. As we drove home Ian said to me, "I really enjoyed today, it feels as though we are getting somewhere at last."

It was soon after this that I decided to start keeping a diary. The following extract was written on December 30th, 1984.

'Awful, dull rainy day. Both feel gloomy and terrified at the amount that has to be done in such a short time. It is so hard to keep "strong", and we both need to feel okay to help each other. I am sure it will all get done but it is not an easy process. It is bound to get easier once we have left our cosy little home and installed ourselves in the caravan. Every so often I ask myself, "Why me? Why can't I just get on with life without letting it all get to me so much?" Then I think about the fields at Molesworth and the fact that they want to build a whole new base there, with all that goes with it, and I am incensed and KNOW I have to do my small bit to try and stop it.'

As Ian was not leaving work until the middle of January, we decided to wait until after Christmas before finding a caravan. We made it known among friends that we were looking for someone to rent the house for six months. The only stipulation was that they would have to rent our cat Lucky, too! She was over thirteen and had been ailing for some time. We wanted her to stay in her own home and garden and moving her would have been out of the question. We were delighted when our friend Mike, rang to say that he was looking for accommodation. He had two cats of his own and would take care of Lucky, too. The timing of his move fitted our plans exactly.

Our dog, Robbie, was coming with us to Molesworth. Robbie is a Shetland sheep dog who was a stray. He had been ill-treated and it took many months before he began to trust us. He could be very defiant and would bark at motorbikes and bicycles. The vet thought he was about two and half years old, although it was only really guess work. He has a lovely nature and seems to know everything we say. He hates riding in the car and always knows when we are going on a journey. He hides in a corner and hopes we will ignore him.

At the beginning of January we advertised in our local paper for a caravan and started receiving phone calls. We looked at a couple of vans in Ipswich that were in a really poor state and decided we would have to widen our search. We visited a dealer in a nearby town who had a yard full of old caravans, most of which had been on holiday sites. Once they become old, the site owners do not really want them as they 'lower the tone' of the place. The owners discover that they have no market value and they have to sell them to firms like this one, for less than a £100. It was a breaker's yard for old vans and it had the mournful air of that kind of place. People's holiday dreams, smart little white and cream homes by the sea, had come to this.

We pushed open the door of one and peeped inside. It looked damp and there were a lot of old newspapers lying on the floor. A mattress lay on a bed-base with a great gaping split in it. We looked into another one and it was the same. They were both probably fifteen years old but they were cheap. They were also a lot bigger than we had thought of having and we wondered how we would get one that size to Molesworth. Our friends Peter and Cynthia James had offered to tow us with their car as it was fitted with a caravan tow bar. There was still the question of whether one of these would stand up to the ride. An old caravan that has not been used for touring tends to get a rusty chassis and the wheels and axles seize up. The journey to Molesworth from Ipswich is the best part of a hundred miles and we had visions of some decrepit old van disintegrating en route.

We discussed prices with the dealer and asked him about other vans, we wondered whether he might be getting more soon. It turned out that there was a time for buying old vans and it wasn't then. Early autumn is the van-buying season, at the end of the holidays. By now most of the decent vans had been snapped up. We learnt that people buy them to live in while they renovate old houses. Farmers use them, builders buy them for site offices or as a place to brew tea or store tools. We left feeling uncertain as to what to do, trying to persuade ourselves that we might be able to live in one of these frail old structures with their leaky roofs, broken windows and ancient linoleum.

The next day we followed up a telephone call and went to see a caravan at a holiday site at Felixstowe. We had a quick look at it but thought it was far too big. All the roads were named after birds. By comparison with most of the mobile homes on the site, number 39 Widgeon was quite small but it was certainly not a touring van. It was even bigger than the ones we had looked at the previous day. When we got home we rang Peter James to ask his advice. Without hesitation he offered to take us the next day, Saturday, to have another look at the van at Felixstowe. We then phoned the owner of the van, who lived in Ipswich, to arrange to pick up the keys.

It snowed hard throughout the night and the garden lay under an inch-thick white blanket. Undeterred, the Jameses picked us up and drove us to Felixstowe and we made our way round the silent lanes of mobile homes, with their little picket fences and stark, bare rose bushes standing black against the snow. We came once more to view number 39 Widgeon. It lay away from the road, tucked out of sight, not quite new enough, modern enough or sufficiently stylish to be on the front row. The roof, door and panels were painted pale blue, the rest painted cream. We pulled on wellingtons and made our way through drifts of snow to the door. We climbed the steps and moved inside.

Not surprisingly it felt icy cold. We had all taken our boots off and our feet soon froze as we padded about opening doors and peering in cupboards. It was well kept. The entrance led into a small kitchen area with sliding doors leading off to the right and left. To the left lay a large room fitted out with solid cupboards in varnished wood. The lower half of the walls were also covered in wood veneer, the upper half was painted cream. The windows were curtained with a flowery print, browns and orange on a white background. The floor in the main room was covered with a brown fitted carpet and a sofa bed at the far end was also covered in a brown material. Near the sliding door to this room the wall appeared to be solid wood. After a few moments we realised that this was in fact a double bed that folded down from the wall. Unlatching the fastenings, we eased it down and found it had a mattress fixed to it. There was also a solid wood partition that folded away against the wall, dividing the half of the room with the bed from the far end where the sofa was.

We wandered back into the kitchen, which was painted white and blue. It was all very neat and clean. Under the sink there was a cupboard full of pots and pans and next to it was a small gas cooker. There were net curtains at the window and a First Aid box was fixed on the wall. The door leading off to the right revealed a pale blue china lavatory, with (as the estate agents say) a low-level cistern. In the back of our minds was the growing awareness that it was all rather bourgeois for a potential Peace Camp residence. Yet its old-fashioned 1950s furnishings had a solidity that we liked compared with more modern caravans, which had jettisoned wood in favour of plastic, chipboard and Formica. It seemed incredible to think that the asking price was only £175. We climbed out into the snow and peered underneath. Peter, who knew more about caravans than either of us, examined the towing mechanism and discovered that the brake leads had been removed. The two enormous tyres were pumped up hard and were almost unworn. We asked him anxiously what he thought.

"It can't be towed, or at least not by me. It's illegal to tow a caravan without brakes. And in any case, it's very big for towing."

We crunched our way back to the car thinking that was the end of the matter. It was, without doubt, a real bargain but it was ruled out by the simple fact that we could not move it. As we drove back towards Ipswich it started to snow again. We discussed going on to the caravan dealer, which was some twelve miles further on past Ipswich, but as the weather grew worse and the car began to slide on the icy surface, we decided that we call a halt to our caravan hunting for that day. Peter and Cynthia dropped us off at home and we made our way back indoors feeling depressed. In a week's time Ian was to leave work and we had agreed that Mike, who was to be our tenant, should move in the following weekend and we still had no caravan to live in at Molesworth.

I decided to ring Tim and Bridie to let them know what was happening. I explained that we now felt that the only answer was to stay with them in their house and start looking locally.

"It looks as if moving a caravan is the real problem. Ian thinks we should look for one near Molesworth, that way we only have to move it a few miles. If there is a place like the one near us, we should be able to pick up something pretty cheap. How would you feel about us staying with you? Do you mind?"

I felt uncomfortable about asking as I am very independent and I hate the thought that I am imposing on people. Tim said they didn't mind at all, but I still felt uneasy. After we had put the phone down we decided we had better tell the caravan's owner that we would not be buying number 39 Widgeon.

I dialled the number and when he answered I started to explain, "It's a lovely caravan, but unfortunately there is no way we could get it to where we want it to go."

I had not told him where we were going as we both felt a little embarrassed about explaining our plans. When he asked where we wanted to take it I said, "Oh, near Cambridge." Then I said, "We've been told that it could go on a lorry but that it would cost a lot of money, much more than we could afford. So, I'm afraid that's that."

But that was not that. I heard him say, "I've got a friend with a low-loader, how would you feel if I could get it moved for you? I could get it done cheaply."

I hesitated, "Oh, I don't know, er... we'd have to think about it, can you hold on a sec?" And I turned to Ian to whisper, "He says he's got a friend who could move it and it won't cost much. What do you think?"

Ian shrugged his shoulders ambiguously, "What am I going to say?" I hissed.

"Say, we'll have to think about it."

I spoke into the receiver again and told him that we wanted time to think and that we would call him back. Putting down the telephone we started to talk about the pros and cons. It suddenly felt very difficult to decide and we came near to quarrelling, but in the end we rang him back to suggest that we went over to see him to discuss a price. We went to the building society and drew out £300 so that if we were able to agree, we could pay there and then. On the way over we talked about what we should say we were doing and I said quite firmly that I thought we should be quite frank about our plans. Ian said, "But supposing he's anti CND? He may not want to go ahead."

"That's a risk we'll have to take."

The caravan owner showed us into his living room and we sat down. We talked about the price; originally he had asked for £175 but we had heard that professional transport costs might be £200. He told us that he had worked in the motor trade but was now retired, and explained that because a friend could move the van, he could offer us an all-in price of £230 including transport to "somewhere near Cambridge". We both felt that it was a very fair offer, but I had to come clean about our intentions.

I took a deep breath and said, "I think there is something you should know first. We are going to live at Molesworth. It's where a new cruise missile base is going to be built near Huntingdon. We're going there to protest. I don't know how you feel about it?"

As I spoke we looked to see the reaction of both him and his wife. We were delighted to find that they seemed to approve and certainly did not want to refuse to sell. We paid over the £230 and left clutching the keys. We both felt elated. We had somewhere to live! On the way home we called at a caravan showroom and bought an Elsan toilet, and some of the very caustic fluid that is used to render the contents harmless. That beautiful blue, low-level loo was not going to be any use where we were going. There would be no mains services such as running water or drains.

We set the date for moving to Molesworth for January 14th, 1985. However, we came up against several difficulties regarding the caravan. We made repeated phone calls to the owner, but he was always evasive about when his friend would be able to undertake the move. In addition, we had visited the caravan site office and discovered that they were not at all happy about the caravan being moved during the bad weather. Eventually, only a few days before we were due to leave our home, the former owner told us that his friend's low-loader was off the road. We were very downcast. In the end we all went to talk to the site manager and try to sort out how we could get the caravan off the site. The site owner relented and agreed to provide a tractor to tow it to the entrance. Now we had to sort out the removal ourselves and this turned out to be an expensive business, costing us more than the price of the caravan itself.

By Sunday January 13th, we realised that it would be another week before we could move to Molesworth. Gradually the house began to take on a new look as we packed many of our things and stored stuff away. Peter James offered to help Ian take a load of our stuff up to Tim and Bridie's home at the Old School House, Clopton, to await our arrival. As Mike started to move in boxes of books and records we felt it was time to leave. We were in effect 'homeless'. Ian's parents asked us to stay with them for a few days and so on January 14th, instead of being in a draughty caravan in the bleak Cambridgeshire countryside, we found ourselves in a comfortable, centrally-heated house – still in Ipswich!

After many telephone calls we managed to book a low-loader from a firm in Colchester. It was to pick up the caravan on the morning of Monday January 21st. After all the rush and tear, we found ourselves with time on our hands. We rang Tim and Bridie and asked if we could come and stay with them for a few days, to 'get the feel of the place'. We stayed four days and whilst there we walked across the fields from the School House to where Rainbow Village had its home. It was a bright, crisp morning and the snow still lay thick on the ground. Making our way across the airfield, we had to cling on to each other as we stepped into deep drifts. Robbie bounded along, disappearing from time to time, the snow almost covering him. He loved to run free, following the scent of hares and rabbits. Intricate patterns of animal and bird tracks criss-crossed our path. Half an hour later we arrived at Rainbow Village.

A tall, auburn-haired man with a straggly ginger beard greeted us. He was wearing a black overcoat held together with a large leather belt, buckled tightly around the waist. It was Sid Rawle, sometimes called the 'king of the hippies'. He had an indeterminate accent that might have had a slight West Country burr. He invited us into his tepee for a cup of tea. The Native American tent was extended by a bender made of bent wood covered in tarpaulins. The small entrance was covered with sacking. Stooping low, we stepped inside and gradually our eyes grew accustomed to the gloom. The floor was covered in pieces of old carpet. We took off our wellingtons and made our way into a circular area where a wood-burning stove gave off a good heat. The stove was made of scrap metal and an assortment of short lengths of metal pipe took the smoke out through the roof. The interior of the roof had pieces of coloured fabric covering the dark tarpaulin. At ground level on one side a glass window in a wooden frame had been built into the structure, which let in a small amount of light. The floor in the living area had a few rugs covering it. Candles were burning and the smell of joss sticks filled the room.

A small boy came in after us asking for a biscuit. He was called Ra, to our ears a rather unusual name, but then he had rather unusual parents. Jules, his mother, found a packet and opening it offered Ra and us a biscuit. Jules was dressed in a floor-length skirt and several jumpers. She was clearly many months pregnant. Jules was very interested in mystical ideas such as ley lines and standing stones, which perhaps explained why her son was named after an Egyptian God. Sid asked us to sit down and handed out mugs of tea. He began to tell us about Rainbow Village, pausing every so often to take a pinch of snuff from a small brass tin that he kept in his pocket. Sid was a great story teller. One incident could be related to another, gradually building up a picture. At the time of our meeting he was rather angry about the way the police had been harassing the Rainbow Villagers out in search of wood. He tried to explain to us the ancient rights of travelling people to search private property for dead wood that could be removed. It was the cutting of live wood that was not allowed. Removing branches from dead elms was quite all right according to Sid, but the police had twice recently arrested people for 'wooding'.

Sid had been living a vagabond existence for at least twenty years. He had been a key figure in the 'flower power' era of the late Sixties and had been instrumental in organising the free festivals in Windsor Park, where according to the tabloid press there was free love and free drugs, as well as free pop music. He was fascinating to listen to. One night he came into our caravan and stayed several hours telling us stories from his past. One saga concerned the island given to Sid and his friends by John Lennon. This tiny island off the coast of Ireland was to have offered the answer to those whose efforts to create the perfect alternative society on the mainland were constantly being thwarted by the laws of property. However the idyll was short-lived. They made a promising start, building homes and growing crops. But the winter was hard and the next spring the crops were poor. People found the almost monastic existence too hard and gradually drifted away. There were tensions and disagreements and of course very little money. The great experiment ended in failure, but this did not dim Sid's enthusiasm for utopian communities.

Now it was Rainbow Village. But the old human problems were the same. Some people felt that there was an elite that tried to determine priorities. They questioned the need for weekly meetings where decisions were made, thinking them a waste of time. They had a place to live. A communal kitchen provided food and somewhere to keep warm. They could draw the dole and buy Special Brew and cannabis. Just before we arrived to live at Molesworth, this small dissenting group had struck at the symbols of power. They had stolen a JCB and smashed a Transit van donated by the Ecology Party and an old caravan that was used as an office and information stand.

We told Sid that we were coming to join them soon and asked where he thought we might park the caravan. "We want to be near to the Peace Chapel and close to the entrance, if that's possible," Ian said.

"I don't see why not," Sid replied. "We'll go and have a look in Peace Lane." We walked together past the collection of coaches and buses and almost to the end of the lane, where a battered white van stood. "This is Brig's old vehicle," Sid said. "We should be able to get it shifted out of the way, how would this suit you?" We were just beside Peace Corner, opposite the gardens and the chapel.

At Peace Corner, the road from Brington to Old Weston ran very close to the edge of the airfield. A track that had once had a metalled surface, now mostly covered in muddy snow, could just be discerned, joining the road at right angles. It was now classed as a bridleway and it ran across the airfield, linking up with Cockbrook Lane, which in turn joined the road between Old Weston and Clopton at a T-junction. At Peace Corner, it was still possible to see the curved line of kerb stones, marking the entrance to the bridleway. Standing at this point, looking towards the base, on the right-hand side, was a triangular area of verge that had been made into a garden of raised flower beds surrounded by low, dry-stone walls. These were Peace Gardens. Behind the gardens, about fifty feet from the road, lay the chapel. On the left-hand side, was the tapered point of a small, triangular field. Walking from the junction, down the bridleway, almost immediately on the left, lay an opening. It was the entrance to Peace Lane, here, running almost parallel to the road. Hedges marked either side of the lane. On the left, the hedge marked the boundary of the small field; on the right was a tall hedge with trees in it, beyond which lay the open fields that comprised Molesworth airfield. Standing just a few yards from the opening, beside the derelict, white Transit van, we looked around us. On either side, trees and hedges, their branches heavy with snow, sparkled in the sunlight. It was just the right spot.

Chapter Five

In Halcyon Spirit

We returned to Ipswich on the Sunday evening, calling at our house to collect things we had forgotten. It felt strange, not a bit like our home. Different pictures hung on the walls and a large, grey settee stood in the sitting room. My only concern now was Lucky. We found her sitting in her usual spot in the garden looking unconcerned. But we were not sorry to leave. Our aim now was to get to Molesworth.

Ian's mother woke us the next morning at 6:45 with a cup of tea. Over breakfast Ian entertained us by recounting a dream: "I was sitting in a railway carriage, talking to J.B. Priestley and Dietrich Bonhoeffer. I was arrested for not paying the fare. I seem to remember I had to put the money in a tin for striking miners. Then I was let off."

We all wondered if this had any significance! We packed the last of our things in the car, now heavily laden with an assortment of pots and pans, leaving a small corner for Robbie. Then Ian tied the bicycles on the roof rack and reassuring his mum and dad that all would be well, we kissed them goodbye and set off for Felixstowe.

We waited in the site office for the low-loader to turn up. It didn't! After about an hour we rang up and found that the driver had had a flat tyre and so it was going to be delayed! It eventually arrived around eleven o'clock. We watched as the driver fixed heavy chains to the caravan and slowly hauled it on to the long trailer. I travelled with the driver and Ian led the way in the Mini.

The weather had turned slightly milder and it was drizzling. We arrived at our destination around lunchtime and the driver manoeuvred the caravan almost into the exact place we had chosen. On the way I had explained to him what we were proposing to do and as he left he wished us luck. Several people living nearby came over to help us. The lane was uneven and we needed to put bricks under the legs to ensure the caravan was level and we could not have managed on our own. The rest of that day was spent bringing our boxes over from The Old School and unpacking. That evening we cooked our first meal on the Calor gas stove. It had two rings on top and a grill but the oven wasn't working. Our only form of heat was from a small, Calor gas fire. It proved to be very efficient, even in the freezing weather that was to come, its only drawback being the condensation it created. That day I wrote in my diary:

'WE ARE HERE, feel quite at home so far, smashing caravan plenty of space and cupboards. Managed to get one of the gas lights working but had to use several candles. I can't believe that we are finally here after all the hitches. "Halcyon Spirit" is in Rainbow Village, Peace Lane, Molesworth. NO CRUISE MISSILES HERE!'

We had decided to name the caravan Halcyon Spirit. The word *halcyon*, meaning calm and peaceful, comes from a kingfisher in Greek mythology that was said to have the power to calm the wind and waves, while it nested on the sea during the winter solstice. It seemed appropriate.

I was aware of Ian climbing over me as I lay in bed. I listened as he filled the kettle from the big, plastic water container in the kitchen. He muttered to himself as he tried to light the Calor gas. I leant across the bed and pulled back the curtain; I could see blue sky through the bare branches of the hawthorn bush.

"Thank goodness, it's not raining!" I called to Ian.

"Do you want some toast? It may take quite a while, though. The burners are all clogged up."

I lay back and looked around the caravan. It had a homely feel about it. We had put up posters and I had stuck photos of the family on the walls. Ian came in through the sliding wooden door.

"I'm freezing; it's taking ages to do. I'm going to put a jumper on," he said.

I giggled as he went back into the kitchen wearing a roll-necked sweater over the red and blue-striped flannelette nightshirt I had bought before we came. His feet were clad in thick, woollen socks. His breath hit the air like clouds of white smoke. At last I heard the kettle start to whistle. Ian came into the room carrying two steaming mugs of coffee. He put them down and went back, returning with two slices of toast. It had taken about twenty minutes. He switched on the radio and climbed back into bed.

We ate our breakfast listening to the *Today* programme on Radio Four. Robbie sat watching us eat, hoping a crumb of toast might fall his way. It felt warm in bed but I wanted to get up. I jumped out and switched on the gas fire, hurriedly pulling on my clothes. I went through to the kitchen to have a wash and discovered the kettle was empty.

"You should have put the kettle on again, after you made the coffee," I said.

As time went on, our morning routine grew more efficient. Some mornings we would have a strip wash. We would bring the red washing-up bowl out of the kitchen and stand it on newspapers on the gate-legged table. Taking it in turns, we would stand naked in front of the fire, washing ourselves in a few inches of hot water. Most mornings the windows were running with condensation and would have to be mopped up. We made the bed and folded it back up against the wall. Each day we had a short act of worship inside the caravan; just a prayer, hymn and a reading. It helped us get through the day in the right spirit.

The first few days living in the caravan seemed full and interesting. We were among many people from all walks of life, all striving to live together in harmony. This was not always easy especially under the harsh weather conditions. We felt ourselves to be a bit 'different' because we had come from a rather conventional background, but we seemed to be accepted. We made lots of cups of tea and coffee and sat and talked with anyone who called in to see us. That first morning Ian used black paint we had brought with us to write the name *Halcyon Spirit* over the door. On the front end he wrote, '*Quakers for Peace*' and drew a Christian CND symbol beside it.

A meeting had been arranged for East Anglian CND groups. Lots of people we knew arrived and we showed them the caravan and asked them in for tea. We discovered that mud was going to be a big problem. Anyone walking about the camp soon found thick mud covering their shoes or boots. When they came in the van we suggested they took off their footwear. Ian wrote out a notice saying that the caravan was an anti-mud zone!

One of our first visitors was Brig Oubridge. In fact he had called the previous evening after we were in bed. It seemed strange talking to this man, who was Caroline Taylor's lover and had meant so much to her in the last few months of her life. He sat on the edge of our bed rolling a very thin cigarette. Leaning forward towards a candle, he lit the roll-up. His eyes were dark beneath black eyebrows. His skin was sallow. As he smoked, from time to time, he stroked his long, black beard. Suddenly, something I said made him laugh and his face became animated, he looked up at me and his eyes twinkled. Brig had lived at a place in South Wales known as Tepee Valley. He had been planning to return there with Caroline when his van was hit by a passing juggernaut. Now he lived in a tepee in Rainbow Village. Brig was very actively involved in the Ecology Party, now more aptly titled the Green Party. We soon realised that, whilst he might reject the need for leaders, Brig was one. He was a born organiser and was forever rushing off to meetings all over the country. When he was away, people would defer decisions, waiting for him to come back.

He asked if he could borrow our car to drive to the Old School and work on the *Molesworth Bulletin*. Ian said he would drive him there and help. The bulletin had been started a few months before. It gave news of what was happening at Molesworth and had built up a circulation of several hundreds. Brig had quite a few duplicating machines with which he managed to create four-colour artwork. When they left, I got out my portable typewriter and wrote letters. I wrote to my mother and Debbie telling them how we were settling in. I wrote to both our local paper and radio station in Ipswich. They had shown great interest in our coming to Molesworth and I thought they would want to know how we were coping with our new lifestyle.

I was so engrossed that I didn't notice that the light was beginning to fade. I prepared a vegetable stew by the light of a candle balanced on the draining board. Our pressure cooker was invaluable, it saved time and gas. Ian had been gone for nearly three hours. He eventually arrived back about six. He had been involved in sorting out a card index system, which Tim and Bridie had devised to record the names of the bulletin subscribers.

Ian tried to light a portable gas lamp, but the jet was blocked. There were also five gas lamps in the van, running off the supply to the cooker. Most of them had no mantles and we only managed to get one of them to light. It was not very bright. We could not see to read. It was clear that we would have to have some other form of lighting if we were going to be there for any length of time. As we were finishing our supper there came a knock and one of our neighbours, John, stuck his head around the door.

"Evening, how are you getting on then?"

"Come in," I said. "We're fine. Would you like a cup of coffee?"

"I'd love a cup of tea," he said, taking off his boots.

I went into the kitchen, carrying a candle and filled the kettle. "Where do you live?" I asked.

"Just down the lane." John removed his glasses, which had steamed up and began polishing them with a piece of tissue. "I deliver the post round the site, that's why they call me Postman John. We used to have a mail box but now the postman brings it to my van."

John stayed for over an hour, telling us where various people lived. Many Rainbow Village residents seemed to have unusual nicknames and we tried to remember them as he spoke about: 'Happy Times Lyn', 'Rainbow Jo', 'Lyn the Bin', 'Cosmic Martin' and 'Carpenter Jim'. The lanes and tracks where they lived had interesting names, too. Brig, Sid and Jules lived in 'Admin Alley', where the 'office work' was done. Some of the other areas were variously called: 'Hassle Free Lane', 'Hawthorn Manor' and 'Bender City'.

Just before we arrived, part of a travelling group called the Peace Convoy had turned up at Molesworth to join Rainbow Village. This group had been on the road for some time. The media had created a very bad image for them. They were said to be unscrupulous, heavily involved in drug dealing and capable of violence. We were somewhat nervous to find them as neighbours. Whatever other people's experiences might have been, we found the Peace Convoy people friendly and easy to get on with. They had arrived in twos and threes over a period of a week. Their strange assortment of coaches, trucks and vans cluttered the entrance to the bridleway. Guarding the vehicles were German Shepherd dogs. The dogs were usually left untied and in the daytime they nosed amongst the rubbish for scraps of food. At night, if one of them was startled by something, the whole pack barked noisily. We kept our distance, though. When Ian walked across the bridleway with Robbie, he discovered he often had two or three other dogs with him. Robbie was wary but the big Alsatians ignored him. One, however, kept thrusting his head at Ian's hand, which he kept tightly in his pocket!

Ian described how, one morning a few days after our arrival, he had got up early, intending to take Robbie for a walk. The sky blushed pink in the dawn light and he could hear music. As he got near to one of the Peace Convoy vehicles, an old fire engine painted blue, he saw that the music was coming from a large P.A. system. The tune was a strange, haunting melody that had been popular the previous year. It was made by an Irish band called 'Clannad'. The sound of their Gaelic harmonies filled the air. The ground was frosted and above the trees the sun was rising, a great red ball. Ian stopped, spellbound, not wanting the moment to pass. Then a man with a great black beard bounded from the fire engine and stood, legs apart facing the rising sun. A cloud of steam began to rise from the ground at his feet and suddenly Ian realised what the man was doing. Still unobserved, Ian walked quietly away, with Robbie trotting silently behind him.

All around the Peace Convoy's vehicles were piles of rubbish: old cans, plastic containers and scrap metal. Getting rid of refuse was a problem. No dustman called. We managed to find an old copper and kept it near the caravan to burn waste paper. One morning I plucked up courage and went over to the motley assortment of vans in the bridleway, to tell the people living there that I wanted to clean the place up. I have to admit that at first I was uneasy about our convoy neighbours. I had never met travelling people and their appearance could be misleading. I climbed up the step at the back of one of the vans and banged on the door. It was opened by the man with a long black beard, wearing an unusual round embroidered hat. I stared inside. A group of men and women were sitting drinking mugs of coffee. They all turned and stared back at me.

"Hello, I'm Jennifer, I live over there," I said, pointing to Halcyon Spirit. "I want to clear up some of the rubbish, but thought I should come to tell you first," I said, feeling quite nervous. "I know it's just me, but I can't bear seeing it all, I hope you don't mind."

The man who introduced himself as Phil seemed to be the leader of the group. He said it was all right as far as they were concerned and I heard someone else say, "I suppose we should do it really."

Later that day, I noticed several of the convoy people gathering up rubbish and burning it on a huge bonfire.

The half-finished chapel was being used for services at the weekends. Tim and Bridie asked us to put a poster in the window, telling people about a candle-light vigil planned to be held in Eirene on the last Sunday in January. It was also the day designated by the World Disarmament Campaign for special services for peace. The light was fading as we stood in Eirene trying to light candles, sheltering them from the wind; a niche in the wall was found where the candles flickered but somehow stayed alight. One or two teenage children from Rainbow Village stood watching and jeering at us. There was a tension now between some of the villagers and those who worshipped in Eirene. It had developed during the winter months and festered like an unhealed sore that no one seemed ready to probe and cleanse.

At first many of the Rainbow Villagers had shared a kind of pride in the chapel and had taken an active part in its construction. Len, a bricklayer, had used his skills to make the arched doorways with their keystones. But then some of the people had wanted a schoolroom built for the children and felt that this should take priority. Eirene, intended to be a meeting place for all, was now seen as the possession of the middle class. Those who were rejecting straight society began to see Eirene as a symbol of the values they were seeking to leave behind. Only a few days previously, a large green van had driven off the road and its owner had parked it just outside the chapel wall. He had then proceeded to strip off the old felt roofing and rotten roof timbers. The debris lay all around the van and the air was frequently filled with the sound of hammering. To those who felt the chapel was sacred, the van was a violation, but nobody felt able to say so. Not for the last time, barriers had developed. But in the attempt to cover up the cracks the subject remained taboo.

It was the end of January when the Roof Fund was launched. The idea was to push forward with the completion of the chapel in time for Easter. CND had agreed to hold a major demonstration at Molesworth on Easter Monday. Tim and Bridie were producing publicity for a week-long work camp in March when construction would be completed. The roof needed expensive timber frames and tiles for cladding. The estimated cost was £1,000. As a publicity stunt, a large sign with a gauge resembling a thermometer was nailed to the wall facing the road. A journalist and photographer from *The Daily Telegraph* spent some time photographing the chapel and the sign, with Bridie wheeling a barrow through the arched doorway. Money was soon pouring in and the red column on the gauge rose daily.

★★★

Before we left Ipswich, Peter James had mentioned that he had an offset printing machine and a paper plate maker he no longer needed. Ian asked him whether we might take it to Molesworth to use in the campaign. Peter agreed and another of our friends brought the two machines over in her car a few days after we arrived. The machines were set up in the School House and Tim and Ian spent several days learning how they worked. Ian cycled over each day, returning later with very black hands. Their first attempts were disastrous, but slowly they learned what to do. Eventually Tim and Ian succeeded in printing a new map of the base. It showed the perimeter and the location of Rainbow Village, the chapel and the School House, but it also showed the way in which Tim dreamed the site might be transformed into a Peace Park. There were 'allotments for Eritrea', an alternative technology area. The old bomb store would be used as a storage place for clothes and medical supplies for Eritrea. The few military buildings were designated as the site of a future School of Peace Studies!

The weather turned very cold again. It was colder than I had ever known. Each morning the Calor gas bottles were frozen up, and we put on as many clothes as possible while we tried to thaw them out. On the January 27th the diary reads:

'The most bitterly cold day I can remember, am sitting with gloves on and all the windows are thick with frost inside. Both gas bottles are frozen. We went to the local church this morning in Old Weston for morning service with Bridie and Tim. Only seven of us in the congregation. The vicar didn't speak to us either going in or coming out. Lots of visitors around today: people from Southend, Muswell Hill, Lambeth, Surrey, Streatham and Battersea. Tim has lent us a paraffin lamp that we have got to work. It's snowing again and staying put. Someone gave us a cheque for £100 for the roof fund. I took it over to the School House. Made phone calls from phone box to the family then sat and read, listening to the radio. VERY cold and windy outside. Almost one week gone already and

what a good and interesting one it has been! We are so lucky to be able to do this, and we thank God so often for having each other and the time to share each other's company and that of others.'

The notice outside the Post Office read: '*Parish Council Meeting, to be held in Village Hall, Old Weston, January 29th, 1984*'.

"Look at this, do you think we should go?" I asked Ian. "They are bound to talk about the Peace Camp. We might get some idea of how people really feel about it."

Ian agreed.

"You're not going like that are you? Don't you think you should change into your decent trousers?"

"I suppose so," he said, taking off his dirty, blue jeans.

Feeling apprehensive, we opened the door of the hall and walked inside. There were rows of wooden chairs laid out, most of them empty. We sat down a few rows from the front, feeling rather prominent. We were early. A white-haired man and a middle-aged woman were on the platform looking through some papers. The man looked up and said, "Good evening!"

"Good evening!" we replied.

"I don't think we have met before," he went on.

"No," I said, "we have only just moved to the area."

"Oh, I see. Do you live in Old Weston?" he queried.

Taking a deep breath I said, "No, Brington." I paused, "We live in a caravan outside the proposed missile base."

There was silence. The man on the stage shuffled his feet, glanced at the women beside him and then back at us. I smiled at him.

"I see," he said. That was all.

The room began to fill up. Several people nodded and smiled at us, as they sat down. I recognised one or two people whom I had seen in the village post office. The local policeman came in and sat down a row behind us. The chairman opened the meeting. There was a long agenda. The most important item was the Peace Camp. What could be done about the bunch of scruffy layabouts who had descended on their village? People all began speaking at once:

"These people are violent."

"They smell."

"They wear dirty clothes."

"How can we get rid of them?"

Voices were raised. Many women said they were frightened. What if one of these people broke into their homes at night? I noticed the couple on the platform looking at us. They were the only people in the room who knew where we were living. A question was directed to the local policeman.

"What can I do if one of them breaks into my house?"

"The law says that a householder may use reasonable force to prevent an intruder committing a crime," came a voice from behind.

Heads swivelled. The questioner went on, "Yes, but what is reasonable force?"

All eyes were on the policeman. "Well, let's say this, if I had a gun in the house, I would use it," came his reply.

Somebody laughed.

Later in the meeting questions were asked about how residents would be affected by construction traffic when building work started on the cruise missile base on their doorstep. I seem to recall there was a long discussion about drainage. One farmer was enthusiastic about the possibility of a new drainage system being paid for by the Ministry of Defence. When the meeting ended, we stood up to leave, feeling completely alone. It came as a welcome surprise, when a man who had been sitting near us, made a point of shaking hands with us.

★★★

We couldn't understand why there seemed to be so many reporters and television people around. We assumed it was because the Government had originally said that the fences would go up in February, though no one really thought that this was a possibility. One day I watched a bizarre scene from the window of the caravan. A television crew had arrived; this was our first encounter with the crew from Anglia Television. They walked across to where the convoy vans were parked and said that they wanted to film them. The camp dwellers refused and pointed across the fields to where other people were living in their tents and tepees. The reporters started off in that direction and then, after walking a short way, turned and started to film the convoy people. Predictably, they reacted violently, shouting abuse at the cameramen. I felt that this confrontation had been deliberately provoked. When the crew went back to their cars I went out and talked to them. I asked them why they had not filmed some of the other people living in the camp. They smiled at me and said that they had come specifically to film the Peace Convoy and had expected and wanted the sort of reaction they had received. I found this whole episode upsetting. There was no doubt in my mind that the media had 'set up' this particular group of people, in a deliberate attempt to 'create' the story they wanted.

On the morning of February 4th, a group of local residents, calling themselves RAMS (Residents Against the Molesworth Settlement), were to have their inaugural meeting. We understood that the landlady of a pub on the other side of the base and a retired major living in a neighbouring village were instrumental in forming the group. The night before the meeting was to take place, we heard that when it was over, a local television crew would be coming to film the Rainbow Villagers for national television. They hoped to capture angry reactions, just as they had a few days earlier. It was obvious they intended to focus attention on the peace convoy again. Ian and I thought it would be a good idea to talk to some of the convoy people and warn them what was likely to happen. The next morning when the crew arrived, all they found was a group of happy people in a carnival spirit, quite willing to give their opinions in a quiet, rational way. They left unable to obtain the sensational, confrontational response that they had been hoping for. That evening the local news showed interviews with the publican, Sid Rawle, Phil the Beard and myself. It did not make the national news.

The filming had a unifying effect on the group. The sun was shining and people joined together to try and level the entrance to Peace Lane. A mound of earth and rubble had been dumped there by the council years before, making it difficult for cars to drive over without their exhaust pipes striking the ground. I provided mugs of tea. The sky was blue and larks sang high above us. It all seemed quite hopeful.

Chapter Six

This is England!

I opened the door of the pub and walked into the saloon bar. It was empty. I stood by the counter for several minutes. A young man came through into the bar.

"I'm sorry, I didn't hear you come in," he said. "What would you like to drink?"

"A half of bitter please."

As I watched him pour it out I asked, "I wonder if it would be possible to speak to the landlady? I am right in thinking she is connected with the RAMS group, aren't I?"

"Oh, you want to see my mother, I'll get her for you. What name shall I say?"

I told him my name and I sat down at one of the small tables, sipping my drink. What on earth was I going to say? Would she throw me out? I waited for what seemed several minutes.

"I'm sorry, we are closed," came a sharp voice.

I stood up and looked at the woman coming towards me. She was well built and had dark, short straight hair. She looked flushed.

"Oh, you've been served." She seemed surprised.

"The door was open so I came in," I told her.

"I am very busy serving meals at the moment, I can't talk to you now," she said brusquely.

"That's quite all right, I don't mind waiting," I replied.

I sat for nearly twenty minutes until she returned.

"Now what can I do for you?" she said, sitting down at the table opposite me. I shook hands with her.

"I'm Jennifer Hartley. My husband and I have come to live in a caravan outside the base."

"I know who you are, Mrs. Hartley."

"I just wanted to introduce myself to you and explain why we have decided to come here. We don't want to cause you any trouble. We are Quakers and Anglicans, and feel deeply about the moral implications involved with building another nuclear missile base."

"We do not want you people living here," she retorted. "If you are against what is happening you have the opportunity of changing things by voting. We live in a democracy. You are breaking the law of the land. I have had to put a sign up on the outside of the pub saying that no one from the Peace Camp is allowed inside. We had some of your people in here once. They smelt terrible." Her tone softened. "I am not saying that you are like that."

"It was not a decision we made easily," I told her. "We prayed about it a great deal before deciding to come."

"Some of my best friends are Quakers," she told me. "What I suggest you do, Mrs Hartley, is go back home and stand for your local council. You are more likely to change things that way. We don't want you here, do you understand?"

"Well, I am sorry that we cannot agree, but I am very grateful to you for giving up your time to talk to me," I said, getting up to go. "No doubt we'll meet again. Goodbye."

The night before that meeting, I had gone with Brig Oubridge to Ipswich. He had been asked to speak to our own CND group. It was the first time I had been back there for a fortnight, though it seemed more like two months! I can remember sitting at the front of the meeting and hearing Brig say, "We don't know when they will move in to erect the fences. It could be tomorrow."

Little did we know! I was not worried; there had never been any doubt in my naive way that somehow the 'Peace Movement' would be able to prevent or delay the fences going up. I was sure that it would take a long time. I believed that people in their thousands would race to Molesworth to try and stop it happening.

Tuesday February 5th, 1985 is a date we will never forget. I had not had much sleep, as it had been 2:30 in the morning before Brig and I had returned from Ipswich. We had arranged to pick up Sid on the way back, but he was in the middle of a long discussion and in no hurry to leave. It had been a warmer day; Ian was helping with some printing at Clopton and I joined him there after my lunchtime meeting at the pub. In the afternoon I typed more letters and talked to Aeddan. Aeddan Penna had arrived at Molesworth late one evening when we were in bed. We offered him a bed for the night. He was an interesting man in his middle twenties and we spent many hours discussing religious ideas with him. He often joined us in our short services in the mornings. That night Aeddan came to supper.

At about nine o'clock, Ian and I walked down the tree-lined road to the phone box to talk to our families. We liked to phone them every few days to reassure them that we were all right and that everything was going well. We both felt tired and were looking forward to an early night. We wandered back slowly. It was a lovely night and there was a full moon. Looking over the fields I noticed something strange.

"Did you see that?" I asked Ian.

"See what?" he said.

"I thought I saw a searchlight right over there," I said, pointing to the far side of the fields. We both stopped and looked, but we didn't anything.

"Perhaps it was a car headlight," Ian said.

When we got back to the camp we wandered over to where we could get a clearer view of the two hangars in the middle of the base. They were surrounded by lights, but I thought there seemed to be more than usual. Ian could see no difference, but he agreed to drive over and see what Tim thought.

Tim opened the door and said, "It's really strange you two should come over, we've had phone calls from different parts of the country saying a large convoy of vehicles is heading this way."

He did not seem unduly worried. There had been several false alarms over the previous few months, but to be on the safe side, we decided to drive on to the middle of the base and have a look around. Bridie stayed by the telephone and we drove off. Tim thought it all looked the same as usual, but as we were driving back a solitary MOD policeman stopped us. Ian wound down the car window.

"What are you doing?" the policeman asked.

I leant over and replied, "We thought that something interesting might be happening."

"Chance would be a fine thing," he said.

We have often wondered whether he was an excellent actor or if he, too, was unaware of what was about to happen.

We drove around to talk to the people at the Peace Camp in Faye Way, asking them to keep a look out for anything unusual. Then we went back to the School House. Bridie was waiting for us. She had just received a call telling her that a convoy of lorries was at Alconbury Weston, only a few miles away. Ian and I realised we had to alert Rainbow Village, so we raced off. Arriving back in Peace Lane, we ran over to the first van we saw and asked the people inside to spread the news that something was about to happen. As we had arranged with Tim and Bridie, we drove back towards the School House. When we approached the junction to Alconbury we met a huge convoy of army lorries, full of soldiers. Somehow Ian managed to accelerate and overtake them. I could feel my heart beating as we passed the leading vehicle. We drove half way down Cockbrook Lane, which was the road they would have to take to get on the base. We knew we had to try and stop it.

What happened immediately afterwards we have already described. After we had tried to block the road and the convoy had continued on its relentless way, we drove back to see what had happened to Tim. He had intended to drive his tractor across the lane, too, but he was still trying to get the tractor to start.

"It's too late, Tim, they are already down the lane, it was impossible to stop it."

Suddenly I remembered Robbie back in Halcyon Spirit.

"Look, we must get back to the other side. Goodness knows what's happening there, we'll see you later."

We jumped back into the car and rushed back, only to be stopped halfway by the police and told to pull off the road.

"We live in a caravan at the base and our dog's there alone. He'll be so frightened. Can we go on?" I asked them.

"You're not going anywhere," came the reply from one of the policemen.

I was nearly in tears, I pleaded with him.

"Will you let me get out of the car and walk to the caravan and bring the dog back here with me?" They flatly refused.

It seemed quite unreasonable. The policemen turned away and started to put red and white traffic cones across the road. Without any warning, Ian put his foot down on the accelerator and before they could stop us, we drove on through the cordon. We had never done anything like it before in our lives, but then the whole situation seemed unreal.

Ian stopped short of the lane where our caravan was parked, as all we could see in front of us was a fleet of white police vans. I got out. All around me were row upon row of policemen, hundreds of them. Keeping my head down, I wove my way in between the blue uniformed figures, trying to reach our front door. It took me a long time to open it my hand was shaking so much. Robbie was delighted to see me. Ian joined me a few minutes later having left the car out on the road. Minutes later there was a loud knock on the door. A policeman stood outside.

"Yes?" I said.

"I have been asked to inform you that you have one hour to leave this site. If you fail to do so you will be removed by six tomorrow morning."

He turned and walked away. I looked at Ian. "What are we going to do? Surely they have to have an eviction order. Anyway we can't move without a low-loader and where would we go? We can't go home."

"I don't know. Let's just wait and see what happens."

Outside there was great activity. Huge earth-moving machines were being driven on to the fields. Arc lights were set up on tall gantries, one right next to our caravan. As each one came on, their cold, white light revealed the scale of the operation. Peace Lane was a solid block of police standing shoulder to shoulder in rows. Their faces were like masks, showing no emotion. From a distance, all that could be seen were the reflective stripes on the back of their jackets. Diesel-driven generators clattered into life. A rhythmic clanging came from the sound of fence posts being hammered into the earth. Dumper trucks were ferrying enormous rolls of barbed wire. The noise of their revving engines, and the strange warning sound they made as they reversed, all contributed to a deafening cacophony. Although we were horrified by the scenes we were witnessing, we knew we must keep strong.

"Let's sing," I said to Ian.

We got out some song sheets that we had used at a Christian CND service and stood on the caravan steps.

"Bind us together, Lord," our voices rang out. The policemen turned and watched us. Some laughed.

Later we walked up Peace Lane. There was a lot of confusion.

"What's happening?" I asked a woman from Rainbow Village.

"They're going to trash us," she said.

Most of Rainbow Village was on Ministry of Defence land and it was clear that the military authorities were going to move them off. Towing vehicles belonging to civilian contractors had moved on to the site, ready to tow away the buses and coaches that wouldn't move under their own steam: buses, vans and coaches that were people's homes. We walked around to where Brig, Sid and Jules lived. Ian had his camera ready with a black and white film in it, which had been given to us by our local newspaper. Bruce Garrard was sitting in Sid's bender eating a bowl of stir-fried vegetables. Ian took his photograph.

It was harrowing watching people packing up their belongings and dismantling benders and tepees. The children shivered, bewildered and frightened. They huddled together, not knowing what was going to happen to them. For some, the unreasonable request to leave within one hour was impossible. Not everyone had their own transport. Others wanted to stay, prepared to be arrested if necessary. People moved about quietly offering each other help. One or two people set fire to their benders rather than leave them standing. The large communal kitchen was set on fire for the same reason. We walked back up the lane and pushed our way through the lines of police to get to the chapel.

"Oh no, look what they're doing to the garden!" I cried.

Soldiers in heavy, black boots were trampling over the beds where the spring bulbs were coming up. A bulldozer was uprooting the trees and I watched in disbelief as a young soldier reached up for a branch and simply tore it down. Rolls of barbed wire were being stretched around posts that encircled the half-finished Eirene, preventing us from getting close to it. Bridie and Tim had managed to walk across the fields and the four of us stood together in silence holding lighted candles. In the caravan I had a beautiful white cyclamen. I took it outside and placed it on the ground, near the fenced-in chapel. An MOD policeman called to me, "I wouldn't leave that there if I were you. It will get trodden on."

"I'll risk it," I told him. "It's a sign of life amongst all this destruction."

Minutes later, another policeman who had heard the conversation beckoned to me. "Shall I put your plant inside the chapel?" he asked.

"Oh, yes please, thank you very much."

It was obvious that even some of the police involved were shocked at the nature and scale of the operation going on around them. One young policeman was fighting back tears. Another, in an aside that I was obviously meant to hear, said, "With the overtime I make tonight I shall be able to have a holiday in Tenerife."

Opposite the caravan, work had begun on constructing the main gate. They were using welding equipment and blue and orange sparks were flying in all directions, creating much noise and activity. The contractors had started to tow off some of the caravans and buses, the homes of Rainbow Village people. Standing by the door of the caravan, we watched as towing vehicles rammed into the back of some of the vans, crushing and denting them. The look on the faces of those driving was full of hatred. How long would it be before we received the same treatment? I was angry. The police standing by were taking no notice.

"Can't you see what they're doing?" I cried out. "This is England! Have you forgotten? Are you just going to stand there and do nothing?"

I was wasting my time; nobody took any notice of me. I went back inside the caravan and wept. And so the night was filled with talking, singing, praying and crying. We felt both strong and helpless at the same time. Where were the press? Why hadn't someone filmed the soldier hacking down the small trees and pulling off the branches with his bare hands? The fields where the winter wheat was growing had become a sea of mud, the wheat beaten into the earth by gigantic wheels. The whole place was being transformed before our eyes.

We went back inside the caravan and put on the kettle. Two or three people had walked over from the Faye Way camp and we asked them in.

"Is anyone hungry?" I asked. "Could any of you eat cheese on toast?"

"Mmm! Yes please."

I started cutting bread and toasting it. I found myself thinking, 'what am I doing making cheese on toast at four in the morning?' I wasn't hungry, I couldn't have eaten anything, but Ian and the others were wolfing it down as fast as I brought it in.

Friends started arriving, despite the road blocks. Bridie and Brig had initiated the telephone tree. The news began to percolate throughout the network of peace groups, telephone calls woke people up as far away as Wales and individuals started to make their way to Molesworth. Alan, who lived near Ely, had come with two other friends. They had parked their VW van about three miles away and, skirting police check points, had made their way to Peace Corner. Alan was a keen photographer and was soon taking pictures of everything. He kept saying, "I don't believe this", over and over again. Roger Spiller, the secretary of East Anglian CND, emerged from the gloom and started asking us what had been going on. Ian had almost finished shooting the roll of black and white film and we were keen to be rid of it, so we asked Roger if he could drop it off at the Bury office of the paper. We were frightened that the police might confiscate it. It was imperative that the film got back to the newspaper, so that they could publish pictures of the scenes we had witnessed.

As night turned to day, newspaper men and TV crews began to arrive. They told us that they, too, had been prevented from getting anywhere near the area, though one reporter had managed to hide in the ditch behind our caravan. The press told us that the Ministry in Whitehall had issued a statement to the media around midnight. It simply stated that the peace camp had been evicted and that a barbed-wire fence had been erected around the perimeter of the Molesworth site. It seemed a little premature. It was almost light and the fence was still going up. Only a few people had actually left. The TV crews were able to interview the Rainbow Villagers and cameras filmed as a group of them left, one leading George the horse, with a goat quietly following along behind. This poignant sight was shown on *Breakfast TV*. The TV crew also filmed the small group keeping a vigil near Eirene. We had been joined by Justin Kenrick and Nick Mills, nicknamed 'Twoboots', who had driven from Machynlleth, near the west coast of Wales. We watched from the steps of the caravan, reluctant to leave it, as they stood in a circle with their arms around each other, singing one song after another.

It grew light; the deadline of six had come and gone and we were still here. We were in a state of great confusion. Were we going to be moved or not? We looked out of the window at the row of local Cambridgeshire policemen who were preventing access to the lane. It was clear that they were more relaxed now, they were chatting to one another. From time to time, one would point and laugh as one of the tow trucks roared past pulling a decrepit old caravan that seemed about to be shaken apart.

"That could be us next," I said to Ian. "I just wish I knew what's going to happen."

"I don't think they can move us without an eviction order. The people they're moving were actually on MOD land. The lane belongs to Cambridgeshire County Council."

We had not realised when we first arrived that we were not parked on Ministry land. It was some days later before we heard that Peace Lane was in fact an old lay-by. Despite Ian's reminder, neither of us was really convinced that we would not be moved.

"Look, I'll go and ask one of those blokes out there if they know. I've been watching and one of them looks quite a decent sort. I've just heard him telling the chap next to him that Quakers are all right!"

Ian made his way outside and went up to the policeman. "Do you know whether we are going to be moved? We can't move the van ourselves; it came on a low-loader. Only I'm worried about the way those contractors are driving, they'll smash the van up."

The man smiled and said, "If you want to know anything you'll have to have a word with my boss. Ask for Superintendent Dean."

Ian thanked him and moved off in search of the senior officer. A few minutes later he was back in the caravan. He looked at me and said,

"I found the Superintendent and he says," Ian stressed the word 'says', "He says that he has no orders to move us."

"Do you believe him?"

"I don't know, but that's what he said."

About eleven or twelve o'clock there was a sudden flurry of activity near the newly-erected main gate. Dozens of reporters and cameramen were running to the spot. I heard someone say, "It's Michael Heseltine!"

"Come on," I shouted to Ian, "let's go and speak to him."

We rushed up to join the throng of media people. There were several plain-clothes police looking anxiously about and as we approached, one said, "That's far enough." He pushed us away from the barrage of reporters. Michael Heseltine had arrived by helicopter and we watched him stride through the gate. He was, of course, wearing the famous flak jacket, and though we have heard various stories about why he was wearing it we still have no idea which is true. We were surprised to see that he had pan stick make-up on his face in an orangey colour, presumably for the television cameras. It didn't go with the flak jacket somehow. We got as near as we could and heard him saying how well he thought the operation had gone and how pleased he was about it.

When he had finished speaking, I called out to him, "Will you have a word with two Quakers?"

He turned on his heel and walked back to the waiting helicopter, followed by his entourage. From that day onward, until the day he resigned, we tried to speak to him, but always in vain.

As the morning wore on Ian checked again with Superintendent Dean and got the same response. Later, I decided I wanted to hear for myself. I searched out the officer. He had a pleasant face with kind eyes. He looked down at me and gave a rueful grin, "As I've told your husband, Mrs Hartley, we have no orders to move you."

I was surprised to hear myself say, "Will you shake hands on that?"

"Certainly," he said, offering his hand.

I shook hands and thanked him and went back to the caravan, still feeling uncertain.

More supporters turned up, including a group of our friends from Ipswich. Reporters came in to take notes and a man from a local radio station was trying to tape an interview. Sid and Jules came in to collect Ra. We had looked after him while they finished their packing. Sid had spent much of the day trying to persuade the police to allow him to move into Peace Lane, but to no avail. Now they were going. We hugged each other. Outside, we said goodbye to Phil the Beard and his friends. There were more hugs. It was hard for any of us to understand why they were leaving while we were allowed to remain. It made us feel uncomfortable. By late afternoon everyone seemed to have gone except us. A few caravans remained in Peace Lane, but these were empty, their owners having left when the army moved in.

At six in the evening we felt brave enough to leave the caravan to take Robbie for a walk. We stepped out through the solid block of policemen to be greeted by Superintendent Dean who said, "You didn't believe me when I said you weren't being moved did you? I hope you haven't been too much inconvenienced. If there is anything you need there are plenty of officers about to help." The ranks parted and Ian, Robbie and I went off down the road.

"I don't believe this. What the hell's going on?" Ian said.

"My head's just going round in circles," I replied.

We looked at each other and laughed nervously, it was all so bizarre. I didn't know whether to laugh or cry, recollecting that it was less than 24 hours since we had been walking back from the phone box. All the Rainbow Villagers had gone. We were on our own now; our only neighbours were the police.

Chapter Seven
We Still Have Fields to Sow

The next few days merged into one. We started to hold short services by the fence near the chapel. Our commitment to Eirene grew. We felt it was important to demonstrate our desire to see it made available as a place of worship and we asked to hold a service in it twice a day at eleven and four. We asked the Ministry of Defence police on duty at the main gate for permission to go inside. Every day they refused and instead we stood outside looking in through the barbed wire.

There were lots of visitors. Once word had spread, people came from all over the country to protest and lend support. A constant stream of reporters wanted interviews, all asked the same questions: "Why were you left...? What are your plans?" In my diary I wrote: *'THIS IS AN INCREDIBLE SITUATION; THE POLICE ARE ONLY LETTING OUR VISITORS IN TWO AT A TIME. It's snowing outside. The police are wet, cold and dejected. Army vehicles and huge trucks etc. are going in and out all the time.'*

To express our feelings about the military-style operation, we made a large poster and pinned it to a wooden board. On it we wrote in large letters: *'A SMALL GROUP OF PEOPLE HAD A VISION OF TRANSFORMING THIS INTO A PLACE OF POSITIVE HOPE AND USEFULNESS FOR HUMANITY. IN THE SPACE OF 24 HOURS THE GOVERNMENT HAS USED THE FULL FORCE OF THE MILITARY AND POLICE TO DESTROY THAT VISION AND MAKE IT INTO A PLACE OF EVIL, A SYMBOL OF DEATH AND DESTRUCTION, WHOSE ONLY PURPOSE IS TO THREATEN THE SURVIVAL OF THE PLANET.'*

Underneath I stuck two colour photos: one of the chapel with flowers and trees, the other showing hundreds of people sowing wheat on the fields. We placed it against the barbed wire fence where it remained for several weeks until one night it mysteriously disappeared.

Finding time to eat was almost impossible with so much going on. We were so tired, but somehow the adrenalin kept us going. One night we had to put a note on the door at about nine o'clock to say we had gone to bed. We just couldn't take any more that day. Sleeping was not easy. Work continued most of the night, bright lights shone straight into the caravan and the droning beat of the generator drummed inside our heads. We still felt very vulnerable, expecting that at any moment we would be ordered to leave. Nick Mills, who had spent some time living at Rainbow Village, was a great support. He moved in with us for a few days. This ensured that if one of us had to go out to get supplies, two of us were always in the caravan, just in case they decided to evict us. Nick is a gentle person with a soft voice and smiling eyes. In times of stress he would pick up oranges and apples and start to juggle with them. We found his presence very calming. We also valued the deepening friendship with Tim and Bridie. Their home, the School House, overflowed with people day and night. Walking across the fields one day as they had always done, to join us for a service, they were arrested. The police kept them sitting in a van out in the bitter cold for five and half hours before they were released, without being charged.

One or two people had started to keep a vigil in the Peace Gardens. I took mugs of tea out to them, offering it also to the MOD police standing by the gate. Only one policeman accepted. The weather had deteriorated. I joined a group from Bradford; we sang and sang in the blinding snow and the biting wind. Tony, a striking miner from Durham, stayed out in the gardens all night. In the morning he told us that a policeman had come over to the campfire and shared his sandwiches and apples with him. We were all in the same boat now. Police stood huddled around braziers, collecting firewood from whatever source they could. Some days, when our gas bottles froze, the police let us boil our kettle on their brazier. Two MOD policewomen went to hospital, suffering from hypothermia.

On the grapevine, we heard that Glenys Kinnock, wife of the Labour Party leader, Neil Kinnock, and Joan Ruddock, CND chairperson, were coming to visit Molesworth. On the Saturday of their intended visit car loads of press people began arriving. They hovered around, clapping their hands and stamping their feet, trying to keep warm. We went outside at eleven for our vigil. The press followed us. ITV filmed us. We couldn't move without a camera being pointed at us. They even brought the cameras inside the caravan and filmed us sitting on the settee, with Robbie lying on the floor beside us, making us feel very foolish. Briefly we came to know what it must be like for those constantly in the public eye and we didn't like it!

When Glenys and Joan arrived, a female TV journalist rushed in saying, "Jennifer, they're here! Look out of the window, will you? We want to film your reaction."

"No! I'd rather not, if you don't mind."

"Oh, come on, it will make a good picture," she said trying to persuade me.

"I'm sorry but I don't really agree with it." I suppose it would have made a good picture but it felt contrived. I don't like playing media games.

Glenys and Joan came inside the caravan. They looked a bit like twins. They both wore a black coat and boots; one wore a red scarf, the other purple. They wanted to know how we had coped on the night of the eviction and listened as we gave them a full account. It was hard to concentrate, though, as cameras were pressed up against the windows. I drew the curtains; it was a private conversation. We had tea out of mugs, and I was conscious of people coming in and out of the caravan all the time they were there, wanting to speak to them. I gave Glenys a letter to take back to Neil Kinnock, and asked them both if they would sign our petition to Cambridgeshire County Council and our visitors' book. They left wishing us good luck in the days ahead.

Phil the Beard and Mick from the convoy came back to see us. Mick copied down the words of the *Desiderata* from a poster on the wall.

'Go placidly amid the noise and the haste and remember what peace there may be in silence. As far as possible without surrender be on good terms with all persons. Speak your truth quietly and clearly, and listen to others, even the dull and ignorant; they too have their story. Avoid loud and aggressive persons, they are vexatious to the spirit. If you compare yourself to others you may become vain and bitter, for always there will be greater and lesser persons than yourself.

'Enjoy your achievements as well as your plans. Keep interested in your career however humble: it is a real possession in the changing fortunes of time. Exercise

caution in your business affairs, for the world is full of trickery. But let this not blind you to what virtue there is; many persons strive for high ideals, and everywhere life is full of heroism. Be yourself, especially do not feign affection. Neither be cynical about love; for in the face of all aridity and disenchantment it is as perennial as the grass. Take kindly to the counsel of the years gracefully surrendering the things of youth.

'*Nurture the strength of spirit to shield you in sudden misfortune. But do not distress yourself with imaginings. Many fears are born of fatigue and loneliness. Beyond a wholesome discipline, be gentle with yourself. You are a child of the universe, no less than the trees and the stars: you have a right to be here. And whether or not it is clear to you, no doubt the universe is unfolding as it should.*

'*Therefore be at peace with God, whatever you conceive him to be; and whatever your labours and aspirations, in the noisy confusion of life, keep peace with your soul. With all its shams, drudgery and broken dreams, it is still a beautiful world. Be cheerful. Strive to be happy.*

'Max Ehrmann.'

Rainbow Village had been moved on from one place to another and were now at Grafham Water on a car park owned by the Water Board. We decided to brave the weather and go and visit them. The roads were very slippery. Everyone seemed pleased to see us and offered us tea and exchanged news. There was a large police presence around their encampment and many feared that the police might find an excuse to move in and break up the group. We drove back, a hair-raising few miles, sliding from one side of the road to the other. Nick had been dog- and caravan-sitting and some friends had joined him and were having hot drinks. I sometimes wonder how many cups of tea and coffee were consumed during our time at Molesworth.

The next day, Sunday, Christian CND was holding a service in the afternoon and Bruce Kent was coming. All morning people began to arrive and soon the police started to get worried. Groups of people standing in the Peace Gardens were asked to move off and over to the other side of the road. They refused and were dragged there. No one had worried on the previous days. Police would not allow anyone to visit our caravan. We could come and go freely, but were also prohibited from entering the gardens near the chapel. Friends from Ipswich arrived, holding aloft our Ipswich Christian CND banner. Metropolitan police lined the road and the entrance. It was freezing cold. Our friend Mabel Baker, a tireless peace campaigner with whom I had once camped at Greenham, came and sat in the caravan. She was allowed through the blockade as she had an arthritic hip, which made it difficult for her to stand for long periods.

When the time came for the service to begin Ian, Mabel and I walked out together. As we neared the gardens, Ian and I walked over to the fence by the chapel, where we always held our vigils. We knelt down on the frozen snow and I read from the *Sermon on the Mount*. An MOD policeman standing inside the barbed wire came over and said, "Please stand up; you'll get frostbite kneeling down there."

Another policeman walked over and handed me a bunch of daffodils. "A woman asked me to give you these," he said.

Ian was reading a prayer out loud as Chief Superintendent Colin Street, who was supervising, came and asked us to get up.

"But we always vigil by the chapel," Ian told him. "Why is today different?"

"Come on now Ian, you know we had an agreement that no-one was allowed on the gardens, be a good chap and get up, otherwise I shall have to have you removed."

We began to sing *Make Me A Channel Of Your Peace*.

"Take these two back to their caravan, will you?" we heard the Chief Superintendent say. "But do it gently."

Clutching my daffodils and with my eyes shut, I continued to sing as we were both dragged back to the caravan. It felt entirely the right thing to do at that time, though in the months to come we were to question our feelings about that kind of civil disobedience. Inside the caravan we collected our thoughts, put on dry clothes, then went outside again to talk to some of our friends on the other side of the police barrier. Several hundred people had gathered, it was an encouraging sight considering the weather was so bitterly cold. Amongst the crowd we noticed Ian's cousin, Paul. We asked if he could come into the caravan but he was not permitted to. Bruce Kent was finally allowed through the cordon after we spoke to one of the senior officers on duty. I even had difficulty in returning to the van myself, as I had changed my coat. The police insisted that, "the woman in the caravan has got a RED coat on." I eventually persuaded them that I was one and the same person, but I had changed my coat when the one I had been wearing got wet.

The next day, my diary entry gives some idea of how busy the days were: *'Woke eight am, everything frozen. Water in flower vase, Robbie's bowl and washing-up bowl all solid. Thick frost on the insides of the windows. Nick took the kettle to the police brazier to heat.*

'George, a local man who has horses on the adjoining field, called to see us to say that he had heard that the MOD wanted to buy his land. He was also upset as a great deal of wood had been taken from his field and he suspected that it had gone on the police fires. We also had visits from John Kiddy, an Anglia television reporter, Tony Scase from BBC Look East, *and a reporter from Reuters in London. Friends from Rainbow Village came and joined in a silent vigil. We received a fruit cake through the post from friends in Ipswich and we shared it with other peace people and the police.*

'The afternoon service was good and several people joined in, including Tim and Bridie and the Bishop of Huntingdon. I wrote lots of letters today, to the base commander, press officer on the base, Cambridgeshire County Council, The Times *and the Guardian newspapers. By evening we were feeling 'all in' and decided what we needed was a bath! John Kiddy had said that we were welcome at his house whenever we liked so we went to the phone box and rang to see if it was convenient. Wonderful, it was! We were made very welcome and watched all the news coverage of the last few days on their video. Very interesting. We seemed to appear several times, can't remember all the interviews as I was in a daze most of the time. A BEAUTIFUL HOT BATH AND HAIRWASH; it was like a miracle. Another very cold night, many degrees below freezing. I pity the poor people outside all night. Have got a paraffin lamp and two Tilley lamps now so have plenty of light. I have got on my longjohns, plus a tee-shirt under my nightie and it's still cold. Bed 12:30pm.'*

The talk with George was interesting. It was the first time that we heard of the MOD's interest in the field behind our caravan. George lived in Brington. He was one of the few people in the village who had been on friendly terms with those camping at Molesworth. As a result, he said he was cold-shouldered by the Brington folk. He was upset by this treatment and anxious about the sale of his field. It appeared that the field was leased to another farmer who was the official tenant. George tried to explain to us that he had done a swap for another piece of land over twenty years previously. This was only the beginning of this story, the ramifications of which were to persist throughout our stay.

★★★

News reached us that Jules and Sid's baby had been born. Jules had hoped to have the baby delivered at Rainbow Village. She had been to the local maternity hospital, Hinchingbrooke, for a check-up and everything seemed to be going well. The baby was due in early February. Many of us had been worried about her on the night of the eviction, but she coped with the sudden need to pull down the beautiful tent and bender and packed up all her possessions with great calm. She had been living in the car park at Grafham Water with Sid and Ra when she went into labour. We visited her the following day and heard about the birth. She and a small group of friends had driven to Hinchingbrooke the night before. She had explained to the staff that she wanted to have a natural birth and the hospital authorities had been co-operative. She was allowed to have her friends with her in a small labour room. They had burnt incense and talked together as her contractions had become more frequent. In the end, she had given birth in a squatting position, under subdued lighting. She had wanted to leave right away but the staff insisted she stayed for a few hours rest. But as soon as possible, Jules was back in the van that was her temporary home. It was here that she excitedly told us the story of Phoebe's birth. Her son, Ra had been named after the Egyptian god of the sun and Phoebe took her name from the moon goddess.

Our days took on a sort of pattern. We talked to all the visitors who came daily, wrote letters, held the twice-daily vigils, shopped, collected water and had conversations with the police standing around outside. Constant rumours circulated that the chapel was going to be pulled down, so we kept a camera at the ready. Because of this threat we slept very lightly and often leapt out of bed to the window, when we heard a machine engine start up. The caravan always seemed to be full of people the first few weeks after the erection of the fence. I coped really well to begin with, but after a while I found it a bit of a strain. My diary entry on February 13th says: *'Had a long think while out walking with Robbie, decided that if I am to be able to carry on here, we are going to have to have more space, or at least a gap to recharge our batteries. Otherwise I feel my energy flow may stop. I still feel fine about staying here and love being in Halcyon Spirit." I told Ian how I felt when I got back and he agreed with me. We had a nice meal with Nick and afterwards he wrote a letter to the local vicar Rev. George North. Nick is going to his grandmother's funeral tomorrow so we will be "on our own". He has been such a support during this uncertain period. He is a lovely person.'*

Tim and Bridie asked us if we would like to go with them, one Sunday evening to the Friends' School in Saffron Walden. They had been asked to speak to the students about Molesworth, the arrangement having been made before the fence went up. Ian's two sons were both at the Friends' School, so it was a good opportunity to see them. Justin offered to take care of Robbie while we were away. It was only eleven days since that awful night and we both were apprehensive about leaving the caravan.

"You're sure you'll be okay, Justin? Help yourself to anything you want, we'll see you later."

Justin smiled and said, "Robbie and I will manage, won't we Robbie?"

Robbie looked up at us, quizzically, thinking someone might be offering him a biscuit. We laughed and walked off to Tim and Bridie's car. As we sped along the dual carriageway towards Cambridge, it felt strange to think that this was the first time we had left Halcyon Spirit. It seemed so difficult, yet now we were doing it. Our thoughts turned to our destination. Ian's sons, Tom and Ollie, were boarders at the Quaker school. We had visited them a few times while they were there and it seemed a friendly place. On Sunday evenings the whole school assembled for meeting, where visiting speakers often addressed them. When we arrived, we unloaded the display boards and made our way to the main hall. The headmaster, John Woods and his deputy, Christine Weston, met us and spoke to Tim, about the theme of his talk.

John Woods explained, "The school will come in and sit in silence for a few minutes, then I will introduce you. After that, you can speak when you feel ready."

The boys and girls were beginning to file in. We noticed Tom and Ollie and they came over to us. They both seemed taller. As they approached they were grinning broadly. Tom said, "You won't speak for too long, will you?"

"We're not speaking, we've just come along for the ride," Ian replied.

Tim said, "Don't worry I wasn't planning to speak for long."

"Good," said Tom. "It's just that when it's over, everyone can relax for the rest of Sunday night. And besides, there's not much sympathy for the Peace Movement. We had a theatre group doing an anti-war show and some of the sixth form were furious. They insisted that to be fair, the school should invite the army in!"

"That seems a funny way of going on for a Quaker school," I said.

Ian joined in with, "I suppose everyone has to rebel, and if the school stands for pacifism, the kids are going to be in favour of war."

"That's it," said Tom. "There are some real fascists in the second year sixth and they set the tone."

Tom was seventeen and in the first year of the sixth form. Later that year he was to become head boy.

Although the school is run by the Religious Society of Friends, to give Quakers their proper title, the majority of pupils are not from Quaker homes. Most of them are boarders, their parents having selected the school because of its good reputation for a liberal education. The head and some of the staff are Friends, but in most respects, the school is quite conventional. Some of the traditional stances of Quakers are reflected in the school, but these attitudes are not thrust upon the pupils.

The Society of Friends came into existence in the seventeenth century at the time of Oliver Cromwell and the Civil War. At the time there was a ferment of religious dissent. All the old ways were being questioned. One group that was quite influential amongst the anti-monarchist army was known as Levellers. As their name suggests, they believed in a more egalitarian society, which aimed to abolish the great class differences. Another group was called the Ranters. Their understanding of religion was that provided they believed in God they could do what they liked. Today they might be called Hippies. Then there were the Anabaptists, who rejected both Roman Catholicism and the more liberal Protestantism current in England. They were most commonly called Puritans, because their strict moral code condemned dancing and singing, as well as drinking. Other people were simply looking for something different. They rejected what they saw as the hypocrisy of the established Church but were not sure what should replace it. They read their Bible avidly and became very familiar with it. Some of these people became known as Seekers. They would meet together in silent prayer, hoping that the Holy Spirit would speak to them.

It was this last group that was most attracted to the preaching of George Fox. Fox was a working-class man from Staffordshire, who had received a religious calling in his youth. Like many of his contemporaries he had gone from church to church, hoping to hear someone whose words found an echo in his own heart. Eventually he realised that none of these men was capable of answering his need and he describes in his journal how he had a sudden intuition that God was speaking directly to him through the Living Christ. Fox preached that everyone could know Christ directly for themselves. He also believed that there was, to use his phrase, 'that of God in everyone'. His teaching appealed to many who were searching, and so began the Religious Society of Friends. They met together in silence and as the silence deepened, one of those present might feel called to speak. Silence would resume until someone else felt he or she had something to say. They did not call these gatherings, services, preferring to describe them as 'meeting for worship'.

From the beginning Friends fell foul of the law; at first, because they spoke out against the established Church and later because of some of their other beliefs. One of the ideas they shared with the Levellers was that it was wrong to pay the usual deference to those in authority. It was customary for a man to remove his hat in the presence of his betters, but this the early Friends refused to do. They also refused the use of courtesy titles. Instead of saying 'sir', or 'mister', they addressed everyone simply by name.

Fox was asked to join the army, but he refused on the grounds that fighting with swords was inconsistent with his understanding of the teaching of Christ. He told the military authorities that he 'believed in one, Jesus Christ, who took away the occasion for all wars'. A few years later the monarchy was restored and there was great suspicion of all the dissenting religious groups. The new authorities saw them all as a breeding ground for revolution and were anxious to suppress them. Many Quakers were sent to prison. It was one of the judges who coined the nickname 'Quaker', after Fox had told him that he should "tremble at the word of the Lord". Members of this new sect were quite prepared to go to prison over a matter of conscience, but felt they had to make it clear to the King that they were utterly opposed to taking up arms against him. A document was drafted and presented to the King, setting out their beliefs and declaring their refusal to fight. This became known as the Peace Testimony and Quakers have continued to this day to take a pacifist position.

Declaration to Charles II, 1661.

'We utterly deny all outward wars and strife and fightings with outward weapons, for any end or under any pretence whatsoever. And this is our testimony to the whole world. The spirit of Christ, by which we are guided, is not changeable, so as once to command us from a thing as evil and again to move unto it; and we do certainly know, and so testify to the world, that the spirit of Christ, which leads us into all Truth, will never move us to fight and war against any man with outward weapons, neither for the kingdom of Christ, nor for the kingdoms of this world.'

That was why Tom's remarks surprised us. It was soon time for the meeting to begin. The Sunday night meeting was one of the few traditions in the school that showed its Quaker heritage. When all the students had taken their seats in the hall silence prevailed for a few minutes. Then Tim stood up to speak. He spoke about the Wheat Project, describing how the land at Molesworth, designated for a missile base, had been dug up; how the wheat had been sown and how a container full of wheat had been shipped to Eritrea. He explained why Eritrea had been chosen as a recipient for the grain: "Not only is it part of a drought-stricken region of Africa, but it is the centre of a long-running civil war," he told them. "As a result, people have not only died from starvation, but also, from the frequent bombing raids which have destroyed the villages and forced the people to live underground."

Tim went on to explain how the war is fuelled both by the Russians and by the Western powers.

"Vast sums of money have poured into Ethiopia, but it has not helped to feed people. It has all been military aid."

Tim kept his talk brief, finishing by telling the pupils that he hoped that a large consignment of grain would be sent to Eritrea from Molesworth at Easter. Peace groups throughout the country were being asked to contribute money or to bring bags of grain with them to the Easter demonstration. Although the fields could no longer grow wheat, the links between disarmament and development could still be made. Tim sat down. Several students came up to look at the display boards we had brought with us, showing photographs of the wheat planting and the journey of the container lorry to the displaced persons camp in

Eritrea. A pupil from the Young Farmers group suggested that land at the school could be used to grow crops for Eritrea.

Afterwards, we were invited to go to Christine Weston's study for coffee, where a few of the senior pupils, including Ollie, joined us. It was good to relax in the comfort of her warm flat for a short time and to listen to comments about the talk. Everyone was appreciative that Tim had kept his talk short and to the point. His emphasis on the links between the arms race and poverty in Africa had gone down well; it seemed to strike a chord. Throughout 1985, the groundswell of popular concern for the plight of those in Ethiopia grew, culminating in the amazing Geldof phenomenon.

***

If the Ministry was worried about public reaction to the destruction of Eirene, civil servants and politicians were unprepared for what followed. A deluge of letters rained down upon them when people realised that the chapel was still standing, albeit under arc lights, behind a triple coil of barbed wire and with police and dogs patrolling it 24 hours a day. In some strange way, the fence and the guards seemed to enhance the potency of its symbolic presence. These were visible, tangible reminders of the brute strength of the nuclear state, which was normally cloaked behind bland assurances and fixed smiles.

Many people wondered why the MOD did not destroy the chapel on the night of February 5th. The Government suffered an extremely bad press, and it is hard to see that it would have been any worse if in addition to hounding out the Rainbow Villagers with their assorted goats, dogs and ponies, they had also demolished the half-finished Eirene. But they were obviously worried about its religious status. Rumour had it that they consulted the Archbishop of Canterbury. They wanted to know whether the chapel had been consecrated, as it would require the permission of the Church and de-consecration before it could be touched. It was not and it could not have been, as the Church must be the owner of land on which an edifice stands before it can be consecrated. However a bishop of the Established Church had blessed the building and therefore some caution was required on the part of Government. It was a sensitive issue. The Church of England was no longer the Conservative Party at prayer. The Bishop of Durham had made no bones about his opposition to the Government's handling of the miners' strike and Robert Runcie, the Archbishop, had offended the

Right by refusing to allow the Falklands Thanksgiving Service to be used as an excuse for gung-ho patriotism.

It took the machinery of state some time to decide how to respond to the letters and petitions. Stony silence prevailed for some six to eight weeks before the carefully crafted and word-processed replies began to trickle out of Whitehall. Our first letter to the Secretary of State, Michael Heseltine, was dated February 11th and the first reply we received from Whitehall was dated May 16th. In fact we received two almost identical replies on consecutive days. Prior to that two Labour MPs, our home constituency member Ken Weetch, and Tony Benn had both forwarded copies of a letter from Lord Trefgarne in response to their enquiries on our behalf. This is the approved method of obtaining information from Government, but Lord Trefgarne, who was Parliamentary Under Secretary for the Armed Forces, was unable to couch a reply until April 23rd. The letters we received from civil servants in May and Trefgarne's letter to the MPs use identical wording. The text of the letter sent direct to us read:

'Thank you for your letter of February 11th 1985. I have been asked to reply.

'The Secretary of State for Defence made a full statement about the recent operation at RAF Molesworth on February 6th. I attach a copy of the Hansard extract for information.

'You raise the question of the building at RAF Molesworth known to some as the 'Peace Chapel'. This building has not been consecrated and was constructed on Ministry of Defence land without the Department's permission or planning consent. We suspect that a number of those involved in the construction of this unauthorised structure were concerned more with its political than its religious use, but also accept that genuine Christians may have been misled into participating in these activities and that many others would be concerned if the building were to be demolished without careful consideration being given to its status. Demolition has been deferred, therefore, while the necessary investigations and consultations take place. There should be no doubt, however, that the Ministry of Defence reserves the right to demolish any unauthorised structure on its land without prior consultation. Moreover, I am afraid that we are not prepared to allow access to the building in the meantime as there is an unacceptable risk that such a concession would be exploited by those whose aims are political rather than religious. There are of course a number of churches in the area who would no doubt welcome new worshippers.

'I hope that this explains the ministry's position.

'Yours sincerely...'

Several points puzzled and annoyed us. Mr Heseltine's speech as recorded by Hansard makes no mention of the Peace Chapel. As to the assertion that, 'a number of those involved in the construction... were concerned more with its political than religious use' and that 'genuine Christians were misled into participating'. Who were these politicos out to mislead Christians? Did the Ministry have evidence to substantiate its claims? Many people were worried at the attempt to create a distinction between religious and political aims. We resent the suggestion of politicians who say that religion should stay out of politics, for it is our religious conviction that calls us to political action.

The daily vigils became part of our life. We had no idea that they would continue, almost without interruption, all the time we were there and beyond. Neither had we worked out a conscious philosophical justification for making these twice-daily acts of worship. It was only later that we began to see them as belonging to the old and rich tradition of the Daily Office that is a central part of the monastic life. In a way that we would still find hard to define, it felt important to maintain these regular times of quiet reflection. It gave us the opportunity to recall why we had come to this desolate place, it renewed our faith and it seemed in itself to be a positive act, which exorcised the very real sense of the presence of evil. Sometimes it felt like the only positive thing we could do and it gave us a fuller understanding of the mysterious power of prayer. For the first time we began to understand the significance of the contemplative way of life. We could see the links between action and reflection and that action needed to be grounded in reflection.

The struggle we had to articulate what this meant to us is illustrated by two poems that Ian wrote.

THOUGHT DURING WORSHIP – MOLESWORTH FEBRUARY 1985

'Their wire can cut my hand but leaves my heart untouched
Their words can catch like razor wire in my consciousness
But the children's stumbling steps on the icy ground
Reaches deeper, plucking at my soul.

For all this, some quiet stream wells from deeper still
And offers consolation, healing and the hope of
New life uncoiling from the earth.
We are but tillers of this soil
Given a heavy task, to care and nurture
This frail globe, spinning in the dark.
We can destroy ourselves and with this much beside
Yet I hold a quiet certainty
Life will go on
Springing fresh from the dead land.'

POWER – MOLESWORTH FEBRUARY 1985

'These grasping machines drag, dredge
Their groans are grating, torturing
The stones.
Steel flanks, flaking yellow paint on
Cast surfaces. Gleaming hydraulic tubes
Jerking.
Lights that flash RED RED.
Cybernetic decisions
Seeming, so, so
Strong, lulling us with their iron mastery.
But our power lies elsewhere
In the fragile rose that grows through
Runway rubble.
From the dark numbness that came
With news of death
The death of a friend, a young mother
Snatched away
A road accident.
The wheat no longer green
That shed its seed
Lying discarded, dormant on the frozen
Mud.
The trampled red stain, the flower
That only yesterday glowed in the hedgerow.
A flickering candle flame
Pulsing, pulsing in the dark.
These kindle the heart

Stir the limbs shaken by black dreams
Bringing new strength
And always, always
The frail vulnerability of an open hand
Trusting, trusting
Ah! That's Love'

We were not the only ones to be strengthened by the vigils, other people obviously felt something, too. Large numbers of visitors came each day. We would explain about the vigil. It was for people of all faiths, indeed for all who loved life. Not all would come to stand by the fence, but most would. Punks and anarchists, families with young children, elderly women and ex-servicemen gathered together. Probably most were nominally Christian, but a few who professed no faith joined others who were Jews or Buddhists.

We explained to newcomers that we asked permission to hold the vigil in the chapel.

"Up until now," we would say, "the Ministry of Defence has always said no, but perhaps it will be different today."

Quietly, we walked over to the big, black gates. One of the policemen on duty would come forward, usually the sergeant, and ask us what we wanted. As they were on two-week tours of duty, they got used to the routine and knew us by name. After exchanging a few pleasantries, one of us would ask whether we might hold a short service in the chapel. Sometimes, a foreign visitor explained where he or she came from and made the request. The answer was always no. The policeman or policewoman would look apologetic and say that they were sorry, but they were afraid they had no orders to allow us access. A short conversation might follow. People often wanted to tell the police why they had come, why they thought they should be allowed into Eirene to pray for peace. Some asked the police why they had to obey their orders. Occasionally, these conversations might carry on for five or ten minutes, before we walked back to the Peace Gardens, to stand silently in a semicircle looking through the barbed wire at the half-built chapel and the fields beyond.

We would offer people the Eirene books and explain that they contained readings and songs that could be used, and that everyone should feel free to speak or sing as the spirit moved them. Sometimes it snowed; frequently it rained. The wind blew, the sun shone, birds sang.

The seasons moved through their cycle, winter gave way to spring, spring to summer. Numbers began to dwindle but the vigils went on, continuing to inspire all who came. The experience could be deeply affecting. It was not uncommon to find someone sobbing and being comforted by a friend. People spoke of their fears and their hopes and we sang the songs that reflected our beliefs:

> 'Though Eden's garden's passed away,
> We still have fields to sow
> With hands to love and hearts to see
> Our trees and children grow.
> Five thousand, thousand, thousand years
> From cell to cell, to cell,
> Life fills our earth, our seas, our heavens
> And shall it end in hell.
> When all these warheads turn to rust
> Until our days are done
> We'll hold our mother earth in trust
> For children yet to come.'

Sung to the tune of 'Amazing Grace', the sound of this song, wafted over the fence, day after day. Inside Eirene they were heard by the MOD police. Mostly, they kept a respectful silence, broken only by the sound of their two-way radio blurting out some new message. A few, of course, seemed to delight in talking and laughing loudly, even telling jokes. But the atmosphere affected even these men, so that after a few days, they too would fall silent as we gathered for prayer on the other side of the wire. It was not unusual for them to come over at the end of the vigil, or at the end of their fortnight on duty, to say that they had valued the experience.

After twenty or thirty minutes, we would all join hands for a moment or two and this marked the end. One day, someone standing at one end of the semicircle thrust a hand into the fence. The person at the other end did the same. Smiling at the policeman standing only a few yards away on the far side of the coiled barbed wire. The invitation was there: 'let us all join hands together'. It was never physically taken up, but the gesture was appreciated. From then on, whoever stood at the end of the line, would hold out a hand to the police on the other side.

Chapter Eight
The Real Thing

One evening, after a particularly hectic day, we had just collapsed to eat our tea when we heard the sound of heavy machinery outside. We looked out and saw a huge crane trundling along. 'This is it,' we thought, 'the chapel is going to be demolished.' We rushed outside and found the person organising operations. We were assured that our worries were unfounded and that all they intended doing was to put concrete blocks across the end of Peace Lane. This they proceeded to do, using the gigantic mobile crane to swing the concrete blocks into position. When they had finished Peace Lane was sealed off with our caravan inside. We wondered if we would be able to get the Mini out, but with some careful manoeuvring we just about managed it. News of all this activity travelled fast and soon Bridie and Tim arrived hot foot from the Old School, as they had heard that Eirene was about to go. The local television cameras also arrived as the rumour spread, then members of nearby peace groups. Finally, a newspaper reporter rang the MOD in London and was told: 'We have no plans to demolish the structure tonight'. We all breathed a sigh of relief once again.

There were also less serious occasions. During the eviction of Rainbow Village some of the pet cats belonging to families living there went missing. It was not surprising considering the noise, lights and chaos. We spotted one of the cats on several occasions. It belonged to Chris and Sheila Craig, who had lived in a coach on land that was now within the perimeter fence. Sheila had come back several days running to call Inkblob, but the poor animal was terrified. The MOD police had put down food for it, but when they had tried to catch it, it had run off. It was a great relief when Sheila arrived one evening firmly clasping

Inkblob. We put Robbie in the kitchen so that the big, black and white cat could have room to move around. I put down milk. Smiling at one another, we watched it lick the saucer dry, purring loudly all the time.

After the incident with the blocks, we were given a CB radio so that in an emergency we could contact Tim and Bridie. They already had the nickname 'Neat and Tidy', so it was an obvious choice for their call sign. Our 'handle' was 'Clean and Friendly'. We never really got the hang of CB; we would stand outside for ages saying, "This is 'Clean and Friendly' calling 'Neat and Tidy', are you receiving me, over?", but we seldom made contact! Frequently, police walking by would eye us suspiciously. Tim and Bridie were remarkable. Bridie took everything in her stride; she was unflappable. Even on the blackest days, she found something that made her laugh. Tim was very enthusiastic, with so much energy that he often worked on a new project till the early hours. He was constantly coming up with new ideas and put many of them into operation with great gusto. His infectious laugh and boundless optimism were a tonic. On the other hand, he would not suffer fools gladly. Tim composes, sings and plays the guitar and he wrote many of the songs we sang during the vigils.

During our stay at Molesworth we grew to love Tim and Bridie very much. I shall never forget one morning in March. I had driven around to fill up the water containers and afterwards joined others at the breakfast table in the Old School. As I got up to leave, Tim announced that he had something important to tell us. A huge grin lit up his face as he announced, "We are pregnant!"

A degree of normality returned. Every day the local milkman called to leave our milk. It always amused me, watching him drive his van down the lane, past all the police. I put my washed, empty bottles outside on the step. It was all very ordinary, providing you didn't look up. The postman also called. Just two days before the fence went up, Carpenter Jim from Rainbow Village had fixed a letter box to the caravan. We had been asked if all the post could come to us, to then pass on to Postman John to distribute. By the time the first post came through the shining metal letter box, we were the only people remaining. I felt rather guilty about that letter box.

The first letter we received in this fashion was a circular advertising, *'protective and decorative wall coating'*. It was delivered by hand, obviously by someone with a sense of humour. Most of the people who wrote to us addressed their letters to USAF Molesworth. One morning during the service, an RAF officer stopped in a car and beckoned to me. I left the group and walked over to him.

"Mrs. Hartley?" he asked.

"Yes, that's me."

He was holding a letter. "Could you tell your friends that this is 'RAF Molesworth' and not 'USAF Molesworth'?"

I looked puzzled. "Pardon?"

"This letter was delivered to the base by mistake. It's addressed to you, care of USAF Molesworth. This is a British base. It causes the Post Office confusion if letters are incorrectly addressed." He passed over the letter, saluted me and returned to his car.

Phil Young had now become our neighbour. He moved into an empty caravan at the end of Peace Lane. Phil had lived at the original Peace Camp, but when that was removed he went to Faye Way. He was a private person and kept himself to himself. Wearing a long dark overcoat, his hair hanging over the collar, his hunched figure would silently pass the window, wheeling a barrow full of firewood. A week after he moved in, the police broke into the caravan and threw him and his pots and pans out onto the lane. Undeterred, he moved back and was never bothered again.

We began to relax, but not for long. Towards the end of February, Ian was approached by a reporter from Hereward Radio. He broke the news that Cambridgeshire County Council were holding a meeting the following week, on February 26th, where they intended to discuss the closure of the lay-by on which the caravan was parked. Piecing together the information we had, it appeared that the Ministry of Defence, or, as it was less euphemistically known in the 1930s, the War Office, acquired the 650 acres of farm land between the villages of Molesworth, Old Weston and Brington by compulsory purchase. On the Eastern side, the B660 provided access to the airfield between Brington and Molesworth. In the Fifties a small section of that road was re-routed to smooth a particularly sharp bend leaving a stretch of disused road beside the perimeter of the base. As in other places, the council used this 'lay-by' as a convenient place to store granite chippings for road repairs. The original peace camp had dubbed this piece of road Peace Lane. It was where we lived.

A large field was split by the new road when it was re-routed and a small, triangular plot now lay between the two roads. This was the field where George kept his ponies. George had already told us that the Ministry was trying to purchase the field. And now we learned they had approached the County Council, as Highway Authority, to close Peace Lane. It was clear the intention was to deprive peacemakers of any site they could use for a permanent witness against the deployment of nuclear missiles at Molesworth.

There and then we decided that we must go to the Council meeting. The following afternoon we had a visit from the County Council solicitor who told us they had received all our petitions and that they would be discussing it at the meeting on Tuesday. We had sent in hundreds of pages of signatures asking the County Council to allow Halcyon Spirit to remain in Peace Lane. Around teatime on the Monday we noticed a huge crane once again. It proceeded to move the blocks that were across Peace Lane over to the sides of the lane. Laughing nervously, we watched as the crane swung a large concrete block dangerously near to the front of the caravan. It turned out that the Council had realised that, technically, the lane was supposed to be open, and in order to save embarrassing questions at the meeting, someone had sent instructions to make sure that the blocks and the huge earth mound at the far end were speedily removed. Later we watched in amazement as a JCB, working at breakneck speed in pitch darkness, moved tons of earth and rubble.

The 26th dawned and we set off for the council meeting in Cambridge. Nick came with us and we sat in the public gallery of the Shire Hall. A specially convened meeting of the Council's Transportation Committee was held at 09:30 in the morning prior to the main Council Meeting. This unusual step was taken in order to push through the closure of Peace Lane as soon as possible. It was the first time I had ever attended a County Council meeting. At that time, the Conservatives had a healthy majority on the Council and were working hand in glove with central Government.

As we took our seats we were given copies of a document, which was also circulated to the Transportation Committee meeting below us. It outlined the requirement to 'stop up' a disused length of highway.

Paragraph 2.2 stated:

'The Ministry of Defence have approached the Council to ask whether the Council would be willing to apply to the Magistrates' Court for an order stopping up the loop. The Ministry would be prepared to pay the Council's costs of making such an application and any consequential expenses.'

Paragraph 3 is also of interest as it sets out the 'History of the Loop', (the words in parenthesis are ours):

'3.1 A Peace Camp was first established on the loop in December 1981. No immediate steps were taken to have the Camp removed from the highway, but concern was expressed about the existence of the Camp on the highway land, in particular, when a substantial semi-permanent wooden building was erected on the loop. [This refers to the original Eirene] The matter was considered by the Transportation Committee at a special meeting on May 14th, 1982. The Committee recommended that legal action should be taken to recover possession of the loop, and this recommendation was accepted by the County Council on May 18th, 1982.

'3.2 The Council obtained an Order of Possession from Huntingdon County Court on November 5th, 1982, but an appeal was lodged against the Order and it could not, therefore, be implemented until July 26th, 1983. On that day the Peace Campers were evicted and all structures, caravans etc. which had been placed on the loop were removed.

'3.3 Later another Camp was established on the loop. The Council has taken no action to evict these campers, and it seems that at least one caravan [Halcyon Spirit!] remains on the loop notwithstanding the recent evictions by the Ministry of Defence at their property.'

The paper went on to explain that Peace Lane remained part of the public highway and could not be enclosed. This explained the frantic activity the night before.

Finally, the paper outlined the legal procedures for stopping up and concluded by explaining:

'Once a highway has been stopped up, ownership of the land normally reverts to the owners of the land adjoining the highway. The owners of the land on each side of the highway own up to the centre of the carriageway on their side of the road. The Ministry hopes ultimately to bring the area of the loop within their property.'

There was some opposition from the Labour and Alliance members, who wanted to know why there was so much haste to close this piece of road. Surely there must be hundreds of similar stretches throughout the county? Perhaps there were pressures other than straightforward highways considerations in this case? The chairman of the committee insisted it was purely a highways matter, and when the vote came it was a foregone conclusion that the ruling Tory group would have a clear majority. However, this was only a recommendation and it had to go before the full council later in the day.

We had previously met members of the Labour and Alliance groups on the council to discuss the issue. They had expressed the hope that they might be able jointly to defeat the ruling group on this matter. The main council meeting convened at 10:30am. As well as the question of closing Peace Lane, we were also interested to see what would happen with two other items. The first was a motion calling for Cambridgeshire to be declared a Nuclear-Free Zone, the second, a motion deploring the way in which the eviction had been handled. Both were proposed by the leader of the Labour group, Mrs Jones.

Looking down from the gallery we saw that all the Labour councillors sat on one side of the chamber, while the Tories were on the other and SDP and Liberal councillors sat in the middle. We sat up excitedly as the county solicitor presented our petition, but whatever hopes we had were soon dashed as the chairman simply dismissed the matter. He told the meeting that the majority of the signatories lived outside the county and that the petition did not reflect the views of local residents. The meeting adjourned for lunch. Janet Jones had invited us to lunch with her. Ian found the prospect of eating with the councillors rather daunting and decided to eat elsewhere. While Nick and I were waiting to collect our lunch, the chairman of the council walked passed me. I was still smarting from the cursory way in which he had dealt with our petition, so I left the queue to confront him. He looked startled as I introduced myself.

"We are very disappointed at the way you dealt with our petition. Surely you must realise that nuclear weapons are a threat to everyone, not just local people? We're representing thousands of people from all over the country and their views should be taken into account."

"I understand your point of view," Mrs. Hartley, he replied, "but we have a duty to the people living in the immediate area. Obviously their feelings have to take precedence as far as we are concerned."

Standing in the corridor after lunch, I noticed Mrs Emily Blatch, the leader of the council. Mrs Blatch was implacably opposed to our presence at the base. I stood by as she spoke to different people, trying to catch her eye. She was smartly dressed in an elegant, two-piece suit, her dark brown hair carefully coiffed. She was holding a large, patent leather handbag.

As she passed me, I said, "Mrs Blatch, could we have a word with you?"

In the short conversation that followed, Mrs Blatch chose to take issue with our claim to act from Christian conviction, insisting that not all Christians shared our view on the evil of nuclear weapons. It was a valid point; perhaps we did come across as self-righteous and unwilling to see another point of view. A few days later, we wrote a letter setting out in detail why we felt we should be allowed to continue the witness and asked her to put our case to the council. We did not get a reply. But we were not alone in thinking that pacifism is a necessary corollary to being a Christian. Kingsley Amis in an essay, *'On Christ's Nature'* writes: *'I am not a pacifist or non-resister myself; I only feel that no Christian who can read has any excuse for not being such.'*

For the afternoon session, we were given tickets to sit downstairs at the back of the council chamber. Hours and hours of council business had to be gone through, most of it extremely boring. Several of the councillors appeared to be sleeping off their leisurely lunch. The recommendation of the Transportation Committee was brought before the full council and was duly accepted. The hoped-for coalition between the Alliance and Labour groups failed to outnumber the Conservative votes. We then waited to hear a motion on Cambridgeshire becoming a Nuclear-Free Zone. It was no real surprise that it was not carried. It became clear that there was little room for individual conscience; when it came to a vote, everyone seemed to vote on strict party lines. The only doubt concerned a few Independents, who were mainly closet Conservatives. The Alliance group was also split on some issues. For example, the Liberals appeared more concerned about the risks of nuclear power than their SDP allies. The motion on the Nuclear-Free Zone was seconded by a Liberal councillor, J.B.F. Brackenbury, who gave a very heartfelt and eloquent appeal to consider the dangers posed by the use of nuclear fuel and nuclear weapons.

The way in which groups voted according to party label was typified by a motion proposed by Chris Bradford, leader of the Alliance group, concerning central Government's plans to introduce value added tax on books. At the time, there was wide public concern about this measure, which was seen as a tax on learning. It was an issue that the education authority had privately condemned, and something that theoretically might have united members of all parties in protest. However, it became clear that certain members of the Conservative group interpreted the motion as being an attack on the Government and were not prepared to consider the rights and wrongs of the issue as such. When the vote came, not one Conservative councillor even abstained, they all voted against the motion.

It was six o'clock before the motion about the February 6th eviction was debated. We were tired and dispirited by what we had seen, but what followed was to shake our faith in the democratic process even further. The motion read:

'That this Council deplores the total lack of consultation with this Authority, the misuse of public resources and police time, and the excessive use of force in moving the peace protestors from their camps near Molesworth.'

We were prepared to see the motion defeated, but before people could vote, a young Tory councillor, G.J. Knowles, stood up to bring an amendment. His amendment was:

'That all words in Motion E after "That this Council" be deleted and replaced by the following words: "…congratulates the Police in removing the so-called 'peace protesters' from their camp near Molesworth and similarly congratulates the Ministry of Defence in speedily erecting a temporary perimeter fence which will enable the later construction of a more substantial barrier."'*

He seemed amused as he read it. Someone questioned the legitimacy of such a move, as under Standing Orders an amendment which negates the motion cannot be accepted. The county solicitor advised that this was true, but the chairman ruled that the amendment was in order. The amendment was carried. Several Labour and Liberal councillors asked that their vote against the substantive motion be recorded because there was no doubt that the original motion had been turned upside down.

I was suddenly aware that Ian was on his feet. In a loud voice he said: "If people want to know why I don't believe in democracy anymore, it's because of people like him!"

Faces turned, an usher started to move towards us, Ian picked up his coat and walked out. I grabbed my things and followed him.

"I wish you'd warned me you were going to do that," I said. Earlier I had whispered to Ian that I wanted to speak and he had argued against it.

"I'm sorry, I didn't know I was going to do it. I was just so angry."

It was seven o'clock; we had been there since nine in the morning. We were depressed and disgusted. We had seen with our own eyes how people had been removed that night. No councillor had visited Molesworth until several days after the eviction. Back at Halcyon Spirit, Helen Trask and Angela Needham had been minding Robbie for us. A young man called Andrew Riddiford, originally from New Zealand, had arrived and was planning to stay a while. He was so kind. Seeing how tired we were, he went into the kitchen and came back holding mugs of tea. Helen told us that there had been lots of visitors while we had been away and we read through a pile of messages that they had left for us. A bunch of daffodils lay on the table and beside them a box of groceries were wrapped in blue tissue paper. A note said they were from a very dear friend, Sister Eileen. At that time we had never met her, we simply knew that she was a Roman Catholic nun who worked with handicapped people near Sudbury in Suffolk. Coming back to such warmth and friendship, we soon revived and resolved to put the meeting behind us and carry on. But the process of implementing the stopping-up order was far from over and there were further ironies to unfold before the law could take its course.

★★★

"There must be people here all the time!" Helen looked at us for affirmation. Her face looked tired but a fierce light shone in her eyes as she spoke. There was something reminiscent of a Native American in her appearance: her sharp features and the fact that her long, grey hair was plaited into pigtails. Helen and her friend Angela, along with Jean Hutchinson, had been amongst the small group that had founded the Peace Camp in December 1981. It must have been a tremendous shock for them when they heard that after three years, the military had at last started to convert Molesworth into a missile base.

Helen and Angela arrived in their old diesel truck known as the Peace Chariot. They were living in Sheffield now, but on hearing the news they had determined to come back to Molesworth. Helen and

Angela were both members of Christian CND and were motivated by their deep religious convictions. Helen was anxious to establish a permanent vigil in the Peace Garden.

"I think it's really important that there's someone out there night and day. I shall stay there myself until others come." Pausing she added, "Another thing, I think the fire should be burning all the time, it's welcoming for visitors."

We nodded our agreement. A great many people were coming up on a daily basis, but what Helen wanted was a continuous presence that was clearly visible.

"It's a good idea," Ian said, "but the weather's so awful. Did you hear about the miner from Durham? It was amazing. He came just after the fence went up. He only had a pair of thin leather shoes and a light mac, but he stayed out there for three days and nights. The police couldn't believe it. Can you see many people doing that? I can't."

Helen looked at Ian and said, "Yes, I know." She paused for a moment before adding, "I shall let people know that I intend to fast until we manage to set up a vigil on a permanent footing."

We did not know what to say. We knew we found it hard enough just living in the caravan. The idea of being outside all the time and not eating as well was more than we could imagine. It would not be the first time that Helen had fasted. Previously she and Angela had both taken part in the 'Fast for Life'. This was an international fast where small groups from different countries simultaneously fasted to draw attention to the arms race. Helen kept up her fast on Peace Corner for many weeks during freezing weather and whenever possible Angela joined her. Eventually other people arrived to take over the permanent vigil.

It was March. Time was going so quickly and so much seemed to happen each day. Every week a number of people were apprehended for scrambling through the wire on to the fields. It could hardly be called a base at this stage, more of a grim-looking fence, which surrounded open, windswept pasture. Alan from Ely and Angie Zelter had gone through the wire to plant willow trees. Both had been arrested. Angie lived in north Norfolk near another military base, RAF Sculthorpe. It was Angie who later came up with the idea of the 'Snowball'.

It was a simple idea; as an act of civil disobedience, two people announced their intention of cutting one strand of wire at Sculthorpe, unless the Government met one of their three requests. A month later, four people would come and repeat the action. If one of the requests was still not met, eight people would cut the fence; it would roll on, growing like a snowball, until one of their requests was met. The three requests were:

'*(1) That Britain votes for multi-lateral nuclear disarmament at the UN and supports the Comprehensive Test Ban Treaty,*

OR

2) that Britain publicly supports the Nuclear Freeze proposals,

OR

3) that Britain takes an independent step towards a freeze or reduction, by returning Cruise, abandoning Trident, or rejecting the storage of chemical weapons.'

We heard news of Angie and Alan's arrest from an MOD policeman who came to the door to give us back the willow trees. He said it seemed a shame for the saplings to die, so perhaps we could plant them somewhere else, but "not inside the fence!"

I found my moods changed from day to day and later from hour to hour. After a morning vigil, when I had felt in good spirits, I suddenly felt depressed and tearful. That particular morning a young policeman, standing inside the chapel had talked loudly while we had been standing quietly in prayer. This felt like a personal attack, especially as I knew many of them well by now. Often this quiet twenty minutes was respected by them. The same afternoon, a reporter from Radio Orwell, our local radio station in Ipswich, came to interview us. I wanted to sound strong and positive, but I was actually near to tears. When we heard it on tape at a later date, it was a relief to hear that we sounded fine. Little did the listeners know!

The March 1st entry in my diary reads, '*Woke at 8:30, listened to 'Desert Island Discs', castaway Anthony Hopkins. He said two things I found really helpful. One was that life is not a rehearsal but the real thing. The other was that we have to think about the journey through life and not just the destination. John Holtom from Hampstead Meeting joined in the morning service. He spoke about camels in the desert, saying that "There are no paths, paths are made by walking." Went to Ipswich to attend Andrew Fyfe's funeral and to see Victoria [our niece] as it was her birthday yesterday. Saw Antony at work. Called*

to see Lucky and she is fine. Bath and hair wash at mum and dad's then straight
back to Molesworth. Tilley lamp runs out of paraffin so straight to bed.'

I thought a lot about the remarks that Anthony Hopkins had made. The thought that this life is our only chance, the only performance, there is no run-through later to correct the errors. His comment about making the most of the journey through life, living each day to the full, rather than thinking that 'one day' we'll do all the things we want to do, gave a whole new perspective to my way of thinking. It was strange how often when we were feeling low in spirit, some words said, either on the radio or by someone visiting, would restore our resolution.

By the time we left Molesworth we had just about become used to the weather. It was dreadful. The mud clung to our wellingtons in thick clods. I used to stand in the puddles, splashing my feet around to try and remove as much as possible before going into the caravan. We put newspaper on the kitchen floor to save the carpet getting too dirty. Every other day we brushed it, creating clouds of dust so thick it was difficult to see from one side of the van the other. Finally we took up the carpet, as Phil said he would like it in his caravan. We bought lino, which was easier to clean, and put down one or two rugs. We took the rugs outside, laid them on the concrete blocks and beat them with a hard-backed brush. The paraffin lamp in the kitchen made the ceiling and walls black. It was a long and tedious job boiling up kettles of water and wiping them clean, but it looked good when it was done, even though we knew within weeks it would want doing again. Once, when the sun was shining I took all the curtains down and washed them. It took ages, and I prayed it wouldn't rain as we would have been rather exposed when we went to bed!

If the inside was difficult to keep clean, the outside was worse. After the fences were put up, litter would collect inside the barbed wire making it impossible to reach by hand. Ian fixed a nail to the end of a long stick and I used it to poke about, trying to pierce the rubbish and remove it. It was a bit reminiscent of a party game and I would be obsessed with each little piece of paper. With great difficulty I would spear a piece on the end of my stick and then very slowly and carefully bring my hand back through the maze of rusty wire, only to have the paper drop off, I would then start the whole procedure again. Visitors often attached photos, posters or messages to the fence and after a while they would blow off and lie in the mud or collect in clumps in the hedgerows. I spent hours trying to get rid of it but it was an impossible task. I got quite cross one day when I looked out of the window and saw the police taking the posters, symbols of hope, off the fence. This particular day the police were dropping all the pieces of paper and wool on the ground. I took them over a black plastic bag to use. They did use it and a short time afterwards a policeman came to the door to return the bag. He was very friendly and we stood talking for a few minutes. With so many visitors coming each day, and with no litter bins, it was not surprising that rubbish collected. The area was very flat and strong winds blew across the open fields, swirling the bits of paper from one place to another.

It was not just the litter left by the peace movement, however. The police on duty were issued with polystyrene cups and plastic spoons. They dropped the cups that would lie around in the mud. I reported it to the sergeant on duty several times and he said he would have a word with the men. Going outside one morning, I looked down on the ground and my blood boiled. A police transit wan was parked in the lane and lying on the ground by the back door were several small packets of sugar, cups and spoons and empty cigarette packets. I knocked on the van window, the police inside stopped playing cards and opened the door.

"I'm simply fed up with trying to keep this place clean," I said. "Look at all this mess you've made! It's not fair, you know, it's always us in the Peace Movement who get the blame for leaving litter and you're equally to blame."

I was very cross. The inspector in charge arrived on the scene when I was in mid flow, wanting to know what the trouble was. I calmly explained to him and he ordered two of the policemen to get out of the transit van to clear up the mess.

Another day, two women from the village of Old Weston came up the road and over to where I was standing. With no warning they launched into an attack on me and the disgusting look of the place. It was pointless trying to tell them that litter worried me, too. If I had indicated for one moment that it was left by people on both sides of the fence, I know what the response would have been.

One Sunday morning early in March, Ian got up at 5:30 and drove to Dunstable to do a live interview for Chiltern Radio. It was for their early morning religious programme. I lay in bed and listened to it, willing him to remember everything he wanted to communicate. It was really good, I clapped at the end, but of course I was biased! I peeped out of the window and, as I guessed, it was bucketing down with rain again. Just before eleven, we put on our waterproof trousers and coats, pulled on our boots and, with our hoods up, we squelched through the mud for our brief act of worship. I stood staring at the half-built chapel, the rain slowly dripping down my neck, thinking what a truly mad world we live in. What on earth was I doing here when I could be at home? A woman spoke. She said she had seen film of children in Africa, children with swollen bellies, dying of starvation. I shuddered. I knew why I was here.

"Can we sing something?" someone asked. "What about 'Walk in the Light'?"

'Good', I thought, 'one of my favourites.' We sang with gusto.

I saw Andrew walking towards us. He came over and quietly told me that the Cambridgeshire police were about to remove the old Commer van in which he had been living in Peace Lane. It had been left after the eviction, as the owners were away. He had moved into it a few weeks earlier. In spite of all our requests to allow it to stay, they hooked it up and towed it over to the other side of the base. The officer in charge that day seemed very edgy, for no apparent reason. He was reluctant to allow anyone on to the gardens, and as soon as people approached the main gate he had a row of police standing in front of it. As luck would have it, Chief Superintendent Colin Street turned up in his car. We had got to know him quite well and liked him. I walked over to say hello to him.

"You haven't asked me in for a cup of tea yet, have you?" he said.

"Well you're very welcome."

He and his deputy made their way to the caravan. I raced ahead, putting newspapers down. I didn't like to ask them to remove their boots, though perhaps I should have done. We were asked what we thought about police tactics during the time we had been there and we gave him a full account of what we had seen, good and bad. I thought it only right to tell them that I agreed with non-violent direct action and we had to differ on this point. It felt good to be taken seriously and we appreciated the fact that we could talk together as rational, reasonable people.

Most of my days seemed to be taken up with writing letters and we spent a fortune on stamps. The previous Christmas, members of our family had given us typing and carbon paper, stamps and envelopes, which were all put to good use. As well as writing letters, we also received a large post. We kept a list of all the letters and cards that were sent to us and another for those we sent. We have kept all the letters and cards we received. The letters are in three lever-arch files, and together with the cards there are 1,205 of them. During our stay at Molesworth we sent 777 letters! It was very frustrating waiting for replies to letters to the Ministry of Defence or to MPs. What I tended to forget was that the wheels of bureaucracy grind very slowly. Our concern about another nuclear base being built was of little importance to the 'powers that be', who had much more 'important' things to think about. However, we did build up an amazing correspondence.

We tried to attend as many local meetings as possible. We went along to one held in the primary school in Brington, where a resident from the Newbury area had come to talk to local people about what it was like living near a nuclear base. We felt very alone, as one by one people stood up to say what they thought of 'protestors'. They were not wanted, they smelt, looked dirty and were abusive. Hardly anyone seemed concerned that the local area was going to undergo enormous changes, or that the life of local residents was going to alter dramatically as a result of heavy vehicles charging up and down their country roads. Few considered the hedges and the trees along the roadsides that would disappear or that house prices would fall. And all this before the base was operational! When that time came there would be all manner of other things to contend with.

One or two people voiced concern about the helicopters flying around constantly. The man from Newbury told the audience that 'the women' were the main problem at Greenham. It was true the police dogs could be annoying when they barked in the night, and the sirens could be heard for miles around when there was an alert. We knew several people attending the meeting and I was keen to stay for a cup of coffee afterwards, to talk to them and introduce myself to the more hostile members of the audience. I wanted them to know that I was a caring, considerate member of society, and that our presence at Molesworth would not give them any cause for concern. But Ian was so affected by all the malevolence that he just wanted to escape. We walked home feeling dejected.

Chapter Nine

A Forceful Woman

Easter was fast approaching and we were nervous of what might happen. The CND was planning a large demonstration and we knew there was very little space available for such a gathering. The farmers had crops coming through in the fields and we were worried about them getting trampled. We needed to know from the CND organisers what provisions were being made to safeguard against this and to alleviate the fears of the local villagers. Because we were in such an isolated position and had to use the public phone most of the time, we seemed to lose touch with the national organisers. A visit to London, therefore, was necessary to meet with those planning the activities at Easter, and also to buy more badges as we were selling many each day to visitors.

I caught a train from Huntingdon and went straight to the CND offices, where I met Ross McKenzie and Tony who were responsible for arranging the Easter demonstration. After talking to them, I realised what a difficult and complicated job they had to do. When I left, I felt more reassured about the whole thing as I could see they were taking great pains to see that everything would go off smoothly. At the same time, I went in to see Barbara Eggleston in the Christian CND office. We agreed that there should be more communication between us. Afterwards, I made my way to Friends House in the Euston Road, where I was able to buy Quaker badges, including some saying 'Bread not Bombs' with a wheat sheaf. I also collected more of the Quaker posters, which decorated the outside of our caravan.

We found these posters to be a great conversation starter and could not help noticing how many of the police stopped and read them while walking down Peace Lane. We changed them fairly frequently so that different messages appeared. I had several favourites: 'World peace will come through the will of ordinary people like yourself'; 'Our greed and our fear are destroying our future'; 'People need water not weapons' and 'The real horror is not that we may be bombed, but that we should ever think of using the bomb on anyone else'. The Quaker Peace Testimony provoked great interest and we were often asked to explain exactly what a Quaker is. So much so, in fact, that we had to supplement our explanations with leaflets about Quaker beliefs.

There are only twelve thousand Quakers in Britain, but their influence seems to be much greater than might be supposed. Time and again we could not help noticing that among the senior police officers the label 'Quaker' was a kind of passport to special treatment. We wondered why this should be. It was a mixed blessing; being singled out sometimes set us apart from our friends.

When I left Friends House I made my way to Blackheath where my daughter Debbie lives. She and her boyfriend Shaun had their own flat, a conversion on the top floor of a Victorian house. Debbie was nearly 22. I climbed the metal steps of Blackheath station and stood by the entrance. "You made it, then," I heard someone say. I turned to see Debbie coming towards me. I thrust a bunch of freesias into her hands and we hugged each other.

I stood back and looked at her. "You look nice, you've had your hair cut differently," I observed.

She has beautiful, deep rich auburn hair. When she was a baby she had a mass of curls. I have kept one of her curls wrapped in tissue paper.

Debbie ran a hot bath for me. She knew the thing I missed most of all was being able to have a bath when I wanted one. She even came in and gave me a glass of red wine while I was soaking! In the evening she cooked a superb meal and I felt pampered. It was lovely!

The next morning I decided to visit the Ministry of Defence in Whitehall to try to find out why they had not replied to any of our letters. I walked up to one of the reception desks and asked if I could speak to the press officer, explaining that I had written many letters and had not even received an acknowledgement, so now I had come in person.

The woman behind the desk said, "I'm sorry, but you have to have an appointment before you can see anyone. I suggest you write in."

"But that's the whole point, I keep writing but no one replies," I reiterated.

"There's nothing more I can do, I'm afraid. I can't give you a pass if you haven't got an appointment."

It was 'Catch 22'; nothing I said made any difference. I sat down on the leather seat in reception and tried to work out if there was anything more I could do. I thought I would have one last try. I got up and walked over to where a well-dressed man was standing by the interior door. I went through it all again and looked at him hopefully.

He thought for a moment and said, "My advice to you is to write a letter."

I left feeling very frustrated.

I returned to Molesworth later that day and in the afternoon our friends, the sisters from Hengrave Hall, came to visit and joined in the afternoon vigil. Hengrave Hall is an Elizabethan manor house, set in parkland near Bury St Edmunds. It is home of the Sisters of the Assumption, a Catholic order dedicated to reconciliation. At Hengrave they live as part of an ecumenical community. The hall functions as a conference centre, with one wing dedicated to young people. Ian and I had spent several weekends there and love the friendly, relaxed atmosphere generated by the sisters. We were delighted to see them; they were a great support to us during our stay. They asked us if we minded their holding their evening office beside the fence. We were pleased to join them. The nuns wore maroon-coloured habits with grey veils. Each had her own missal with brightly coloured ribbons, marking the texts for the day.

At six o'clock each evening the MOD police changed shift. A single-decker bus would drive up to Peace Corner carrying the night shift. They disembarked some clutching newspapers, some carrier bags. The day shift had been looking at their watches and was eager to leave. It was a long day from six in the morning to six at night. Good-natured banter would pass between them as their paths crossed. This particular evening I felt sorry for the ones leaving. The bus that was to collect them didn't turn up. They clustered around Peace Corner, some sitting on the dry-stone wall, others walking out in the road to see if the transport was on its way. They looked fed up and dejected. I went out and talked to some of them, offering cups of tea. Three-quarters of an hour later the bus arrived.

That evening, an incident happened that I am not likely to forget. I decided to drive down to Old Weston to ring my mother. I parked the car opposite the phone box and got out. To my horror, the car started to roll backwards. It was on a slight hill. I held on to the open door with all my strength, but the car was gathering speed all the time. Finally, I had to let go and watch in utter disbelief as the car ran down the hill, veered off towards the other side of the road and came to a halt in the car park of the village hall, having ploughed through the picket fence. For a moment I couldn't move, then I glanced around to see if anyone had seen what happened. Nobody was about. I ran down to the car. The back bumper was dented and the door wouldn't close properly.

I drove back to the caravan to break the news to Ian. Then I went out to the police transit van to report what I had done. I was very distressed.

"Goodness knows what the villagers will say; you know what they think of us."

A policeman leaned out of the van and grinned at me. "Don't worry, love, we like you!"

It was nice of him to say so, but it did not make me feel any better. He suggested that we go back to the hall to report the broken fence. Ian came with me and, feeling very nervous, we pushed open the door of the hall and went in. There was a meeting going on and I had to interrupt the speaker on the platform. Heads turned and looked at me as I explained what had happened. The man on the platform came to the back of the hall and took down all the details. We told him we would, of course, pay all the costs involved in repairing the broken fence and I kept apologising over and over again. I was very embarrassed. Several weeks later, a local farmer arrived in his pony and trap to give me a bill for £60. I handed him a cheque there and then.

★★★

We were pleased when two women from the Pacific came to visit Molesworth. They had been asked to come over to this country by women from Greenham. Their story was horrifying and so little was known about it by people over here. We were ashamed to have to admit that we had not realised the tremendous costs being borne by the people of the Pacific as a result of nuclear testing. They told us in detail of the awful consequences: large populations forced to leave their homes; the high incidence of cancers and babies born with gross deformities, many were simply lumps of bone and jelly. One of the women came from Micronesia and the other was a Maori from New Zealand. For her this injustice was just the latest in a whole line of such incidents inflicted on native populations. We began to realise that before nuclear weapons like cruise ever get deployed, millions of innocent people have already experienced their obscene effects. As our own country had been one of those to use the Pacific for nuclear tests, the women left us feeling guilty by association for the crimes perpetrated in our name.

On March 15th, listening to the radio, we heard the news that the Belgian Government had agreed to deploy sixteen cruise missiles by the end of the month. It was with a heavy heart that I went out to stand by the fence for the morning vigil. I felt upset and angry and this was not helped by the fact that the police inside the chapel were particularly noisy. They often remained quiet while we stood there.

I decided to say something to them afterwards. "Excuse me." I tried to attract their attention and they looked up and walked over.

"I hope you won't mind me saying this, but you were terribly noisy this morning while we were having our vigil. I know you may not agree with the way we do things, but it's only for a short time and it means a lot to people."

"Sorry about that, it certainly wasn't intentional, we'll try not to let it happen again," one of the MOD policemen said, adding, "I've been meaning to ask you, what exactly is a Quaker?"

I fumbled in my mac pocket and brought out a crumpled leaflet entitled 'What Quakers Believe'. "Do you want this?" I asked him, holding it up. He nodded and I passed it through the barbed wire, our hands just meeting.

"Thanks, I'll read this when I'm off duty." We then went on to have a conversation about drugs, 'hooligans', Gorbachev and the Pacific. There was nothing I enjoyed better than a conversation with people who had a viewpoint different from mine, and it was obvious that they, too, enjoyed the chance to air their opinions.

By now the 'Easter Wheat Campaign' was gathering momentum. We heard that a coach load of Welsh supporters was coming to Molesworth later in the day, to bring a contribution of wheat and blankets for Eritrea. During the previous month we had been asking visitors to sign a petition, a different one from ours to the County Council. Copies had been taken away and others had been sent out by post to groups. A large number of these sheets had now been returned and Tim, Bridie and others thought it would be a good time to hand them in to the base commander. The petition read: *'We, the undersigned, are shaken and horrified by the militarisation of a large field at Molesworth, Cambridgeshire, including a peace settlement and an All Faiths Peace Chapel. We urge you to take all possible steps to return the fields to productive, peaceful purposes, and immediately to allow access to "Eirene" the Peace Chapel for all to witness for Peace.'*

The coach pulled up at Peace Corner and everyone piled out carrying sacks of grain and bundles of blankets. They formed a human chain across the gardens, passing their gifts from one to another until the gardens were covered. The petitions had been taped together so that they formed a huge roll of signatures stretching many yards. We had arranged with MOD police and the RAF to present the petition to a senior officer, and had been told they would only allow two people to go on the base to deliver it. Bridie and I stood by the gate as the officer on duty opened it for us, and then for the first time ever we walked through it.

We were escorted to a small portable building not far from the gate, where a rather nervous Flight Lieutenant was waiting to receive us. We gave him the petition and also a daffodil, which seemed apt as we were told his name was Jones. (Had he been specially chosen for the occasion, I wondered?) We asked him to see that the petition was forwarded to Michael Heseltine, and he said he would pass it on but he did not know how high it would go. When we asked if we could hold a service inside the chapel, he refused saying he had no information regarding the chapel. Bridie asked if the materials for building the roof of Eirene could be placed inside the chapel until such time as we could complete the building.

Flt. Lt. Jones looked uncomfortable as he replied, "The chapel is the property of the Ministry of Defence."

When we rejoined the others we formed a huge circle outside the gates and held a service. A Welsh minister read from the Bible in his own language and in true Welsh tradition we sang heartily, our voices carrying across the fields. At the end of the service everyone was given a daffodil, which they used to decorate the ugly, black main gates, transforming them. As we waved goodbye to our Welsh friends it began to snow.

***

Another weekend was upon us, though it was hard to distinguish between weekdays and weekends anymore. For some time we had been writing to John Major, the local Conservative MP, and had arranged to meet him that Saturday. He was speaking to a public meeting at the primary school in Brington village, about a mile away from Peace Corner, and we were to see him afterwards. We sat through the meeting, hearing again of the anxiety and anger felt by many of those present.

The villagers were particularly concerned about the forthcoming Easter demonstration and someone had obtained a copy of a paper called *Class War*, extracts of which were read out. The article was full of obscene and violent suggestions, and very far removed from anything almost anyone in the peace movement would have agreed with. Once again we just had to sit and listen feeling very uncomfortable. At the end of the meeting John Major was in demand and we had to wait for a long time before he was free to see us. He apologised when he finally showed us into the headmaster's study. Before this meeting we had seen him on television and formed the impression that he was not a very forceful man. We thought we would have no difficulty in making him understand our views. We were proved wrong. As the discussion progressed it became clear that he relished debate and could quote vast numbers of facts and figures. For him the nuclear issue was all a question of the numbers game. Neither Ian nor I are confident talking about statistics and could not compete at this level. We believe that nuclear weapons are evil and that this is a moral argument. It was tough going trying to bridge the gap between these two ways of thinking. We came away dissatisfied, feeling that a good opportunity had been lost.

Early on the morning of Mothering Sunday, an RAF officer called at the caravan to deliver a letter acknowledging receipt of the petitions. The week was full of incident. We heard on the radio that the MOD had agreed to sell off some land, including the land on which the chapel stood. The rumour was that a local farmer would buy the chapel land and demolish the building. It would have saved the MOD any embarrassing publicity and it all seemed quite feasible. In the middle of the week, we went to Chesterfield to give a talk to the CND group and at the weekend we drove to Stratford-on-Avon to open a Peace Day. Both were round trips of several hundred miles and, thankfully, the old Mini didn't let us down. We were woken up early one morning by Helen Trask with the news that Tim and Bridie were ploughing up an MOD field on the other side of the base, ready to plant more wheat. We cycled over to see if we could help. When we arrived the police were trying to convince them that it was NOT MOD land but belonged to a local farmer. This ploy did not work and the ploughing continued. Sheepishly, the police returned an hour later to say that it WAS MOD land and they must either leave or be arrested.

We couldn't stay long as we were expecting Ian's parents to visit us for the first time. They spent the previous night at Papworth, visiting the couple that had given accommodation to Ian's mother while his father was having major heart surgery in 1981. It was a very cold day and they stood with us at the vigil surveying the bleak surroundings with dismay. Afterwards, Ian's father remarked that it reminded him of his time in a German prisoner of war camp. Mum and Dad said they would like to take us out for a pub lunch. We suggested going to Oundle, the small market town famous for its public school and ancient stone buildings. We had only just ordered a drink when Dad collapsed in terrible pain. The landlord rang for a local doctor who arrived very quickly. By this time the pain had increased and Dad was lying down on a bench in great distress. The doctor advised that he should go to hospital and sent for an ambulance. We followed on in the car to Peterborough District Hospital; after an examination, they diagnosed a stone in the kidney. The doctor suggested he returned to Ipswich to report to his local hospital as they had all his notes. Ian drove them back to Ipswich and stayed for a few days until the crisis was over. We had been looking forward to their visit so much and what should have been a really happy day turned out instead to be one of great anxiety.

That evening I was on my own. I stood outside talking to visitors and to the police. A policeman standing on duty near the front of the caravan asked if I had any dry newspapers for them to use to light the fire in their brazier. I took them out a pile. Later, when I had taken

Robbie out for his late night walk I found I had locked myself out. How I had done this remains a mystery. I felt a bit foolish when, after all else failed I had to ask the same policeman for help. Two policemen came and unscrewed the window catches on the little room we used for a toilet and I watched with baited breath as one of them squeezed through the small opening, hoping that he would not lower himself into our bucket of pee! All was well and he came out of the front door grinning.

"One good turn deserves another," he said.

Ian went away again later in the year and I repeated the same trick!

I was in the middle of typing a letter when Tim arrived on his bike to say that Rainbow Village were at the top of Cockbrook Lane trying to get back to Molesworth. I wanted to see what was happening, so grabbing my bike Tim and I rode across the bridleway together. Approaching the top of the lane we could see a crowd of people. Caravans and buses were strewn along the Clopton road. Police were milling around, directing towing vehicles to move them off the road. Local farmers had gathered at the corner of Cockbrook Lane, very agitated, calling out and shaking fists. Tim and I talked to some of the Rainbow Villagers, who were unsure about what would happen to them. Some of the vehicles had managed to park off the road but were stuck in thick mud. Others had parked at an angle across the road. No traffic could move in either direction. It was utter chaos. There wasn't much I could do to help so I returned to Halcyon Spirit. During the afternoon I looked outside and saw a huge police presence at Peace Corner. I went out to ask what was going on. I was told they were expecting Rainbow Village to return. The caravan was surrounded by police.

At that moment I had to leave to pick Ian up from the station in Huntingdon, on his return from Ipswich. He had travelled from London with Nick and I told them about what was going on as we drove back. We went straight to the Old School to drop Nick off. He dropped his bag and went back up the road to see what was happening to Rainbow Village. Several of the coaches and vans were still in the road, though by now some had been moved on. We watched the local news on television with Bridie and Tim and the incident was given a lot of coverage. On our way back to Peace Corner, we noticed even more people standing around the top of Cockbrook Lane, and Nick and

Mallen called out to us to say there had been an accident. The police wouldn't let us stop to hear what had happened; they waved us on.

Back at the caravan, we put it out of our minds, anxious to catch up on each other's news. Getting up to draw the curtains I noticed that once again loads of police were around.

"I'm going out to see what's happening," I told Ian. Immediately I was conscious of a change in the atmosphere; it felt very tense.

"Can you tell me what's going on?" I asked one of the police.

"One of your lot has run someone over, the chap's dying in hospital. Your bloke's been charged with attempted murder."

"WHAT!" I exclaimed. "I can't believe that, you must have got it wrong." I looked back at the policeman shaking my head, but he gave me a long, cold stare. We were very distressed. What he had said couldn't be true, it had to be a mistake.

"I wish someone would come and tell us what really happened," I said to Ian.

"They will. You'll just have to be patient."

Eventually, Mallen, Tim and Andy came over to give us their version of the story. Apparently, a man working for the breakdown service had crawled under the bus belonging to Chris and Sheila, to release the hook and chain used to tow the vehicle out of the mud. Chris, who was sitting in the driving seat, responding to various instructions being shouted at him, thought someone told him to slowly move forward. He did so, not realising that the man was still underneath the bus. With all the noise and confusion it was understandable how the accident occurred. Chris was pulled from the bus and arrested. Sheila asked everyone to sign a card for the injured man in hospital. Later, we heard that his spleen had been removed. It was a long time before he was fully recovered and a long time before this case was closed. We had found Chris to be a gentle, caring person and the whole affair was a nightmarish experience, which left its mark, not only on him, but on Sheila and their young son, as well.

★★★

We were beginning to feel the strain of living at Molesworth. In the days following the accident, it was clear that our relationship with the police had suffered a severe setback. I found talking to them difficult.

Every day was hectic; sitting for a moment in quiet was impossible. If we were not talking to visitors, we were catching up with the mounting correspondence. On average we received six or seven letters a day and one day we had fourteen. Apart from answering these, we tried to send regular letters to Michael Heseltine. We sent him bundles of our petition, each containing thirty or forty sheets of signatures. The packages we posted by recorded delivery. I still have the receipts, five in all. He never replied. We also wrote to Cambridgeshire County Council, the base commander, local police, various church people and Members of Parliament.

We enjoyed meeting visitors, but as time went on it became difficult to answer the same questions in a spontaneous way. Many people were seeing Molesworth for the first time and needed somewhere to sit and talk. Inviting them into the caravan for a cup of tea helped to release the anger and emotion they felt. I see from my diary that I was starting to get edgy with Ian. I remember feeling very cross with him when he decided to 'sort out' the correspondence file that I had been keeping in order. He can usually tell when I am annoyed about something as I become cool and don't say very much. After a little while he starts probing and my anger pours out and I end up in tears.

It was not really surprising that our tempers began to fray. We both knew that we were under great pressure and the run up to Easter added to this. Although we still felt we were in the right place, we knew we could do with a brief change of scenery. Our sleep pattern was often disrupted by the constant noise outside from the generator and the transit vans coming and going. One night a policeman knocked on the door to ask our names. As the police were well aware of our names by then, it seemed a strange request.

"Ah well, I'm a dog handler," he said. "I need the names in case you need any help during the night."

I spent the night thinking that 'something' was going to happen, but nothing did, not that night anyway!

The next morning a police inspector came to the door to tell us that the army was going to put new wire round the Peace Chapel.

"You know what'll happen to all the bulbs, don't you?" Ian said.

"Oh, no, they won't touch them will they?"

We had watched the daffodils grow taller each day, having struggled to survive the hard winter. Soon they would flower.

"I think I'll sit outside and watch to see they don't damage them," I told Ian.

I took a stool and put it by the chapel. An army officer and about a dozen young soldiers were preparing to remove the existing barbed wire. I went over to address the commanding officer. "Would you ask your men to be careful not to tread on any of the bulbs, there are lots coming up inside the wire, and it won't be long before they come out."

He turned and spoke to the group of young lads. I made my way back to sit on the stool. They were careful, but one soldier did start to put his boot down on a daffodil.

"Please watch where you're putting your foot!" I called out to him.

"Get off those flowers, boy!" the voice of the sergeant boomed out.

The soldier looked down at his feet, then at me, "I'm sorry," he said.

When the new wire was in place I got up, not a single bulb had been destroyed.

I knew I had to get away. Ian had agreed to speak at the Friends Meeting House in Cambridge the following day, so we took the opportunity of going to Ipswich for a couple of days' rest. I was surprised and embarrassed when my father-in-law showed me an account of the daffodil saga in that day's *Guardian* newspaper.

'EASTER AT THE SHARP END'

(The Guardian, March 29th, 1985*)*

'There was a bizarre scene yesterday outside one of the gates of Molesworth cruise missile base. A young Royal Engineer replacing a section of fencing nearly stepped on the inch-high green shoots of some daffodils when he was shouted at by Jennifer Hartley, a Quaker, who lives in a caravan there.

"'Mind the plants!" she called - she is a forceful woman.

"'Oh, sorry," the soldier mumbled, as if his mother had just ticked him off. Carefully he arranged the roll of razor wire, so as not to damage the daffodils planted in a circle near their shelter by the protestors; in ten days' time the blooms will open amongst the sharpened coils, causing many photographs to be taken.

But then Molesworth has become a bizarre place as thousands of CND members are likely to find on the Easter demonstrations next weekend.'

The article went on to describe the conditions at Molesworth for police and the protesters, the 'Easter Wheat Fund' and the reaction of people in the area to the coming demonstration.

It was lovely to soak in a hot bath and forget about the mud and fences for a little while. We returned to Molesworth refreshed, but uncertain whether we had the reserves to get through the next week. It was now the Monday before Easter and media interest about the demonstration was mounting. As soon as we got back, an interviewer from the BBC Radio 4 *Today* programme arrived. He wanted to know our feelings about the rising apprehension of local residents and what we, and others living around the base, thought might happen. This was very difficult for us as we were getting increasingly concerned. How were such vast numbers of people going to fit into the limited space around Molesworth? We had to choose our words carefully as we wanted to be as positive as possible without being unrealistic, and were well aware that what we said could be distorted. We were encouraged by the fact that when the Assistant Chief Constable of Cambridgeshire, Alan Ratcliffe, appeared on the local television news, he had spoken in a calm and reassuring way, showing no bias whatsoever. Now all we could do was wait. In two weeks' time it would all be over and we would know if people's fears were justified or not.

Caroline Taylor and her daughter Lucy

Tim and Bridie Milne Wallis with Emily

The caravan leaving site in Felixstowe, January 21ˢᵗ, 1985

Halcyon Spirit in its new home in Peace Lane, January 24ᵗʰ, 1985

Eirene All Faiths Peace Chapel, appealing for funds for the roof

*Outside the main gate at Greenham Common, wearing 'the hat'. Robbie only
visiting, March 28th, 1983*

The day of my court case in Ipswich, holding up my statement, February 6th, 1984

Night of the army invasion, February 5th, 1985

Part of the huge military and police presence, early morning, February 6th, 1985

Arctic conditions on the front, February 1985

It really was that cold! Christian CND service, February 10th, 1985

Our only neighbours in Peace Lane, February 1985

Bruce Kent at Christian CND service, February 10th, 1985

Glenys Kinnock (C) and Joan Ruddock (R) visiting us. I've had no sleep for nights and it shows, February 9th, 1985

MOD police 'guarding' Eirene

Asking permission to be allowed to hold our daily acts of worship in the chapel

Blessing the Easter wheat for the Eritrea project. (From left to right) Ross, Bridie and Julian, April 2nd 1985

The 'Bread not Bombs' mural painted by Ross Wallis and helpers, Easter 1985

Rainbow over Peace Gardens, Easter 1985

Easter Demonstration from the air (Photo by permission 'The Times/NI Syndication')

Robbie and Halcyon Spirit

Halcyon Spirit from the church field

Photo that appeared in the local paper

'Now the green blade riseth'

The badge seller

The board we put up on the wire of the fenced-in chapel

Tony Dumper, Bishop of Dudley, at the Anglican Pacifist Fellowship, 'Beating the Bounds', Whitsun 1985

Labour MPs visit, April 24th, 1985

Four Welsh ministers from the Welsh Fellowship of Reconciliation with their wives. (From left to right) Islwyn Lake, John Tudor, John Owen, Pryderi Jones, 24th April, 1985

Jennifer, Ian, Bridie, Ian and Tim visit the Ministry of Defence in London, July 1st, 1985

'Hiroshima Day', August 6ᵗʰ, 1985

(From left to right) The Rev. Alf Willetts, Lord George Macleod of Fuinary with Gordon Roe, Bishop of Huntingdon, 'Eirene Day', September 1ˢᵗ, 1985

Lord George Macleod of Fuinary, founder of the Iona Community, visits us in Halcyon Spirit

The cross being erected in Peace Lane, October 20th, 1985

Hibakusha (survivors of the Hiroshima and Nagasaki bombs) attending the service to erect the cross, October 20th, 1985

Mallen in Peace Lane with Robbie

The ash tree and a three-hundred year-old hedge are destroyed and replaced over night with a new fence November 1985

Eirene demolished by MOD workmen, April 14ᵗʰ, 1986

You can't kill the Spirit!

Halcyon Spirit leaves Molesworth for Upper Heyford

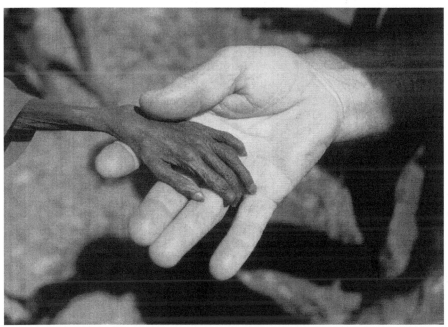

'Inasmuch as you have done it to the least of these my brethren, you have done it unto me.' Matthew 25. 40

Lambeth Palace, SE1 7JU.

26th February 1985

Dear Mr. and Mrs. Hartley,

Thank you for your letter dated 23rd February.

The Archbishop is concerned about this matter, and
continues to keep in close touch with those bishops who
are directly involved with the sale of the land at
Molesworth.

The Archbishop is confident that the Bishop of
Peterborough, in making his decision on the sale, has
taken into account all the relevant factors, including the
wishes of the local people.

Yours sincerely,

Wilfrid Grenville-Grey
Secretary to the Archbishop
for Public Affairs

Mr. and Mrs. Ian Hartley,
Quakers for Peace Caravan,
Halcyon Spirit,
Peace Corner,
Old Weston Road,
Brington,
Near Molesworth,
Cambridgeshire,   PE17 5SE

Lambeth Palace, SE1 7JU.

19th February 1985

Dear Mr. and Mrs. Hartley,

The Archbishop has asked me to thank you for
your letter dated 7th February, and to reply on his behalf.

With regard to the recent events at Molesworth,
the Archbishop feels that this is an area under the
responsibility of the Bishop of Ely. Both the Bishop of
Ely and the Bishop of Huntingdon have, in their different
ways, cautioned the Government over this matter, and I
believe that because of their efforts, the Chapel, even
though it is on Ministry of Defence land, has not been
demolished, as the Government originally planned.

The Archbishop believes that nuclear deterrence
can only be justified if we use the time it gives us to
achieve steps in disarmament. He plans to say more about
peace making in the context of the 40th Anniversary of the
founding of the United Nations, when he leads a debate in
the House of Lords later this year.

Yours sincerely,

Wilfrid Grenville-Grey
Secretary to the Archbishop
for Public Affairs

Mr. and Mrs. Ian Hartley,
Halcyon Spirit,
Peace Lane,
Peace Corner,
Old Weston Road,
Outside USAF Molesworth,
Brington,
Cambridge

From Tony Benn MP

25 March 1985

Dear Lemmster + Ian

Many thanks.

Millions - including

me - start your

concern + respect

your stand.

I will see how

visits could be

arranged

yrs Tony Benn

·From: John Major M.P.

HOUSE OF COMMONS
LONDON SWIA OAA

21 March 1985.

Dear Mr.and Mrs. Hartley,

Thank you for your letter which follows on our meeting last Saturday.

The Ministry of Defence will be replying to your letter as soon as possible but they have a considerable backlog of correspondence at present. Insofar as the "Peace Chapel" is concerned, no decisions have yet been taken although, at some future date, the Ministry proposes to dispose of this land. It is not yet clear when decisions on this matter will be finalised.

I am very pleased that we were able to find some points of agreement last Saturday and I found our exchange of views to be most useful. I remain unreconciled to the plans for mass demonstrations (as I believe you are) but I hope that no serious damage or injury will be caused at Easter.

Yours sincerely,

John Major

Mr. & Mrs. Hartley
Peace Corner
Old WEston Road
Brington
Nr. Molesworth PE175SE

MAX MADDEN MP (LABOUR)
HOUSE OF COMMONS
LONDON SW1A OAA

01 - 219 - 3414 (Office)
01 - 219 - 6248 (Secretary)

1st May 1985

Mr and Mrs Hartley
The Caravan
Molesworth
CAMBS

Dear Mr and Mrs Hartley,

It was very good to meet with you both last week: my only regret
is that the insanity of cruise missiles compels you to live in a
caravan at Molesworth.

I attach an exchange which took place yesterday in the House of
Commons and I was very sorry there seems to be no willingness on
the part of the Government to allow the Chapel to be built and
people to attend services there.

I have written to Ken Weetch and I hope he will be able to find time
soon to pop down to see you.

Meantime, can I thank you and your colleagues again for your very kind
reception last week.

With all best wishes,

Yours sincerely,

MAX MADDEN MP
BRADFORD WEST.

'Halcyon Spirit'

11th May 1985

Dear Mr. Kinnock,

Back in February your wife visited us here at Molesworth with Joan Ruddock from national CND. I thought that I would write to you to let you know that we are still here outside the gates of the proposed Cruise Missile Base, witnessing for peace.

We had a visit the other week from 10 Labour MPs who came to see for themselves this enormous 'white elephant' which one cannot help feeling Molesworth is. We maintain a good relationship with the police on duty here both civil and MOD. We also try to 'build bridges' with the local residents who are very opposed to peace protesters and who will in the coming months find their lives more and more disrupted as building work starts on the base. Since the Easter demonstration we have found that local feelings towards us have become much improved as the fears whipped up by a few people did not materialize and we are making several friends locally.

I know that I am an idealist but I have this dream that your party will win the next election and that you will reverse the decision to deploy Cruise at Molesworth and instead turn the whole area into a Peace park. It could contain gardens, a tree farm, a place for open air concerts, a farm area for children to visit and teenagers to run and work on. The ideas are numerous. It could be a positive alternative as was already happening before the 'invasion' took place. Is it just a dream? or could it really happen?

We intend to continue our witness here for as long as is possible or until they allow a permanent peace presence here at the base. We continue to hold twice daily acts of worship for all faiths outside the barbed wire chapel and sincerely hope that one day the government will allow us to finnish building it as the fund for the roof is already complete so we can order the materials any time.

If there is anything that you can do to try and help us to gain access to the 'Eirene' Peace Chapel we would be most grateful.

Yours very sincerely, and best wishes to your wife,

Jennifer and Ian Hartley,
Quakers for Peace Caravan.

HOUSE OF COMMONS
LONDON SWIA OAA

The Office of the Leader of

the Opposition

22 May 1985

Dear Jennifer and Ian,

Thank you very much for your letter. Some of my
colleagues who called on you a few weeks ago have
told me of your visit and they have also, of course,
raised the various questions with Ministers.

Your hope that we'll make Molesworth redundant as
a base is not a dream. It is going to happen
because we are going to win the Election and we
are going to get rid of the cruise missiles.
Naturally that victory will require a lot of work
and a lot of votes but we are certainly heading
in the right direction.

The dignity and sincerity of your activities at
Molesworth are an important ingredient in efforts
to focus attention on cruise and the way in which
it is not just a menacing weapon but a threat to
the values and conduct of our society. I send you
good wishes in your efforts and will see that the
matter of access of the peace chapel is taken up
again.

Kind regards,

Neil Kinnock MP

Jennifer & Ian Hartley
Quakers for Peace Caravan
"Peace Corner"
Old Weston Road
Brington
near Molesworth
Cambs. PE17 5SE

From: John Major M.P.

HOUSE OF COMMONS
LONDON SWIA OAA

16 May 1985.

Dear Mr. and Mrs. Hartley,

Thank youfor your letter which I received tody and for taking the
trouble to write to me. I am sorry that my letter did not arrive in time.

I entirely agree with you that we must all do everything we can to
ensure that the community can live in harmony, despite opposing views, and
I shall certainly continue to do what I can to try to achieve this.

I, too, have found our conversations interesting and helpful and
I am very grateful to you for your offer to act as a channel of communication
with the peace movement. I will certainly contact you should a need for
such a channel arise.

With kind regards.

Yours sincerely,

John Major

Mr. & Mrs. Hartley
Halcyon Spirit
Peace Corner
Old Weston Road
Brington
Nr. Molesworth PE175SE

THE RT. HON. DAVID STEEL, M.P.

HOUSE OF COMMONS
LONDON SW1A 0AA

21st August 1985.

Dear Mr. & Mrs. Hartley,

I write in the absence of David Steel for the
Parliamentary Recess to thank you for your letter of
9th August.

Regretfully Mr. Steel is presently on holiday but
he will see your letter and enclosures for information
on his return and I am sure he will be impressed by your
dedication to the cause of peace.

Yours sincerely,

Miss B. Miles
Private Office.

Mr. & Mrs. I. Hartley,
"Peace Corner",
Old Weston Road,
Brington,
Nr. Molesworth,
Cambs. PE17 5SE.

BUCKINGHAM PALACE

11th December, 1985

Dear Mr Hartley.

The Queen has commanded me to thank you
for your letter of 3rd December about Cruise
Missiles at Molesworth and your future plans to
visit India.

You may like to know that Her Majesty's
mail goes straight to her desk each day.

Yours sincerely

Robert Fellowes

Mrs. Ian Hartley.

HOUSE OF COMMONS
LONDON SW1A 0AA

12th January 1989.

Dear Mrs. Hartley,

Thank you very much for your letter which I received today and which I have read with interest. I do indeed recall you and your husband and am most impressed by all that you have done since you left Molesworth. I share your concern about mental illness and am glad to know that you are now working in this very challenging but rewarding field.

I appreciate your concern about the future of the fencing around Molesworth and I am in fact discussing this with the Secretary of State for Defence to see if it is possible to consider removing it.

Thank you also for your good wishes which I much appreciate and warmly reciprocate to you both.

Yours sincerely,

Mrs. Hartley
4 Arthurs Terrace
Ipswich
IP4 2NN

Chapter Ten

No Roast Potatoes

Hand-painted banners on the theme of 'Bread not Bombs' decorated the schoolroom walls. Ross McKenzie was there to give journalists the timetable for the Easter demonstration and to answer questions that arose. Tim spoke about the 'Wheat for Eritrea' project and was supported by a representative from the Eritrean Relief Organisation in London. James Firebrace from War on Want, who had written a book on Eritrea, also contributed to the discussion. The large room was crowded with supporters and journalists. Television crews had switched on their bright lights. The CND was holding its press conference at the Old School.

Earlier at Peace Corner, the television crews had filmed as the Bishop of Huntingdon had joined with Bruce Kent, Barbara Egglestone and others of us to bless six bags of wheat. This was a symbolic action; a whole lorry load of grain was waiting to begin to its journey to Eritrea. When the press conference was over we all went outside to watch the last bags of wheat being loaded on to the lorry. We waved as it moved off on the first stage of its journey from Molesworth to Eritrea.

The build-up to Easter had started. Hardly any people had arrived yet outside the caravan, but the press were already wandering about looking for a story. We told them that it was not until Easter Monday that thousands of people were expected. The media seemed to be expecting some sort of trouble or excitement, but they were disappointed as it was very quiet.

At the vigil on Maundy Thursday we shared bread and passed some through the wire to the policemen on duty who took and ate it. There were several speakers. Tim talked about the 'divisions and boundaries' that separate people. Andrew, who we all now called Andy, looked upset. Suddenly he moved forward and pushed his way through the razor wire and sat down in the middle of it, holding his hand out to the policeman. He sat for several hours, finally being pulled out and arrested. Later, when he went to court he contested that the land he was sitting on was in fact council land and not owned by the MOD. This was later proved true by plans and maps. The MOD had to take down the barbed wire fence around the chapel and move it several feet back, which meant that we could stand much nearer to the chapel.

On Good Friday we shared hot cross buns with the police and the campers. It was a fine day and I walked Robbie across the bridleway. During the afternoon vigil I happened to look up and to my surprise saw Debbie and Shaun walking towards me. I couldn't believe it. There were times when I completely forgot I was a mother. Being in the caravan outside the base seemed to be all-consuming and I needed to be reminded that life existed outside Molesworth. After their first visit in February, I never imagined they would come again.

They had stayed overnight on that occasion and we had driven into Thrapston, seven miles away, and bought a Chinese takeaway. The food was washed down with a bottle of Valpolicella that Debbie and Shaun had given us. We asked the officer in charge of the Cambridgeshire police if they would let Shaun park his red Cortina near the caravan. At the time, the police had orders not to allow anyone to park on the road near Peace Corner. The place they designated for parking was over a mile and half away, near Old Weston. We managed to wheedle a concession; the car could be left about four hundred yards further up the road near the other end of Peace Lane.

Shaun and Ian unloaded the sleeping bags and a couple of holdalls, then Shaun locked up the car. It was a squeeze, sleeping four in Halcyon Spirit, but we were all feeling in a good mood. We giggled a lot as we pulled down the bed and opened up the settee. With the lamp turned off, we lay in the darkness listening to the police coming and going and to the remorseless 'chug, chug' of the generator. Debbie treated the whole thing as an adventure and I went to sleep feeling pleased that the visit had been a success.

We did not go out the next morning until we had eaten a leisurely breakfast. While Ian took Robbie for his morning walk, Shaun and

Debbie packed up and took their luggage to where they had left the car. A few minutes later they were back. I realised at once that something was wrong. Shaun's face was very pale.

Debbie spoke. "Someone's bashed in the roof of the car."

Shaun added, "There are footprints on the bonnet. They must have jumped up and down on the roof."

"Oh, no!" I wanted to cry. I was angry and sad at the same time. "How could anyone do that without the police noticing, they're everywhere?" We had heard tales of people having aerials bent and wing mirrors snapped off, but I kept asking myself why this had to happen to Debbie and Shaun. "I'll come and have a look, then I'll find the inspector," I said, and as I spoke I pulled on my wellingtons and grabbed my coat.

The smart red car now had a large dent in the roof. The police came to look. I found the duty inspector, a different one from the previous day. He was polite but unhelpful.

"I'm afraid there's not much we can do. We will need statements from you and the registered owner. I've called up our forensic chap and he'll be along shortly. But I doubt we'll ever find who did it."

"I just don't understand how it could have happened. There are dozens of police around all the time. I asked if we could park the car beside the caravan. That wasn't allowed, but I was assured that it would be all right where it is. Yet in full view someone has walked over the roof and jumped up and down on it!"

Shaun and Debbie sat waiting for a policeman to take down their statements. It was lunchtime before the forensic man came and all he was able to tell us was that the footprint was a size seven, the tread marks suggested a boot rather than a shoe. This was hardly enough to track down the culprit. When Debbie and Shaun finally left on that afternoon, I was sure that they would not return. But here they were, smiling at us. We hugged and kissed each other and walked over to the caravan.

Deep in conversation, we drank coffee and caught up on each other's news. They were spending Easter with Shaun's parents in Hertfordshire and had decided to call in on us as a surprise. We looked at their latest photographs and Ian cooked a supper of savoury rice, omelette and salad. While we were eating, John Kiddy from Anglia

Television made a social call. He had brought daffodils from his garden. Debbie gave me an Easter egg before they left. The visit had only been for a few hours, but I was very happy, mostly because the incident with the car had not discouraged them from coming back to this desolate spot.

We waved them off at Peace Corner and then went over to the campfire to talk to one or two visitors who had arrived. A middle-aged couple were setting out their things near the gardens. They had travelled from Cowbridge in Wales and were intending to sleep out in the open all night. We were to meet them again. To show their personal opposition to Molesworth, they came once a month on a Friday night and slept at Peace Corner.

Easter Saturday we woke to find hundreds of policeman stationed around Peace Corner and the gardens. They were in a line along the bridleway too. We just couldn't understand why there should be so many when the marchers were not arriving until Sunday afternoon and the main demonstration was not until Monday. No more than twenty peace people were around. During the day a few more people arrived and a group gathered around the fire on the gardens in the evening. Someone had a guitar and we all sang old Sixties songs, which the MOD policeman nearby seemed to enjoy as they were calling out requests.

Easter Sunday was wet. One by one the marchers, coming from different areas arrived at Peace Corner. They were carrying banners and playing instruments. Bruce Kent wheeled a barrow with a bag of wheat, his contribution for Eritrea. Everyone seemed relaxed and happy, though many had been walking for days in very unpredictable weather. In the evening a candlelight vigil was held on the gardens and people sat on plastic bags or on the stone walls, holding candles and singing. It was raining on and off and not very warm, but this did not dampen their spirits. At one o'clock in the morning we went to bed. The vigil continued all night. From time to time, tucked up under the blankets, we could hear snatches of peace songs.

Easter Monday began quietly. It had been raining hard all night and outside, where the water had not formed enormous puddles; the ground was thick wet mud like treacle. Slowly the gardens, the lane and the bridleway began to fill as more and more people arrived. The coaches were parked a long way from the base and not everyone was able to walk the seven miles around the perimeter. Nevertheless, thousands made it to Peace Corner. The bridleway was a solid, seething mass of women, men and children, all carrying pennants in vivid colours. Later, at one o'clock, hand bells rang and the pennants were pushed firmly into the soft mud. All around the fence, along the road and in the gardens was a sea of rainbow colours, waving gently, in stark contrast to the cold, grey steel fence. The atmosphere was like a carnival, in spite of the rain and despite the fact that many people had mud caked up to their knees and most were soaking wet.

In the caravan we were virtual prisoners. We opened the windows and sold badges, songbooks and leaflets. We answered questions and gave instructions on how to find the press tent, the camping area and the loos. The kettle was never off the boil. One or two people came to the window asking for tea and sandwiches. We politely pointed out that we were not the catering van that was further down the lane. The caravan did have its uses. One woman had an epileptic fit and was brought inside to recover. An elderly man, wearing his war medals, had walked so far in the dreadful conditions that his back was hurting. He had a rest and a cup of tea. Two young mothers asked if they could come inside to breast feed their babies. They sat calmly amidst the hubbub outside, with their little ones peacefully sucking and snorting.

I have never known such a hectic day. People were knocking on the door, on the windows on every side, asking questions. As fast as one moved away, another moved up. It was obvious that as the caravan was at the top of the lane, near the entrance, many thought we were a public information point. Hour after hour the long column of protestors walked past the van: men with children on their shoulders, old-age pensioners with walking sticks, young and old together braving the elements. Just as suddenly as the crowd had grown in the morning, it now began to dwindle. It was time for the seething mass of demonstrators to make their long way back to the coaches. We were exhausted but relieved it had all gone so well. There had been no damage to any of the farmers' fields and the fears and worries of the local people had been unfounded. It had been a resounding success.

We slept well and woke with the sun streaming in the windows. Bridie and Tim, with Peter, Bridie's brother, picked us up at ten o'clock to go to London. We had been invited to be on a television chat show at Thames Television. Others invited to take part were local people from Molesworth and Greenham, the RAMS (the Residents Against

Molesworth Settlement), LOCAM (another group of local people from around Molesworth), CND supporters and Greenham women. As soon as we got into the studio we realised that the programme was designed to be confrontational. The various factions were seated in different blocks. The questions were aimed to whip up feelings and make divisions, not to create understanding. The real issues were not discussed and hardly anyone had the opportunity to speak.

When the 30-minute live programme ended, we were shown upstairs and into three separate rooms where wine and lunch were provided. I could not understand at all why we had to be segregated. It seemed to me important that we all took this unique opportunity to talk to one another and discuss our differences. So, with my plate of food in hand and in the company of another woman, I opened the adjoining door and walked into the next room. In that room were the RAMS group and local Greenham and Molesworth residents.

I walked up to a group of people standing together in the middle of the room, smiled and said, "I thought I would come and join you, it seems silly all to be separated when we have the chance to talk to each other."

A tall man wearing a pin-striped suit immediately launched an attack. He warned me, saying, "If ever there is another demonstration like yesterday in our area, we will use violence, we will smash you."

I was completely taken aback and mumbling that I had not realised they would object to some of us joining them, I began to retreat towards the door to the other room. The man's voice called after me loudly, "You can see the sort of people they are, barging into OUR room."

As we got to the door two men stopped me and said, "We don't mind you being here."

Their faces were familiar and I felt sure they lived near Molesworth. It was a relief that at last someone wanted to talk. We stood with them discussing the programme when the door opened and a woman from Thames Television came in. She put her hand on my shoulder and said in a patronising voice, "Would you please go back into the CND room, you are not supposed to be in here."

I was incensed. "Why can't we all be together?" I asked.

"These people especially requested a room on their own," was the reply.

So now I knew. I went back into the room feeling like a second-class citizen. As a protest I refused to finish my lunch. I regretted it later as I love roast potatoes and I hadn't eaten any for ages. I found the whole episode upsetting. Afterwards I wrote a letter to Thames Television, in which I said I thought they should be trying to bridge divisions, not create them.

The day ended on a good note, though, as we attended an Eirene concert at St. James's Piccadilly, in which Bridie and Tim were singing.

Chapter Eleven
Blue Irises

The rehearsal had been underway for over an hour. The unaccompanied voices, singing in harmony, reverberated in the church. Michael Harp picked up his dulcimer and the tinkling melody rolled around the building. I was tired, it had been a long day, but the music was soothing. The song ended; Tim and Bridie and Michael stood discussing the programme for the concert, they seemed pleased with the way the rehearsal had gone.

"We're going to take a break now."

I looked at Ian who was sitting next to me in the wooden pew. He whispered, "Shall we get a breath of fresh air?"

I nodded. Instead of making for the door that led on to Piccadilly, we walked out of the other exit and found ourselves in a square. In the centre were iron railings and trees. We crossed over and walked round. In front of us, lying on the ground was a bouquet of flowers. Next to the flowers, a small plaque stated that on this spot PC Yvonne Fletcher had died. In my mind, I saw a newspaper photograph of a policewoman's hat lying on the ground. We stood staring down at the flowers, daffodils and blue irises wrapped in cellophane. Moisture had gathered in fine droplets on the under surface of the wrapping. I wanted to cry.

It was then we realised just how much our attitude to the police had changed. I thought of the conversation I had had on the previous day, Easter Monday, with Superintendent Dean. The noise had begun around eleven. Three large metal skips stood by the entrance to Peace Lane, put there to collect the rubbish after the demonstration. Four or five young men were hitting one of the skips with sticks or metal bars. Each pursued his own rhythm, creating a complex dissonant pattern of sound. It was loud, threatening and aggressive and it went on for several hours without a break. Now and again I looked out of the caravan window and there seemed to me a kind of frenzy in the movement of the drummers, as if they were imitating tribal ritual. I felt that it was in some way designed to incite the crowd to violence and it worried me. How could I concentrate? Someone was asking me where the Christian CND service was being held.

"As far as I know it's in Molesworth village."

"Are you selling tea here?"

"What time is the service?"

"Hello, Jennifer!" I looked around only to see our friends from Ipswich, Pete, Keith, Adam, Steve and Angie, clustered around the doorway.

"It's at 1:30, but it's a long walk, you'll never get there in time. No, sorry we don't sell tea, try up the lane. Come in all of you, if you can get in, it's all go here." I had a dull ache in my head.

"Excuse me." Another head appeared through the window.

"You'll have to answer this one, Ian," I said, "the noise is driving me crazy and I'm going to see if I can get them to stop."

I made my way across to where the noise was coming from. It was so loud. I went up to each person in turn, asking if they would stop. Some stopped just long enough to find out what I wanted. The noise continued unabated. After a few minutes, I walked away. I saw Superintendent Dean. He gave his usual genial smile and asked how things were going.

I was angry. "Can't you do anything to stop that banging? I'm sure they're deliberately trying to whip people up."

He started to explain, "I think it's far better to leave them. If I send my men in, then straightaway other people will get involved. Someone will say the police are picking on them and before you know there'll be an ugly incident."

I knew he was right. I remembered other occasions where the officer in charge had caused more trouble by intervening. Once, a protestor had got through the fence and the inspector on duty had decided to clear everyone from the Peace Garden. He had antagonised a lot of law-abiding people, who could not understand why the police had all linked arms and pushed them onto the road. I had seen a woman of sixty in tears, shouting at a policeman that he had no right to behave like that.

Looking back, there were two aspects to our developing relationship with the police. One was the way in which we observed policing tactics in operation. The incident with the skips was one of these. The other aspect was the way in which we came to know individual officers through long conversations with them. We came to understand better their tactics and began to realise that some were much better at crowd control than others. Through conversations with men like Superintendent Michael Dean, Chief Superintendent Colin Street and the Assistant Chief Constable of Cambridgeshire, Alan Ratcliffe, we saw that some senior officers had a high regard for civil liberties. Time and again they said, and demonstrated by their actions, that they respected the right of peaceful protest.

One day, Alan Ratcliffe stopped as he was driving past Peace Lane. It was a quiet time, we were sitting outside on our own and he strode over to us. We started to talk about the Easter demonstration. We had written to him afterwards saying how well we thought the police had handled the situation around Peace Corner, during the demonstration. We said how much we felt his television appearance, just prior to the demonstration, had helped to cool the anxiety of local residents.

One of us mentioned 'Class War', a group of extremists who advocated violent opposition to the nuclear state. They had come to Molesworth at Easter to sell their literature. Mr Ratcliffe said that he thought it was a pity that small groups like this brought discredit to the peace movement. We talked about the way television editors always looked out for shots of confrontation between police and demonstrators. Ian was amused when he used the phrase, 'a certain element', to describe the fringe groups; it seemed a favourite euphemism with a number of policemen.

It was fascinating to hear a senior officer talking about tactics. He told us that before coming to Cambridgeshire he had been in the 'Met'. The Metropolitan Police has a reputation for being very hard, even amongst other forces. Indeed, the Met had been at Molesworth and we had heard some reports of their rough handling. To illustrate this point about fringe groups and the media, he told us a story about a demonstration he had policed in London. A march had taken place along an agreed route and it had all gone off very smoothly. Also, as agreed, a small group were allowed to go into Downing Street to present a petition at Number Ten. The whole event was filmed for TV, but just as the crowd were dispersing at the end, a few people jumped over the barriers at the entrance to Downing Street and sat in the road. The police moved in and carried them off to waiting Transit vans. That night on TV the only coverage of the demonstration were shots of the police hauling people away who had jumped over the barricades. We listened with opened minds.

The other way in which we came to a closer understanding was through conversation with ordinary police officers. I had always made a point of talking to the police on demonstrations, but it was not until we were living side by side with them that my understanding really grew. In those first bitterly cold days after the fence went up, we got to know the civilian police. They huddled around an old oil drum burning anything they could find to keep warm. The Miners' Strike was approaching its *denouement* and many of the police had spent weeks travelling up to Yorkshire. They talked to us about their feelings quite freely. Many of them hated policing the strike. They resented spending time away from home, even though the overtime was good. Not that they had a great deal of sympathy with the miners. More than once I heard a story of the way a group of strikers had smashed up the home of a working miner. The story would be told to show that such people did not deserve our sympathy; they had taken the law into their own hands and they intimidated women and children.

What the police we spoke to at that time particularly resented was the feeling that they were 'in the middle' and that the Government was using them for political purposes.

One man said to me: "I joined the police to serve the community. I wanted to be a village bobby, a community policeman. Being here or at Corton Wood isn't what I joined up for. I've hardly seen my wife and kiddie since Christmas."

Most police officers didn't seem to blame us for the fact they were spending hours out in the cold doing very little, apart from playing cards in the back of the white transit vans. However misguided they thought we were, they respected our stance; we were doing what we thought was right.

In those cold February days when the chill factor brought the temperature down to -23°C, cases of hypothermia occurred among the MOD police. Ministry of Defence police guard all defence establishments and they are under direct control of the Ministry, not accountable to any local authority. At very short notice, some two hundred men and women found they had been seconded from their home base in order to police Molesworth. They were given accommodation in the large, draughty hangars. Shifts were twelve hours, from six until six. They told us that their day began at 3:30 in the morning as breakfast was at four, lunch at 11:30 and tea, the last meal of the day, at four in the afternoon. Although they had a bar and recreation facilities, they usually went to bed by nine o'clock, as they had to be up so early. The tour of duty lasted two weeks.

At first men and women were not kitted out for the arctic conditions. No proper footwear was issued and only regulation uniform was permitted. It was far tougher for them than for the civilian police as they seemed much more tied by bureaucratic procedures. It was two weeks before the order came down issuing more suitable clothing. Conditions in the hangar were poor; not only was it cold but dusty, too. Many people succumbed to respiratory infections. We heard about all this by talking to officers on different occasions. We would stand peering at each other through the barbed wire, often joking that the police seemed virtually to be prisoners. It was too near the truth.

Surveillance helicopters still flew overhead all day long. One evening when were taking Robbie out for his bedtime walk, one followed us up the road. It flew just above the trees, the beating sound of its blades making a tremendous noise as it hovered. The trees bent over and dead leaves rose and swirled in the air. A bright white searchlight shone down on us. It was an unnerving experience.

Two Rainbow Villagers were arrested for taking dead elm out of a nearby wood that was owned by a local farmer. It was a confusing issue. Soon after the fence went up, when the weather was bitterly cold, we had watched from the caravan window as two policeman climbed through into George's field to collect wood to burn on their brazier. I could understand their needing it, no adequate fuel had been provided at that time. They had to keep warm somehow. But if it was all right for them to take wood from private property without permission, why wasn't it also all right for Rainbow Villagers to do so? They also needed to keep warm.

When 'Carpenter' Jim and 'Happy Times' Lyn appeared in court, I agreed to go and say what I had seen, in the hope that their charges would be dropped. I had reservations as I personally had nothing against the police, quite the reverse in fact. I was trying to 'build bridges' between us. But I felt it was the right thing to do. Jim's case was dismissed without my having to give evidence. Lyn was fined £25. My statement was dismissed, as it was apparently only 'hearsay'. I was telling the whole truth though!

A huge clamour of protest greeted the Cambridgeshire police's introduction of special car permits for local residents. The National Council of Civil Liberties took up the cause, but the passes were issued. The intention was to allow access to the B660 only to pass holders. By the time the passes were available and local people had displayed them on their windscreens, the initial flurry of hundreds of protesters coming daily had dwindled to twenty or thirty. The police rarely used the passes as a means of preventing access to Peace Corner. Counterfeit copies of the yellow passes soon began appearing. It would have been a difficult law to enforce. Parking restrictions were enforced and these made life difficult as we found out when Debbie came, but the situation never became like the Miners' Strike, where busloads of demonstrators were prevented from getting anywhere near the picket lines. Only once did we hear of a coach being stopped before it reached the base. Coaches used to drop people off on the corner and collect them at a prearranged time. Car owners parked a quarter of an hour's walk away in Old Weston.

For the first few months after the fence went up, hundreds of police patrolled Molesworth. A local shopkeeper drove up in his van each day selling newspapers, cigarettes and sweets. I used to take my place in the queue, passing the time of day with the policeman next to me. I found it interesting to see how many copies of *The Sun* newspaper were sold. We read *The Guardian*. I used to buy one of the only two copies he had. I would joke loudly as I walked away, "Are we the only people who read a decent newspaper?"

They always took it in good part. At weekends a mobile van supplying hot drinks and snacks was provided for the police, but they didn't mind anyone else using it. It even had chips, but we were only tempted twice.

On International Women's Day, a woman asked one of the MOD police guarding the chapel if he would put a lighted candle inside. Much to our surprise, he did so. Another time we asked if a vase of daffodils could be put in the chapel. A policeman reached through the wire, taking it from me and placing it on top of the pillar. The sergeant watching from the main gate came over and told him to take it down and return it.

We enjoyed talking to the police, especially the MOD police standing 'guarding' the Peace Chapel. We got to know some of them well. Working the night shift in all weathers must have been hard. We used to take out fruit cake and hot drinks to pass around to protesters and police alike. We were particularly touched one evening when, at the end of a fortnightly period, one of the night shift called me over and handed me a card. On the front it had a picture of a kingfisher and a butterfly. Inside it said, 'To Jennifer and Ian, from the night shift chapel, best wishes'. They had all signed their names and written the dates they had been on duty at Molesworth.

The same faces turned up time and time again, back for another two-week stint. They seemed to dislike it intensely and counted the days when they could be back home again. We made friends with one MOD sergeant at the Main Gate. When we first met him his manner was decidedly cool towards us. Each day we asked him for permission to use the chapel and gradually his attitude changed. He was looking forward to going back home to his wife and family. Ian painted a picture of the chapel for him, which we gave him on his last day. He seemed pleased. We never saw him again. Cards made from a sketch Ian had done of the chapel had on the inside cover, 'It is better to light one candle than to curse the darkness'. We tried to give a card to each of the police who had been stationed in the chapel when they left to go home. I wrote a message in each one saying, 'Thank you for taking care of our Peace Chapel!' These words were written with some irony.

One afternoon there was a knock on the caravan door and a female MOD inspector and sergeant stood outside. The inspector said she wanted to say goodbye to us without a fence between us. They asked if they could buy badges to take home to their children. We sold them several each, as well as cards of the chapel. The MOD inspector took a badge out of her lapel and gave it to me. It was a Rupert Bear pin and is sold to raise funds for the wives and families of the RUC shot in Northern Ireland. As they left, they shook hands with us and said they hoped they wouldn't be back as it was 'soul-destroying'. After that we often sold badges to the police, Ministry of Defence and civilian.

What did we talk to the police about? There was little we didn't talk about. Many evenings, I would wander over to the fence by Eirene and start a conversation. We used to talk about our families, our children in particular, and places that we had visited in common. I became friendly with three men from South Wales. Another pair came from the Lake District. That was a good starting point. I recalled a holiday Ian and I had spent in Wasdale. Sometimes the subject turned to a man's family. One had recently got divorced, another had problems with a teenage daughter. The ISSUE would raise its head in due course and more often than not we would find points of agreement. Breaking down stereotypes and building bridges seemed important to us. One night Ian and I were both talking to one of the men from South Wales. I'll call him David. We started talking about the threat of nuclear war and the way children react to it.

David said, "I know. My boy is nine years old. He knows what I do. One night he's watching telly and there's this documentary about cruise missiles. He says to me, 'Dad, why do you have to work at that place? It's wrong; they could blow up the world.' What do you say, eh? What do you say when your own son says that?"

Neither Ian nor I said anything; there was nothing to say.

Chapter Twelve
An Amicable Relationship

Mallen bounced up grinning. He was soaked to the skin. All he was wearing was a worn, brown leather windcheater over a shirt and jumper. His trousers and shoes were drenched. I don't think he had a coat, I had only ever seen him in that same jacket, but he seemed quite oblivious to the cold. The sleet had caused his glasses to mist over and as we talked he took them off and wiped them.

At the time, he was staying at the School House for a few days which turned into a few weeks. He was supposed to be doing a degree at the Bradford College of Art, but the lure of Molesworth kept him coming back. By the end of April, we had come to know him well and we respected his carefully thought out, clearly expressed views. It came as a shock when I discovered he was the same age as my son Antony. Mallen was just called Mallen. He had been born with a quite conventional name, but had changed it by deed poll. I never asked him why he had chosen that name, but he was bound to have had a good reason. It did cause the police some confusion. He would be addressed as, 'Mr Mallen' or they would say, "Mallen what? What's your surname?", and he would patiently and politely explain that he was simply Mallen.

He first visited Molesworth in the spring of 1984, when the first wheat was sown. Like us, he was attracted by what Tim and Bridie were doing. Mallen had read a lot more than either Ian or I about non-violence, but like us he had a great respect for Gandhi. It was typical of Mallen that he used Gandhi's obscure middle name for the central character in a story he was writing. It was part of his final exhibition work at Bradford, and he was not only writing but also illustrating a short fable about ants. The hero was called Karamchand. Mallen's talent as a graphic artist was put to good use on the *Molesworth Bulletin*. For this he produced an immaculately drawn cartoon strip that was gently satirical. Sometimes the target was the Peace Movement while on another occasion it was the MP, John Major. The MP, normally a mild-mannered, bespectacled 'John Minor', is called to do something about the Peace Campers at RAF Molebury. Suddenly he rips open his shirt to reveal a Superman logo as he declares, "When duty calls I am also MAJOR DISASTER, scourge of peaceniks and lefties throughout the land!"

Easter seemed a long time ago; it was nearly the end of April. The pennants had turned to limp wet rags and had been deposited in plastic bags. The Wheat Fund had raised £24,000 to buy grain for Eritrea which was already on its way to Africa, thanks to the help of War on Want and Band Aid. The piles of blankets had been tied and bagged and sent to the Save the Children Fund. Quakers from Wells-next-the-Sea on the North Norfolk coast had offered us accommodation in their holiday flat at the Meeting House, and we spent a week walking the dunes at Burnham Overy Staithe and the salt marshes at Stiffkey. Robbie had bounded around the deserted white sands like a puppy. We lay, sheltered from the wind, in the spiky Marram Grass, looking up at the clouds racing across the sky and we forgot about barbed wire, arc lights, generators and police dogs.

Mallen sat watching as we opened the post. A lot of letters had arrived in the eight days we were away. Things were changing at Molesworth. Since Easter, Helen's hope that a permanent vigil would be set up in the Peace Gardens had become a reality. She had made an appeal for Gore-Tex sleeping bags like the ones the women at Greenham used. The material, though completely waterproof, breathes and thus obviates condensation on the inside. With a sleeping bag that's warm inside, it is possible to stay out in all weather. And now a small group was doing just that.

We heard that Labour MPs were coming to visit Molesworth the following day, but the details were uncertain. When Andy came over to borrow the car the next morning, to drive to Peterborough Court, he said the MPs were coming at 11:30. It was a beautiful spring day. As we went out for our vigil, I noticed that the film crew from Anglia Television were unpacking their gear from an estate car. By now we knew them well and I went over to see if they had more information about who was coming. But they knew no more than we did. Another car drew up, emblazoned with a Hereward Radio motif. From yet another car, a man emerged clutching a spiral-bound notebook. He announced he was from the *Cambridge Evening News*.

"Excuse me," he said to us, "Can you tell me what's happening?"

Ian laughed, "I'm afraid nobody seems to know!"

We were standing with four respectably dressed women from Sheringham Meeting who had arrived a few minutes earlier. John Gregg and Jonathan, two of the group living on Peace Corner joined us. We walked over to the MOD policeman at the gate. He was anxiously trying to read the number plates of the cars that had pulled up.

"You're going to be on telly again," Ian said.

"Oh, I'd better make sure they get my best side," he replied.

"What's going on then, you expecting visitors?"

We told him what we knew and then asked if we could go inside the chapel to hold the vigil. After getting the habitual negative response, we walked back to stand in the gardens. Jeanne Steinhardt and Sidney Dunnicliff from Wellingborough joined us. They, and others from Wellingborough, made the 50-mile round trip to Molesworth every Wednesday morning. We stood in silence, watching the birds on the other side of the wire. I noticed two yellowhammers. They were busy searching for crumbs on the ground that had been beaten flat by the police walking up and down. Clinker and ash had been tipped out of the brazier and lay in an untidy heap near the chapel archway. I was aware of movement behind me. I turned around and saw that about half a dozen men in suits were getting out of cars. The others noticed too. Ian took Jeanne's hand, to signal the vigil was over. The women from Sheringham, John, Sidney, Jonathan and I joined hands. We stood, smiling at each other a moment longer before breaking away.

I recognised Ian Mikardo, but no other faces were familiar to Ian or me. Ten MPs came, among them Gavin Strang, Ann Clwyd and Max Madden, all members of the Parliamentary Labour Party's CND Group. They wandered around looking at the fence and talking to police. Someone was asked to move a car that was obstructing the entrance and was arguing about why this was necessary.

I looked at Ian. "Shall I offer them a cup of tea?"

Finding as many mugs as I could muster, I loaded a tray and stepped out into the sunshine. The MPs stood by the caravan in groups talking to reporters. Gavin Strang was a few yards further off, near the gate, giving an interview to Anglia TV. I moved among them handing out mugs of tea. I noticed that I had given one MP our SDP mug. It had appeared in the caravan with another commemorating Prince Charles' wedding. We didn't know where they had come from.

I approached the young Labour MP as he put the cup to his lips. He was unaware of the slogan painted all over it.

"Don't let the cameras see what your drinking from, they'd love it," I said, smiling broadly.

He looked puzzled, uncertain of what I was talking about, then screwed up his eyes reading the inscription on the mug. A look of mock horror crossed his face. He tried to hide the mug inside his jacket as several of his colleagues laughed, one reaching for his camera.

News of the MPs' visit had reached the ears of Ratepayers Against Molesworth Settlement and two of their most active members, the landlady from a local pub and a Brington parish councillor, now turned up wanting to know what these Labour Party politicians were up to.

"Hello!" I said, moving up to the councillor, "I'd like you to meet some members of Parliament." As we walked back to join the MPs I said, "This is a Brington parish councillor, he's a local villager."

We knew him quite well, having attended to Parish Council meetings at the School in Brington. I left him in a deep and animated conversation with Max Madden, the Member for Bradford West. The parliamentarians stayed for two hours and before leaving they presented a cheque of £50 for the 'Easter Wheat Campaign'.

Veronica came that day. She is one of our closest friends in two senses: she lives just around the corner from our home in Ipswich and she is very dear to both Ian and me. She had driven up from Ipswich with a friend and it was their first sight of a missile base. Like most people, they were shocked by the forbidding appearance and could not understand how we seemed to take it for granted. It reminded them of a concentration camp – and they were seeing it on a good day! We had our lunch out in Peace Lane, sitting on striped canvas garden chairs, a few feet from the fence. We must have looked a bit like those people who picnic in motorway lay-bys.

It was a day for seeing old friends and making links between the past and the present. Julius the husband of Lesley, my friend from Derby, arrived and sat with us. Lesley now called herself Leah. I remember how, on a joint visit to Greenham, we had sat and talked about what we would like to be called if we could change our names. I chose Fern, which seemed appropriate sitting amongst the golden, rusty bracken. It didn't catch on, but Lesley's choice of Leah did and she has been known as Leah ever since. A group from Bristol brought Diana Francis, whom we last met in the old Abbey at Bonnecombe, attending the International Fellowship of Reconciliation conference. Diana had been elected president of IFOR at Bonnecombe. She is a Quaker. We sat on the grass verge reminiscing, thankful for the high hedge that obscured all the military trappings that lay behind it. It was a warm afternoon with hardly any breeze. After the four o'clock vigil, I walked back to the car with Veronica and her friend, another Jennifer.

"Thanks for the cake and flowers, see you again soon, take care, love to the family," I called out as they drove off.

I walked back slowly. The little copse that lay just down the road was coming to life. Shyly emerging from the shaded, grassy floor of the wood were celandines and bluebells. In the ditch, clumps of yellow cowslips grew in profusion. A surge of hope went through me. Surely they could never really bring nuclear missiles here?

★★★

Was it this feeling of hope that prompted me to re-pot some geraniums and wash the kitchen curtains? And was it this same feeling that prompted Ian not only to empty our toilet bucket, but also the one in the small tent down the lane, provided for visitors?

Neither of us found the toilet arrangements easy. The Elsan stood in the little room to the right of the kitchen; there was no difficulty in using it, that wasn't the problem. The problem was what to do with the contents when it was full. At first, we emptied it into the long drops dug by the Rainbow Villagers. They stood in the middle of the fields partly concealed by a canvas windbreak. I was pleased not to have to use them as they were a bit exposed. With the fields fenced in, we had to find another site. Ian discovered a small field on the opposite side of the road, a few hundred yards from the caravan. It belonged to the Ministry and once Nissen huts had stood on it. Now all that remained under the long grass, thistles and brambles, was evidence of the concrete bases on which the huts had stood. The field was obscured from the road by a fifteen-foot hedge. When the eviction took place, the army had dug ditches at the two entrances to prevent vehicles driving on to it. Ian took a spade and dug a small 'shit pit' in one corner of the field. Every week, he carried the blue bucket down the road. Later, the hole was enlarged when Peace Corner acquired another Elsan toilet. Our friends on Peace Corner preferred to trundle their bucket down the road in a wheelbarrow. The police and RAF, normally ever vigilant, never queried these journeys - perhaps they turned a blind eye?

A handful of people were now living permanently in the Peace Gardens. Someone would arrive, stay a few days and move on, others stayed longer. It was a hard existence, with no shelter from the strong winds that blew, day in, day out. Cooking was done over a wood fire and at night they slept in waterproof sleeping bags. The police refused to allow tents or any 'permanent structure' to be built, but gradually a kind of shelter grew. It started as a piece of wattle fencing and little by little was embellished with canvas and polythene. If it became too 'tent-like' for the police, they would come and demand that it be taken down.

★★★

I don't know what happened to Whitsun. Now we have the 'Spring Bank Holiday' on the first weekend in May and 'Whit Monday' is May Day. It was a beautiful morning. Neither of us was in a hurry to get up, we looked at the hawthorn just outside the window. It was covered in blossom. I lay thinking about the previous day; so many people had taken part in the afternoon vigil. I had spoken about Ann Francis, a vicar's wife from Wales. A friend of hers, Sonia, who also came from Wales, had made a little garden in the barbed wire fence, behind a hedge where the cowslips grew. Sonia had dug a small patch of earth and planted clumps of bulbs and flowers. On a piece of wood, she wrote that it was for Ann Francis, who was in prison. Ann had been given a year's sentence for criminal damage at Greenham Common. It seemed a harsh sentence. Later, I showed people where to find the garden. You had to walk down the road, cross a ditch and climb through a gap in the hedge. On the other side was the 'fence' of coils of old barbed wire going rusty. In between the strands lay the small circular patch of cultivated earth. The young plants were wilting in the sun, so I fetched water in a milk bottle to revive them. It was strangely moving.

Today the Anglican Pacifist Fellowship (APF) was coming to 'Beat the Bounds'. We were not sure what this meant or what they would do. All we knew was that they were starting off from Molesworth village and walking to Peace Corner. They were not expected until one o'clock. The radio news bulletins were full of talk about the celebrations being planned for the fortieth anniversary of V.E. Day. I couldn't understand why the Russians were being excluded. Then they had been our allies, now they were our enemies. The Germans were now our friends. Our politicians in the 1940s had talked of the gallantry of the Russian Army and the fortitude of the Russian people in their struggle against the evil Nazi regime. Now, the British Government was trying to blot out that memory, it didn't fit into the current picture. I tried to put this into words during the morning vigil.

The morning passed in a leisurely way. Tom, another New Zealander who had been living at Molesworth from time to time, had brought his sister Vicki to see what it was like. Tom was wearing cut-down jeans and a tee-shirt. He sat on the ground, with his arms hugging his knees. Vicki and I sat on chairs while Ian was perched on a log. Vicki was asking questions about the base.

"It might be a good idea to put the table out, there should be lots of people around," I suggested to Ian.

He pulled out the old card table from under the van. We used it to display badges, leaflets and cards to sell. He set it up beside the caravan. Soon Ian was doing a steady trade selling Molesworth badges. We had other badges, produced by the Quakers, which seemed to be popular, but most people liked to have a badge that mentioned Molesworth. We still had a few that were made for Rainbow Village that Brig had sold us. They showed a *Wind in the Willows* mole holding a placard, saying 'No Cruise'. Quite a crowd had gathered.

'They're coming! They're coming!' said a little boy, running up to his mother.

I stood up and hurried across to the road. Coming towards me I could see a procession of clerics, all looking splendid. White surplices over black cassocks blew like sails in the breeze. In front, a middle-aged man carried a large wooden cross. Another figure was swinging a smoking censer as he walked. There was an air of incongruity about it all as they walked beside the high, welded mesh fence, with its coil of gleaming razor wire shimmering on top. Inside, the uniformed police with their black-peaked caps stared in disbelief. A dog handler pulled sharply on the lead of his German Shepherd as it began barking.

Behind the clergy in their vestments came others, lay people, dressed in sweaters, anoraks and jeans. The crowd milled around the black gate, with its barbed wire and row of black crosses on top. The sun shone, the sky was blue and the Peace Gardens were beginning to bloom. It was time to eat. For once the ground was dry. The crowd was hungry having just walked some four miles around the fence. In the gardens small groups of people sat about laughing and talking, others clustered on the gravel in Peace Lane, happily munching sandwiches. Thermos flasks appeared. Little children ran around exploring and dogs sniffed at paper bags looking for remnants of packed lunches. It reminded me of a church outing.

'Beating the Bounds', we discovered, was an old tradition of the church dating back to medieval times. The priest and parishioners would walk the parish boundary at Rogationtide, blessing the land and praying for a good harvest. The APF had planned its trip to Molesworth the year before. The members hoped to bless the land that had been ploughed and planted with wheat. Now the fields were behind fences, but we could see, as it says in the old hymn, 'Love is come again, like wheat that springs up green. The title of the hymn is *Now the Green Blade Riseth*. Words: J. M. Crum (1928) Music: traditional French carol harmonised by Martin Shaw (1928).

When everyone was refreshed, a service was held. Someone circulated hymn sheets; we were all in good voice. The Bishop of Dudley, Tony Dumper, gave the blessing. Some stood with bowed heads, others sat on the rubble walls of the flower beds. The bishop stood in the middle of the gardens on a makeshift platform, made from two wooden pallets, given to the camp for firewood. Behind him lay the imprisoned chapel. His arm was outstretched in the sign of blessing. For a moment it was quiet, then we sang a final hymn. The procession re-formed on the road and moved on, making its way to the church in Old Weston.

Bridie and Tim had agreed to help provide a barbecue at the home of farmer Robert Ward in Molesworth. Ian and I drove over later in the afternoon. Children were jumping off bales of straw in the barn and taking turns to sit on the tractor. A queue of people collected baked potatoes and cheese, while Tim was ladling out soup into plastic cups.

The sun was still shining and it felt warm in the sheltered farmyard. We sat on the grass and talked to Bridie's family. The Wallis clan were Annette and Oscar, Bridie's mother and father, her sister Jo and husband, Alf, and their two daughters, Hannah and Naomi, plus one of her brothers, Peter.

Tim and Bridie flopped down on the grass beside us.

I smiled. "You must be really tired, but it's been good to see so many people."

"Yes it's been great," Tim replied.

Ian, who had been daydreaming, sat up. "What's tomorrow?"

"Tuesday. May 7th," said Bridie.

"It's tomorrow we have to go to court," he announced.

★★★

The courthouse in Huntingdon was by then familiar to us. We arrived promptly at 9:45 that Tuesday morning. Neil Davidson, our solicitor, was already there. It was the day that the Stopping-up Order was to be heard by the magistrates. Neil ushered us into one of the courtrooms. There were no magistrates, no ushers. A young man in a grey suit who was holding a bundle of papers was the sole occupant of the room. He greeted Neil.

On the Thursday before, the local government elections had been held and the Conservatives had lost their overall majority on Cambridgeshire County Council. Naturally, the implications of this took a while to sink in. The Alliance now held the balance of power in a 'hung' council. Tuesday was effectively the first working day for the new administration as Monday had been a Bank Holiday. Meetings had been held between the leaders of the three groups, but no new committees had yet been appointed. Unbeknown to us, the County Solicitor had raised the question of the Stopping up Order for the closure of Peace Lane, with the leaders of the three groups and asked if they wanted to proceed. The Labour group were in favour of throwing the whole thing out, the Conservatives wanted to go ahead as planned, but the Alliance decided that a postponement was desirable, in order that the issue could be re-examined by the new council.

The young man in the grey suit was a representative of the county solicitor. He briefly conferred with Neil who told us that the matter was to be postponed indefinitely, pending a new Transportation Committee being chosen. The question would then be referred to them for new recommendations! We walked out of the court, asking Neil to explain how it would be likely to affect us.

"As I see it, it means you're still technically on the highway, until this goes through. That means the police could charge you with Obstruction of the Highway, if they felt so inclined."

"But that's nothing new, is it?" Ian asked.

"Quite right, they could petition you for that at any time under the Road Traffic Act."

"But they haven't so far, so why should they now?" I wanted to know. I felt the sense of relief I had experienced at the news of the postponement vanishing.

Neil smiled and said, "There's no reason to suppose they will."

"Unless," Ian carried on, "they hadn't bothered before because they knew the road closure was coming up. Now they may feel they have to act."

"Would you like me to write another letter to the Chief Constable?" Neil said, sensing our anxiety. He whipped out his little Dictaphone and began dictating: "To the Chief Constable... Dear Sir, we have been instructed by our clients..."

It was tremendously reassuring to hear Neil simply dash off a letter there and then. I don't know what we would have done without him. We had first met him in February. Tim and Bridie knew Neil and his wife Denise, who was prominent in the local residents' group called Local Concern about Molesworth Base. (LOCAMB) were a more moderate group than the RAMS. Neil took on the defence of a number of the Rainbow Villagers, it was all legal aid work and we suspect he made little money out of it. He had been acting for us since mid-February. His first action was to write to the Chief Constable and try to establish whether they were planning to act against us. The reply from Mr Radcliffe had reassured us when he stated, '*We do not, however, propose taking any action against your clients at this stage.*' The last sentence made us smile. It read: '*We realise that Mr and Mrs Hartley are genuine peace protestors and our officers have what we term an amicable relationship with them.*'

The letter Neil wrote on May 7th received another reassuring response from the Assistant Chief Constable. It spoke of the uncertainty surrounding the future status of the land, and went on to say it was difficult to be definite but reiterated the promise to give Neil adequate notice, should we be required to move. The question of the future of the land certainly did remain a mystery. We knew that the original intention of the MOD was to buy the field behind the caravan where George kept his horses, but we had been staggered to discover that the land owner was not a local farmer but the Church of England.

We later learned that it consisted of a parcel of Glebe Land, and although the local parishes were all within the Diocese of Ely, this field was owned by the Diocese of Peterborough. The Diocesan Board of Finance had received an offer of around £2,000 from the Ministry of Defence for these 1.6 acres. There is little doubt that they would have accepted the offer had the deal remained secret. Unfortunately for the MOD, the news leaked out and the Diocesan Board received several offers in excess of the original bid. Even then, because of the provisions of the Glebe Land Act, the Church was not bound to accept the highest offer and still showed an inclination to proceed with the sale to the Ministry. The irony here was that this Act had been introduced in the 1970s in order to prevent land speculators with large incomes outbidding tenants and worthy local enterprises, when Glebe Land came up for sale.

Christian CND was one of the groups that had made a bid for the land. When they heard that the sale might still go through, they decided to take legal action and at a cost of some £6,000 took the case to the High Court to try to obtain an injunction preventing the sale. There were two pillars to the Christian CND case. The Reverend Robin Anstey, a vicar in the diocese, agreed to stand as the plaintiff because the case was technically, as distinct from morally, based on the argument that if the land was sold for less than the highest bid, his stipend would be affected. In addition the resolution of General Synod at the conclusion of the Church and the Bomb debate was cited. A clear majority had come out firmly against first-use nuclear weapons. Cruise missiles are part of NATO's so-called flexible response. They travel slowly and are designed to strike at hardened missile silos in a pre-emptive action and so are clearly intended to be used first.

On April 17th a ruling was given. The court upheld Christian CND's case and the church agreed to call off the sale and to proceed only at some later date, if the purchaser met these two criteria, i.e. that the offer was the highest received and that the use made of the land would not be in conflict with the policy of General Synod in respect of first-use nuclear weapons. This was not the end of the story; the possibility remained that the Ministry could submit a higher bid and that the members of the Diocesan Board of Finance could refute the argument about 'no first use'.

We sat pondering all this over a cup of coffee in a snack bar. Ian said he felt jittery. It was the feeling of uncertainty and fear that behind closed doors moves could be afoot that we knew nothing about.

★★★

"Today is the fortieth anniversary of V.E. Day," the radio announcer intoned. Lying in bed, listening to the news, I decided to write something about the war. With breakfast cleared away, I put the typewriter on the table and typed out:

'May 8ᵗʰ, 1985, MOLESWORTH

'Today is the fortieth anniversary of the ending of the Second World War in Europe.

'Both the First World War and the Second World War were horrific, and left children fatherless, women without husbands and sweethearts, and many people maimed and destroyed mentally and physically for life.

'We talk of violence in our society today; war is the ultimate violence.

'We are here to bear witness to the fact that war must not occur again as the outcome would be more devastating than any war fought in the history of humanity.

'We ask you to join us today in our act of worship to pray for world peace, and for people to have the courage and trust to live together with people in all countries in tolerance and co-operation.'

In a notebook, Ian jotted down his impressions of that day; he did not keep a diary, but occasionally made notes about things that were on his mind. He wrote:

'We listened to the service from Westminster Abbey. There were a lot of references to peace, readings from Isaiah about the lamb lying down with the lion and [Micah] beating swords into ploughshares.

In our service earlier J. spoke about her father who had been through World War I and who had been marked for life, unable to talk about it. Showing emotion (which he obviously felt) not being manly. Tom spoke about the conscientious objectors of both world wars who were imprisoned for their beliefs.

'J. has written a piece about today asking the police to join us in our service. It was very inspiring and I felt very moved when she read it out first to the MOD police sergeant and then to the Cambs police in their transit van.

'During the service I thought about how the world could avoid future conflict. It seems that fear, greed and selfishness on an individual level is matched on a national level by similar vices.

'Just finished reading The Abolition *by Jonathan Schell. He explains that the need to preserve national sovereignty is what has driven countries to threaten their neighbour. If you want peace prepare for war. Deterrence is the ultimate in war preparation, which paradoxically makes actual fighting wars an anachronism.'*

On the next page of his notebook, Ian had written a summary of the main argument in the book, in which the author rejects the idea that peace could come through world government. At the foot of the page he had written:

'Nothing about the morality of terror as a means of maintaining peace (in this context, peace = status quo). Tim has been thinking about the idea of achieving disarmament through world government. His idea is to help build an alternative infrastructure that points the way, acts as a model for world government.

'1:30pm. At this point my reverie was interrupted by the action of the Nottingham Moles who got into the base. Some twenty people, I think. They climbed on to watch towers. It certainly changed the atmosphere. All the MOD police began rushing about. Driving round very fast in their vans. Dogs and handlers running here, there and everywhere.'

The Nottingham group's non-violent, direct action, which incidentally was filmed for Channel Four's *Diverse Reports*, was clearly in Ian's mind, when on the next page of his notebook, after outlining what Neil said about the road closure, he continues:

'It's difficult to retain a sane perspective on what we are doing here. How long will we be allowed to continue? Are we doing enough? Should we do something that would lead to arrest? When others do NVDA (non-violent direct action) we rationalise our own inaction on the grounds that it would jeopardise our position. But I think we both feel somewhat unsettled by other people doing it and I think I

could easily do something - not from a sense that it was right/useful etc., but simply because it felt as if I was <u>doing</u> something. Tom was very good on Monday - he said that our presence here was v. important and that we helped to create a relaxed and easy atmosphere. I wish I could always feel that this was enough. I think Jennifer is far more positive than I am - witness her action today in producing a statement for the police for V.E. day. This felt very good and empowering to me but what had I done? What do I do?'

I too had spent some considerable time thinking about NVDA. Although I was not against it in principle, I felt that at that time it was not the right thing for me to be doing. I had tried to build up a good relationship with the police on duty and knew that many of them were in sympathy with our views. Deliberately to break the law at a time when there were so many good opportunities for real dialogue seemed counter-productive.

Something happened two days later that made us think more about law breaking and civil disobedience. We had a visit from four Welsh ministers.

Chapter Thirteen

Tangnefedd, Heddwch, Cariad

'*A carload of ministers representing the Welsh Fellowship of Reconciliation called Cymdeithas y Cymod, are visiting Molesworth this Friday, 10th May... We intend to perform a "symbolic action", including the release of a dove to carry a message to Wales. We'd like to meet you or any others who share our Christian pacifist convictions, to exchange greetings and prayer together...*

Shalom, John Tudor.'

Four ministers arrived. A grey-haired man in a heavy overcoat introduced himself as John Tudor. He had a big, square jaw and when he smiled, his lips were lightly pressed together. His eyes had a mischievous twinkle as he introduced his co-conspirators. Islwyn Lake, a Congregational minister from Machynlleth and the oldest of the group, had been a conscientious objector in the Second World War. Pryderi Jones, a younger-looking man with dark hair, was minister of a chapel in Wrexham. Finally, John Owen from Ruithin was shorter and about the same age as Pryderi. He, like the other John and Pryderi, was a Welsh Presbyterian minister. They sat in the caravan eating their sandwiches and telling us what they intended to do. When we had heard their plan, we decided to hold the vigil at twelve and combine it with their action.

Just before twelve we went outside. We all stood in a semicircle with Bridie, Tim and Michael Lawler from the Gandhi Foundation. The ministers sang a hymn in Welsh and then took turns to read from the Bible. After a prayer, Pryderi picked up a small cardboard box and opened the flap revealing a grey and white pigeon. He held the box aloft and the bird swept out and upwards over the chapel fence, away into the distance, soaring up into the sky. We watched as it disappeared from sight. Then the ministers walked forward to the fence and took out a large white banner with the sign of the Welsh Fellowship of Reconciliation painted on it in red. Together, they hung it on the wire. Other cardboard placards were produced, with texts from the scriptures in Welsh, such as '*they shall beat their swords into ploughshares*'. These were hung alongside the banner. An MOD policeman came over and asked them to remove them saying that it was illegal to put anything on the fence.

"We have nearly finished," John told him. "There is just one further act we wish to carry out."

We waited a few moments while the ministers spoke in low voices to one another, then John Tudor opened his coat and took out a long pair of old wire cutters. I had noticed the end of the cutters hanging below the hem of his coat and had waited with bated breath to see if the police also noticed. Moving forward as one, the ministers all took hold of the handles. Pushing down they tried to cut one strand of wire. The cutters were blunt; they wouldn't cut. They tried again. Ian took a photograph with Islwyn's camera. The MOD policeman was radioing control to report an incident. The Cambridgeshire police, watching from their transit van, were at first unaware of what was going on. The ministers drew back. The wire was still intact. We were all unsure what action the police would take.

"The cutters were completely blunt," John Tudor was saying. "A local farmer lent them to us; I'll have words with him when I get back!"

The two policemen who walked over to speak to the ministers, seemed very uncertain about what they should do. They had called headquarters and were awaiting instructions. The message came through. Arrest them! It was all very civilised and friendly. The ministers were escorted into the back of the van.

"Good luck, hope they don't keep you too long," I called out as the van slowly drove away to Huntingdon Police station. Out of the back window they smiled and waved.

Tim went to Huntingdon in his car to fetch them. They had been kept in separate cells for many hours. We were disappointed not to be at Peace Corner to welcome them back, but we had arranged to visit John Major, the MP. A letter we received from John Owen a few days later helped fill in the picture as it contained a photocopy of his charge sheet. It read as follows:

177

'Person charged... John Owen.

'That you on Friday May 10th, 1985, at RAF Molesworth in the County of Cambridgeshire, had in your custody or under your control a pair of wire cutters, intending without lawful excuse to use it to damage certain property, namely the perimeter fence, belonging to the Ministry of Defence.

Contrary to Sec.3. Criminal Damage Act 1971.

'That you on Friday May 10th, 1985, at RAF Molesworth in the County of Cambridgeshire, without lawful authority or permission displayed a sign on the perimeter fence at RAF Molesworth.

Contrary to Byelaw 2 (i) R.A.F. Molesworth Byelaws, 1985.'

The charge sheet bore the date and the time, 18.00 hours, six hours after their arrest. The date set for the court appearance in Huntingdon was May 30th. The other three ministers received the same charges and court date.

Ian had arranged to be at a meeting in London and was unable to attend the court hearing, but several others from Peace Corner and I were able to go to lend our support. The ministers, wearing suits, stood together in a row in the dock. Individually they read out their carefully composed statements.

John Tudor spoke slowly and clearly, "I plead guilty."

After a pause he continued.

"Because the substance of these two charges is not in dispute, I have no LEGAL defence. To attempt to fight a court case would be a waste of time and energy for all of us, a diversion from the real issue.

"It is true that four of us together placed a Christian banner and some Scripture texts on the barbed wire belonging to the Ministry of Defence in a field in Cambridgeshire. It is true that we intended to cut one strand of the barbed wire. I would add that the crimes were committed at noon during an act of worship attended by six other members of the general public, and watched by a large number of policemen guarding the Peace Chapel."

He talked for a few more minutes and finishing by saying, *"...I thank the court for the opportunity to say a further few words. We are ordained Nonconformist ministers, family men, people of a good standing, academically well qualified, members of a profession especially honoured in Wales. To be arrested, held in police custody for nearly six hours, and to stand before this court accused of*

178

crime is new to each of us... We are not four vandals or eccentrics prepared to flout the law of this country. In fact we belong to two church traditions, which have consistently and repeatedly condemned the deployment of nuclear weapons by our country as a means of defence... I question the legality of such monstrous weapons. I renounce them. I oppose their siting here or anywhere in our country. The Peace Chapel, Eirene, is a symbol of renewal and hope, and should be allowed to flourish as an alternative possibility for us all. We try to follow the Prince of Peace. Mr. Chairman, I am guilty, and remain unrepentant."

Each took a slightly different line of argument; Pryderi Jones concluded his short speech by saying, *"...We have been accused of the intention of damaging Ministry of Defence property. I am not playing with words when I say that we also are Ministers of Defence, concerned with a greater damage. God compels us to defend the innocent, the creation and life itself. But we defend by proclaiming and following a Christ whose way is that of reconciliation, (when walls of conflict are broken down) of peace, (which always means preparation for peace, not war) and justice, (which means a world where resources are shared for the benefit of all.) Our actions – our symbolic action – you may disagree with, but not our Master. Our responsibility and calling is to obey Him and no one else. We have given this court our apology for any inconvenience. But we cannot offer you our regret or our guilt."*

Islwyn, standing erect and speaking softly, yet clearly, with a lilting Welsh accent, made another point: *"...That which is to be established at Molesworth would be described officially as a form of defence and there are those who would justify the use of nuclear missiles in a time of crisis. Nevertheless, Molesworth represents a threat to destroy life on an unprecedented scale. The enemy towards whom we point our missiles are people like us – some strong and vigorous and others old and sick; workers in factories, babies in prams or in the womb; children at school... We agreed to make our witness by joining in the daily act of worship at Peace Corner and by means of three symbolic actions, namely the liberating of a dove; placing Christian messages on the fence and making clear our intention to cut a piece of wire. This action was all the more meaningful to us as it took place not at the perimeter fence, but at the small separate fence that now keeps worshippers outside the place of worship. I would maintain that what could legally be considered a punishable offence was a small attempt to proclaim and uphold Christian values in a dangerously violent age."*

John Owen's turn came.

"...The Government believes that nuclear arms have kept the peace for 40 years, yet, more local wars have been fought during that period than in any other corresponding period in the world's history. I cannot reconcile this policy with the

Christian Gospel of love. As a theological student, I became more convinced each day that the way of Jesus was the way of life, and that his way of love was the way to peace, for the individual and for mankind as a whole... May I conclude with a question for you to consider before you come to your verdict? Which act really endangers the peace, the cutting of a wire in a fence, or the building of a cruise missile base for 64 cruise missiles, each one of them fifteen times as effective as the bomb dropped on Hiroshima, which killed two hundred thousand people and is still killing people today? And a quotation in Welsh by the Welsh poet, Waldo Williams:

'Pa werth na thry yn wawd

Pan laddo dyn frawd?'

"This literally translated means:

'What value that does not change to mockery

When man kills his brother?'

"I thank you for the opportunity to explain the motives behind my actions."

As each man spoke, the court room had been very quiet. I had to resist an impulse to applaud when they finished speaking. Each statement had been delivered with great eloquence. Now the three magistrates, seated at the raised wooden bench, began to confer in whispers, then the sentence was read. For attempting to cut the fence, fine £10 each. For hanging banners on the fence, fine £10 each. In addition, each man was ordered to pay costs of £7.

★★★

It was not the last we heard of the case. John Tudor sent me a copy of a letter he had sent to the officer in charge of the property store at the police station in Huntingdon. In it he requested that the confiscated FOR banner should be returned and asked if I could collect it for him. I heard a few weeks later that the items were ready for collection. I signed a form and the policeman handed over the offending banner and placards.

Meanwhile, local magistrates' courts in Wales were asked to collect the £27 fine that had been imposed on each of the ministers. Each man refused to pay. In the case of the Congregational minister, the Reverend Islwyn Lake, the magistrates at Machynlleth imposed a penalty of one day's imprisonment. Islwyn spent the remainder of that day in police cells and he was released in the evening. In the case of the other three who are all Presbyterians, on the refusal to pay, an Attachment of Earnings Order was imposed on their 'employer' namely, the Presbyterian Church of Wales. We knew the courts had the power to order an employer to deduct fines from an employee's salary, but in our experience it had been a rarely used remedy. By a strange coincidence, though, it had been used in the case of another Welsh Presbyterian known to both Ian and me and also to John Tudor. Her name was Awell Irene.

It was in April when Awell Irene and a friend called David, who has since become her husband, camped for the weekend at Molesworth. We chatted with them shortly after they arrived and felt an immediate rapport. I guessed they were in their late twenties or early thirties. David was quiet and thoughtful, the son of an Anglican clergyman. Awell Irene had dropped her surname and she was simply known by her two first names. The word 'Awell' means 'breeze' and 'Irene' has the same root as Eirene, the Greek word for 'peace'. A peaceful breeze, she was also very vivacious. We discovered that she was employed by the Welsh Presbyterians as a community worker in North Wales.

We rarely bought a newspaper as it meant a trip into Kimbolton. The van that used to deliver papers had stopped calling. That Sunday, Ian had gone off and returned with a copy of *The Observer*. Turning a page I came across the headline, '*THE UNLIKELY MARTYR FROM THE VICARAGE*'. The article was about Anne Francis. It was the first we had heard about her sentence.

"Ian, come and read this, it's terrible," I called out.

I just couldn't believe it. She had been at Molesworth only a few weeks previously and had come to the caravan to see us. I felt very upset. As it was almost eleven, on impulse I took the newspaper with me, thinking I might refer to it during the vigil. Awell Irene and David joined us by the fence and after a few minutes, I started to read the newspaper account out loud.

"In what the peace movement sees as the start of a legal crackdown on its members, a vicar's wife this weekend begins a twelve-month jail sentence for causing £120 worth of damage to the Greenham Common perimeter fence. Anne Francis, 44 year-old mother of four grown-up children, was found guilty at Aylesbury Crown Court last week of two charges of criminal damage... Mrs Francis, from Llantilio Pertholey, near Abergavenny, had denied the charges. She

said it was 'a righteous act, not an act of damage.' She had shown the jury a video film of the effects of the two nuclear bombs dropped on Japan in 1945...

"According to her husband, the Rev. Donald Francis... 'if the severity of the sentence makes her a martyr it will be a role she will adopt' with some reluctance.

"The daughter of a Newport steelworker, Mrs Francis has been a convinced Christian pacifist since her teens. Her involvement has intensified over the past three years, reflecting a belief that time is short and the nuclear danger immediate..."

It ended with another quote from her husband saying, *"It will be Christmas before she comes out"*. Anne appealed against the sentence and it was commuted to six months.

Later that day, Awell Irene walked across the fields, following the line of the outer fence. Finding a remote spot, with only a single roll of barbed wire, she scrambled through. She had taken with her a pot of red paint and a pair of wire cutters. With the red paint, she wrote large letters on one of the steel doors, set at intervals in the welded mesh security fence. Awell Irene painted the Welsh words, 'Tangnefedd, Heddwch and Cariad'. The first two mean 'peace', the third means 'love'. After that, she cut a hole through the welded steel wire and waited to give herself up. It was some time before a policeman on patrol found her and arrested her. David came and told us that she had been arrested, but it was not until the following day we heard all about it, as she was not released until the early hours of the morning. As she told us what she had done, she looked calm and relaxed. Something, she explained, in the story of Anne Francis had triggered off a compulsion to take the action she had. The newspaper account I had read aloud had filled her with anger, sadness and a great sense of injustice.

When we heard that the court had ordered the Welsh Presbyterian Church to pay the fines of the three ministers, we knew that this was what had happened to Awell Irene and that she had been powerless to prevent it. But there was a new twist to the ministers' tale. What followed is described in a letter John Tudor wrote to us afterwards: *'It is to the great credit of the officers of the General Assembly of the Presbyterian Church that they vigorously refused to comply with the court orders. The legal ground of their unwillingness to comply was that ministers' stipends cannot be regarded as 'earnings' in accordance with the terms of the Attachment of Earnings Act. In other words, in law, the officers of the Presbyterian Church of Wales are not employers of ministers of religion, merely agents who collect donations from individual ministers' congregations for disbursement. The magistrates' courts, in the cases of the three men, adjourned their decisions on the matter for months, pending the publication of a case being heard in the House of Lords about that time. This happy coincidence served the ministers well, since the House of Lords' judgement proved favourable. This other case totally vindicated the Presbyterian Church of Wales' refusal to obey the Attachment of Earnings Order in their three cases.*

'*The unanimous judgement of the five Appeal Judges in the House of Lords Appeal Case, Colin Davies versus Presbyterian Church of Wales, hinged on whether a minister had a Contract of Service legally binding or not. This historic and binding judgement found that he had not. A minister is bound to his church not by any contract but by conscience. He is not employed. Therefore in the case of John Tudor, Pryderi Jones and John Owen their stipends cannot be regarded as earnings from which fines can be subtracted by other servants of the church on the bidding of the court.*'

The whole process was to take almost twelve months and created a great deal of publicity, especially in Wales. Eventually though, the time came for the three men to go to court once more, this time to face prison sentences. They were quite determined to face this consequence, but fate intervened in the shape of some supporters. John Owen was sentenced to seven days in prison; however, members of his congregation paid the fine rather than see their minister go to jail. In the case of the other two, anonymous donors paid the fines without their further appearance in court.

In an article Ian wrote for a magazine first published that spring, called *Dialogue and Resistance*, he tried to put into words his thoughts about 'Non-Violence'. He described some of the various activities that people were calling 'non-violent direct action'. There was what Ian called the 'up-and-over' school: those who secretly get inside bases, plant trees, cut fences, partly in order to demonstrate lax security; then there was the '*kamikaze*' approach of those, like the Snowballers, who announced their intentions in advance and were sometimes arrested before they had cut one strand of fencing. Ian spoke of other factors, some emphasizing that it was not what you did, but the spirit in which it was done. But he asked where this feeling of rightness came from? He raised the question of whether illegality was a necessary component and suggested that law-breaking was not an end in itself. What was more important was demonstrating an alternative to war and setting an agenda to do so. The article concluded: '*I hope that I have outlined... some of the questions we ought to be asking. What follows are a few more positive thoughts. First, I think non-violence must come from a desire to live out the truth, acting from a deep sense of injustice and the desire to create a more equitable and peaceful society. It is also about working for change within others. How many others, I'm not sure - it maybe that we can only hope to change others through personal interactions, which is necessarily limiting. It seems that we are often stampeded into ill-considered actions from our consciousness that we stand on the edge of the abyss... Somehow we have to live with that consciousness and at the same time act with love, which means acting as if we had all the time in the world.*

'How did Jesus, the carpenter's son from Galilee, so inspire his followers with the purity and faithfulness of his witness that they went on to spread that message around the world? However much that Gospel has been betrayed down through history, the essential, subversive message is still there for each new generation to find... this gospel inspires my action... It is the experiential Christ that is my touchstone for non-violence. An important disclosure made by Jesus concerns the nature of power. There is no way to peace, peace is the way. If we contrast the power of the state with power of non-violence, it seems that the state's power rests on numbers and money, whereas the power of non-violence relies on symbols that stir the heart. The ultimate symbol of this kind is, for me, the crucifixion of Jesus. Our strength lies in our weakness. As Paul says, "this is a stumbling block to the Jews and folly to the Gentiles."'

★★★

In the middle of May I was ill for a week. It was then that I missed the privacy of my home and my own comfortable bed. It wasn't the first time I had suffered with the virus, but this time it was worse. I had developed a sick headache on the journey back from Sawtry after our meeting with John Major. Knowing it had been a long and eventful day, I ignored it and went to bed. I woke the next day feeling very dizzy. I stayed indoors all day, doing very little, though I did type four urgent letters, one being to Neil Kinnock. The dizzy feeling got worse, and as a last resort I took some of the pills my doctor in Ipswich had given me on a previous occasion. My legs and ankles ached and when I moved it felt as though I was on board a ship in a stormy sea. The floor moved and I couldn't seem to walk straight.

Paul Johns, then the chair of Christian CND, came to see us and I sat trying to take in what he was saying, my head going around in circles. When he had left I asked Ian to ring and make an appointment with the local doctor in Kimbolton. The doctor filled in a form as I was only a temporary patient.

"What's your address Mrs Hartley?" he asked.

'Here goes', I thought. "Well actually, my husband and I are living in a caravan outside the proposed cruise missile base at Molesworth." I looked straight at him trying to gauge his reaction.

"Are you really? Well, I am a member of the Medical Campaign Against Nuclear Weapons, so I fully support what you're doing."

I couldn't believe it. He examined me and said my symptoms of a dry throat, giddiness, nausea, pains in the limbs and strong urine were consistent with Labyrinthitis, an infection of the inner ear, and it was this that was affecting my balance. He prescribed tablets that he thought would help.

I stayed in bed all the following day. It was the first time I had been in bed in daytime while at the caravan and it felt very strange, so public, but as I was feeling ill I didn't give it much thought. I found it difficult to lift my head from the pillow without the room spinning. One or two of the police had asked Ian where I was, as I hadn't been at the vigils. Opening the caravan door to a knock, Ian found Superintendent Dean outside.

"I understand that Jennifer isn't feeling well, how is she?" he asked Ian.

"Come in, I'm sure she'd be pleased to see you," Ian replied opening the sliding door from the kitchen to the main room.

Lying in the bed that took up nearly half the room, I felt slightly foolish as the Superintendent stepped inside and towered over me. He stopped and talked to us for about half an hour and seemed genuinely concerned about me. I appreciated his visit.

The virus recurred in June, coming on very suddenly. The night before we had been to a midsummer's party at the home of John and Rosemary Kiddy, the people who had kindly offered us the use of their bathroom. I wondered if it was the loud music or the wine I had drunk that had triggered it off. I was unable to stand up and was violently sick, all very difficult with no flush loo or running water. It didn't last so long this time, although I felt unwell for a week or so. Margaret, a member of Bishop's Stortford CND, offered to give me some reflexology treatment. I had no idea what it was. She explained that it involved massaging the feet as each part of the foot corresponds in some way with different organs in the body. As she moved her fingers over the fleshy pad underneath the middle toes, I experienced a sharp pain, it was the area related to the ear! Since then I haven't had another bout of the virus, though I still get dizzy, sick headaches every so often.

I was not the only one who required medical treatment. Robbie developed a rash underneath his limbs and sore patches appeared. We took him to a vet in St. Ives where they treated him week after week with ointment, injections and pills. His whole system seemed to be affected and he woke us up, needing to go outside almost every night for over three weeks. We are now fairly certain that all his trouble stemmed from a nervous condition. It wasn't much fun for him at Molesworth, although he never complained. The mud and wet made his coat filthy and drying him after each walk was almost impossible.

Ian has never been much good as a nurse, but then he says I'm a pretty awful patient! When I was ill, it was predictable he would soon feel depressed. That day in May when Superintendent Dean visited was a case in point. The weather was awful. I had written at the end of the diary entry for that day, in capital letters, 'RAIN, RAIN AND MORE B. RAIN!' The wind blew at gale force that night and at 2:30 the banging of the window woke me up. I dozed on and off until five o'clock. Then Robbie started pacing up and down, a sure sign he wanted to go outside. I woke Ian up and he was very cross when I suggested that he took Robbie outside, as I was still feeling sick and giddy. He jumped out of bed and shut the dog in the kitchen, hoping he would go back to sleep. I knew that wouldn't work, so in the end I got up and dressed and took Robbie up the lane and back.

In the morning, Ian was feeling low and guilty about losing his temper.

"I sometimes wonder what on earth I'm doing here," he said to me. "I don't seem to know where I'm going anymore, I've had enough of this place."

I couldn't think of anything to say to reassure him. I was feeling far from strong myself. At eleven, Ian went out to the vigil alone. I could see from the window that two people had joined him. Afterwards he invited them into the caravan. Jeanne Barton was a Quaker from Leicester, who had brought with her an American guest called John

Suchard. He was a tall, big-framed man with a gaunt but tranquil face. He explained that he was part of a group of American peace activists called the Ploughshares Eight. We knew about the group; they were Catholics and after careful and prayerful preparation, they had entered a missile manufacturing plant in a town with the unlikely name of King of Prussia. Once inside, they had poured blood over blueprints and hammered the nosecone of a warhead. The eight were arrested and sentenced to prison; when John visited us the case was still on appeal. It was hard to believe, looking at this mild-mannered man, that he could have done it.

We were talking about why we had come to Molesworth, when John suddenly said he would like to give us something. Looking at Ian he took a small card out of his pocket and gave it to him.

"It's a prayer by Thomas Merton; I know you'll like it."

Ian read the words on the card then turned to me.

"I don't believe it, read this Jennifer."

"Why don't you read it out loud?" I suggested.

"Shall I?" he enquired, looking at us. "All right then." And he began to read: "*My Lord God, I have no idea where I am going. I do not see the road ahead of me. I cannot know for certain where it will end. Nor do I really know myself, and the fact that I think that I am following your will does not mean that I am actually doing so. But I believe that the desire to please you does in fact please you. And I hope I have that desire in all that I am doing. I hope that I will never do anything apart from that desire. And I know that if I do this you will lead me by the right road, though I may know nothing about it. Therefore will I trust you always though I may seem to be lost and in the shadow of death. I will not fear, for you are ever with me, and you will never leave me to face my perils alone.*'"

We had first heard of Thomas Merton when we were at the IFOR Council in France. We had been given a little book on the American Trappist monk, written by Jim Forest, secretary of the International Fellowship. It was called *Thomas Merton on Peacemaking* and was largely composed of letters Merton had written to Jim, especially during the Vietnam War. The book had struck a chord, or to use a phrase coined by George Fox, 'it had spoken to our condition'.

John Suchard turning up that day was, to borrow an idea from Rabbi Lionel Blue, like the appearance of an angel. A little while ago, Ian read Lionel Blue's autobiography, *A Backdoor to Heaven*. Like his

187

radio broadcasts on *Thought for the Day*, the book combines humour with a serious message. One chapter is titled *Angels on Horseback*. In it, the Rabbi says that as a Jewish child he never heard fairy tales; instead he had angels. But *'my angels had no haloes or wings and wore no nighties. They were the mal'achim, the angeloi, the messengers one encounters in one's life who were sent by God.'* For Lionel Blue, one was a Yiddish-speaking horse, another was a char woman and a third a Carmelite nun. For Ian, John Suchard was just such a messenger.

★★★

Ian said goodbye to me and drove back to Molesworth. It was the first time since we left our home in January, that Ian and I were to be apart for any length of time. It was the third week in May and I had come to Leigh-on-Sea to look after my mother for a week, while my sister was away. Ian returned to Halcyon Spirit where he had a busy week. When I returned, I was intrigued to see what he had written in the diary. There were references to Leicester city councillors and Bruce Kent having visited and the fact that it was 'Bread not Bombs' week.

To mark the week, Bridie and Tim had, with others, organised leafleting and vigils in some of the nearby towns. A slide show was arranged on the wheat project and local people had been invited. Before going away, I had been delegated the task of inviting the major from RAMS group to attend the event. The major lived in a beautiful thatched cottage in the village of Bythorn. I was a bit nervous as I went up to the door and knocked. There was no reply so I began to walk away, but looking back I saw the door opening.

"Yes, do you want something?" The man standing in the door way had a kindly face. I went back up the path.

"I don't know if you know me, my name is Jennifer Hartley, I live in a caravan outside the base."

"Oh, yes, I know who you are," the major said.

"I have been asked to invite you to a slide show at the School House. It's 'Bread not Bombs' week and we thought you might be interested to see some slides about the consignment of wheat that was sent from Molesworth to Eritrea."

"No, I wouldn't be interested and I am just about to play tennis, so I really can't stop to talk to you now."

I went on, "I have also brought you a copy of the latest *Molesworth Bulletin* as we feel it's only right that you should see it."

He didn't look very pleased. "If I take it I shall only tear it up," he told me.

The major looked about sixty, was softly spoken, and I could imagine him as someone's grandfather. I felt I wanted to explain our presence at Molesworth. He said he never talked about anything political, but listened as I said my reasons for being there sprang from my beliefs as a Christian and because I thought that nuclear weapons were immoral. He replied that we were breaking the law of the land, and asked how we would feel about people coming and setting up home in our back garden. If we wanted to change things then we should do it through the ballot box. I must have stayed talking for at least ten minutes and by the end of the conversation we were both laughing.

I was frustrated to learn that while I had been at Leigh, Bruce Kent and a group of well-known peace campaigners, including Pat Arrowsmith, Air Commodore Alistair Mackie and the Euro MP, Carol Tongue, had come to the base in order to hand out a specially composed leaflet. The leaflet was addressed to 'Members of the Armed Forces'. It stated that all nuclear weapons were illegal under international law, quoting various protocols, conventions and the fact that Nazi war criminals were unable to use the plea that 'they were only obeying orders' as a defence. It went on to say that the military manuals make it clear that complicity in crimes against humanity is unlawful. It ended with these words: 'You must, of course, obey lawful orders. That is your sworn duty.

We urge you, however, to refuse to obey illegal orders such as those requiring you to guard, maintain or transport any nuclear weapons of first use such as cruise missiles.'

The signatories included others who were not present, among them, Bishop Trevor Huddleston, Dora Russell and historian E.P. Thompson. It sounded as if it must have been quite tense as the participants were aware they might be charged with 'Incitement to Disaffection', which roughly translated means encouraging the troops not to fight. Lots of press and TV people came, but no arrests were made.

I was pleased to see that Ian had written a poem. He wrote in the diary that it had been inspired by a conversation he had with the Reverend Reg Macklin, the Rural Dean. We liked Reg very much; he had a difficult job. He was under pressure from all sides to come out strongly on the issue of the base. He could see the justice in many different arguments, but refused to come out firmly one way or another. Ian had tried to explain that despite appearances to the contrary, what was going on at Molesworth was a crime against humanity, which was potentially just as life threatening as the building of gas chambers.

'No cause for alarm
Yes, they are building the gas chamber in there
Yes, they have plans for the incinerator
No, they will not sift the bones for gold
No, the skin will not be fit for parchment.
Did they clamour to pull down the barbed wire at Belsen?
Did they sit in front of the lorries at Dachau?
Did they meekly enter Auschwitz?
Architects drew plans
Contractors provided cement
The soldiers built fences
The women and children listened to the tannoyed music
And calmly filed into the waiting shower baths.
These are not death camps
These are public utilities
These are not to be used
This will not happen
This is keeping the peace
This is the home in which we live
This is the house that Jack and Susan built.
All things are well
All manner of things are well
We know best
We know the cost
This is not war, this is peace
There will be no holocaust
There will be no genocide
Eat your breakfast, drink your coffee.
This is a public service announcement
Close your doors, shut the windows

> *Put out the light, put out the cat*
> *Run a nice warm bath...'*

Looking through the post, my eye caught the familiar green crest on buff-coloured paper that announced a letter from the House of Commons. It was a response to the letter I had written to Neil Kinnock earlier in the month. In it I had written: '*I know that I am an idealist, but I have this dream that your party will win the next election and you will reverse the decision to deploy cruise at Molesworth and instead turn the whole area into a peace park. It could contain gardens, a tree farm, a place for open air concerts, a farm area for children to visit... It could be a positive alternative as was happening before the "invasion" took place.*'

'*Is it a dream?*' I had asked, 'or could it really happen?'

I scanned the reply from the Office of the Leader of the Opposition.

'*Dear Jennifer and Ian,*

'*Thank you very much for your letter. Some of my colleagues who called on you a few weeks ago have told me of your (sic) visit and they have also, of course, raised the various questions with ministers.*

'*Your hope that we'll make Molesworth redundant as a base is not a dream. It is going to happen because we are going to win the Election and we are going to get rid of cruise missiles. Naturally, that victory will require a lot of work and a lot of votes, but we are certainly heading in the right direction.*

'*The dignity and sincerity of your activities at Molesworth are important ingredients in efforts to focus attention on cruise, and the way in which it is not just a menacing weapon but a threat to the values and conduct of our society. I send you good wishes in your efforts and will see that the matter of access of the Peace Chapel is taken up again.*

'*Kind regards,*

'*Neil Kinnock.'*

It was the kind of letter we thought we ought to keep safely in case we ever wanted to hold Mr Kinnock to his promise at a later date. I'm not a member of any political party, but as I consider nuclear disarmament the most important and urgent issue in the world today, I would support any party prepared to take steps to remove the threat of a nuclear catastrophe.

Chapter Fourteen

Save Eirene!

I was convinced the only reason that the Peace Chapel was still standing was because scores of people continued writing letters, admonishing the MOD for not allowing access. I spoke about this at one of our regular liaison meetings at the School House. Such meetings brought together those living at the Peace Camp in Faye Way, the folk on Peace Corner, Tim and Bridie and representatives from some of the local groups. Jeanne Steinhardt usually came from Wellingborough and was a regular participant at the vigils, so we knew she shared our concern for Eirene. We decided to form an Eirene working group to look at ways of continuing to keep Eirene in the limelight.

Our first idea was prompted by something Neil, our solicitor, said. We had asked him whether we could do anything legally to prevent the MOD demolishing the chapel.

"Well, you could put up a public notice, claiming the building belongs to you, and requesting that no action be taken to destroy it, without reference to yourselves."

"But we don't own it," Ian said.

"Yes, but you could claim to represent those who built it. They provided the materials and it was built by their labour." Neil glanced at me, adding, "I'm not saying it would work."

"But it's worth a try, yes?"

"Yes, I think so, it can do no harm. Well, I must be off." And with that, Neil climbed into the battered, old, dark green Mini van that he travelled about in. It seemed an incongruous mode of transport for a solicitor, but then Neil was no ordinary solicitor, despite his pin-striped grey suit. His office was decorated with South Sea Island fans and a photograph of a be-wigged Neil shaking hands with the Queen, palm trees in the background. Before coming to Cambridgeshire, he had represented the Crown on a remote tropical island.

We discussed what he had said with Jeanne. We had gone to Wellingborough to visit her for the first time. Jeanne and her husband Mark lived in a large Victorian house called 'Delos'. It was a family home, but theirs was a remarkable family. As well as two young children of their own, they lived with five or six mentally handicapped adults and Jeanne's grown-up daughters by a previous marriage. Down the road, they had another house, with a mixture of helpers and handicapped people living as a family. Not content with these responsibilities, Jeanne and Mark had started a wholefood shop, which gave employment to some of those living at 'Delos'. Jeanne still found time to devote to Molesworth. Originally from Glasgow, she still retained a distinctive Scots accent. She thought the idea of a notice sounded good and encouraged us to pursue it. We decided it must be a well-built sign that looked official, and that it should be erected in the garden near to Eirene. Jeanne suggested we write an appeal in the next *Molesworth Bulletin*, asking for offers of help.

As I was typing out a piece to go into the *Bulletin* the next morning, a group from Bishop's Stortford CND arrived. Charles Barnett came in and introduced himself. He was an upright, well-spoken man and could easily be mistaken for a retired army captain. I told him about the sign and the appeal.

"I think we might me able to help you here," he said. "Wait a minute, I'll call Jimmy." He went outside, returning a few minutes later with another man. "This is Jimmy; he's very good at carpentry. I've had a word with him and he says he will be pleased to make the sign."

"Is that right?" I questioned, looking at Jimmy.

"Yes, it shouldn't be too difficult. If you give me all the dimensions and let us know how much you want to spend, I'll be happy to do it."

"That's marvellous, thank you." I couldn't believe it. I tore up my typewritten appeal.

"What's more," Charles went on to say, "I think I can safely say that Bishop's Stortford CND branch will bear all the costs of the materials. I shall have to clear it with the group, but I don't envisage any problems."

Tim and two or three other people were collating the pages of the *Bulletin*. We went over to tell him the good news. He stopped what he was doing so that together we could discuss the wording to go on the sign. We had decided that it should give a short history of the chapel, as well as declaring our ownership and the request to be notified before it was tampered with. John Hutchinson was the obvious choice to do the sign writing. John was married to Jean, one of the founders of the Molesworth Camp. A trained graphic artist, he now owned a picture gallery in nearby St. Ives. John had produced a marvellous pictorial chronicle of the Peace Camp, and more to the point, he had made the original hand-painted sign for the Peace Campers back in 1981. John readily agreed to do the calligraphy.

June 22nd was chosen as the day to erect the sign and we wrote to the press and television companies, inviting them to come to the unveiling ceremony at noon that day. Charles and Jimmy arrived at 10:30 in the morning with the signboard in two pieces in the back of the car. They also brought the cement and sand needed to secure the posts. Other members of the group arrived, and before long quite a large crowd were standing near the gardens. The police started eyeing the proceeding suspiciously. Charles acted as foreman calling out orders, and soon three men were digging two deep holes for the posts and shovelling the mud onto a plastic sheet. We had deliberated for some time where would be the best place to put the sign, as we wanted it to be seen by as many people as possible.

"Have you got permission in writing from the council to put this sign up?" a voice asked me. I turned around. A Cambridgeshire policeman stood beside me.

"As a matter of fact, I discussed it with a councillor yesterday when he called to see me," I replied, a bit taken aback. It was fortuitous that the day before, Cambridgeshire County councillor, Michael Evelegh, chose to visit Molesworth. An Alliance member, he was the new chairman of the Transportation Committee, and had come to see Peace Lane as the matter of the road closure was once more on the agenda. I had happened to mention that the next day we were putting up the sign in the gardens. It had seemed a good idea as the land did belong to the County Council.

"Can you give me the name of this councillor, Mrs Hartley? We will need to contact him to make sure everything is in order."

I was beginning to get a bit worried, but tried not to let it show. "Chris Bradford is the leader of the Council, he would be the person to speak to," I told the officer.

"Right," he said. "Thank you," and walked back to the stationary police van parked on the side of the road. I watched him go to the front of the van and speak into the radio. I hurried across to where Charles was standing. Keeping my voice low I said, "I think they are going to try and stop us. Can you work any faster?" Charles spoke to the men mixing cement, explaining the problem. More people joined in to help and within a quarter of an hour the sign was up for all to see.

We waited until twelve-fifteen, hoping the press would turn up, but they didn't so we went ahead with the unveiling ceremony. Jimmy had borrowed a green velvet cloth belonging to his mother, which was draped over the sign. Ian and I uncovered it. It looked splendid. Jimmy had fashioned it beautifully. The board had been carefully varnished, bringing out the pattern of the grain. John had painted the wording in clear, well-formed white lettering. It read: *'Eirene (Eye-re-knee is the New Testament Greek word for Peace)'*

'The original Eirene was a wooden structure built in the Spring of 1982 by the People's Peace Camp. After their eviction to Warren Lane, a second Eirene was begun using runway rubble left on the site of the peace camp. The corner stone was laid by Satish Kumar on April 14th 1984, after informing the Ministry of Defence who made no objections to the plans.

'Hundreds of people helped to build the chapel leaving personal treasures in the walls. On September 2nd 1984, the chapel was dedicated by the Bishop of Huntingdon and members of other faiths.

Construction stopped during the winter, whilst money was raised for the roof. Even without a roof Eirene was regularly used for worship until the night of February 5th when the MOD enclosed the chapel with barbed wire. The roof fund reached its target in March but permission to complete the building was refused.

'Interfaith acts of worship are held in the gardens every day at 11.00am and 4.00pm.

'Eirene is owned by the many people who gave their time and energy and materials in building it, and no alteration should be made to its present state without the prior permission of the stewards of Eirene acting on behalf of the owners.

'The stewards of Eirene. c/o Halcyon Spirit, Peace Corner, Old Weston Rd, Brington, Cambs.'

I then read out a prepared statement: "We dedicate this board to all those who have been involved with the idea of Eirene, from its conception through to today. We intend to move the board nearer to the building once we have regained access to the chapel. We also intend to put the roof on (the fund for which is in the bank), so that people of all faiths may have the opportunity to pray for world peace at this place that is preparing for war.

"We would like to thank Bishops Stortford CND, especially Jimmy, for constructing and donating the board and John Hutchinson for his fine sign-writing."

Over the course of the next few days we noticed several police officers walk over to read the sign. We were uncertain what the reaction would be, but the only comment made to us was how nice they thought it looked!

***

What could we do next? How could we find out what was going on in the minds of the men and women in Whitehall? Thousands of people from all over Britain had signed petitions and many batches had been sent to Michael Heseltine at the Ministry of Defence in London. Now we wrote requesting a meeting, to allow us to put our point of view to him. It had been widely publicised that the local group calling itself Residents Against the Molesworth Settlement (RAMS) had met him, so it seemed quite fair to us that we should have the same opportunity.

Our letters always received a negative response and, in fact, we had no reply at all to six letters we wrote. In one I even included a poem:

'Dear Michael Heseltine,
I wish I knew what we could do
To get a letter back from you.
Five times we've written, with no reply
Is it worth another try?
We want to witness in Peace Lane,

But will you let us here remain?
We smile and sing and pray for peace
And talk to visitors and police.
We protest very peacefully
Which is allowed in a democracy,
So, more petitions to you we send.
We trust that they will not offend.
All we ask is a sign from you
That our requests are getting through
PLEASE Michael take this in good part,
And prove like us you have a heart!'

The letter continued.

'We believe that we are here at Molesworth for a very serious reason. Up to now we have written to you in a responsible and civil manner. As yet, you have not answered. It would be very helpful and useful to us to know what your response is to our petitions and letters. We look forward to hearing from you in the near future.'

This brought no response, so in desperation we wrote to a man called Malcolm Lingwood, a civil servant at the MOD. We had got his name from the Member of Parliament for the local constituency, John Major. In the course of a conversation with John Major at one of his surgeries in Sawtry, he had mentioned that he had spoken to this civil servant, whose job it was to answer all the letters from people protesting about MOD policy. Perhaps he was the man to contact. If he was the person responsible for answering our letters we might be successful if we wrote to him personally.

By late June, we decided that we must make a bigger effort to see Michael Heseltine in person. We decided to write a letter in conjunction with Tim and Bridie Wallis formally requesting a meeting. We said that we wanted to discuss the Peace Chapel and also other matters relating to Molesworth. We decided to wait for a few days to see if we had a reply. If we heard nothing I would telephone Michael Heseltine's secretary. I managed to get the phone number from Lord Trefgarne's office. He was the then Minister of State for Defence Support. There was no response to the letter, so I made the call and spoke to a man called James Calvert. I explained that we had asked to have a meeting with Michael Heseltine and that we had not had any reply. I told him that we and many others had written hundreds of letters to Michael Heseltine and also sent thousands of petitions requesting assurances that the Peace Chapel would not be demolished, and that now we wanted to meet him in person to see if we could work out some sort of compromise. He said that he would look into the matter and we would hear in due course.

We still received no reply so I rang again. I spoke to the same man and yet again he stalled, so I explained that the four of us would be coming to London the following Monday and would call at the MOD to see Michael Heseltine. We then debated among ourselves as to the right course of action. We all felt that we had conducted ourselves in a correct way and that our request was not unreasonable. All the letters we had written had been polite and we had waited for many months to get some assurance from the MOD regarding the future of the chapel. We decided to write a press release and send it to all the national and local papers saying that we had contacted the Minister for Defence, asking for an assurance that they would not demolish the chapel until we had the opportunity of putting our views to him. It took us all morning typing and addressing envelopes, but we felt it had been worthwhile. We also decided to make a banner to take up to London with us saying 'SAVE THE EIRENE ALL-FAITHS PEACE CHAPEL, MOLESWORTH'. It was painted in all colours of the rainbow on a piece of pale blue sheeting.

Ian and I had arranged to stay the last weekend in June with my daughter Debbie and her boyfriend, Shaun, at their flat in Blackheath. We arrived in the late afternoon and were made welcome. They had prepared a meal for us and we enjoyed the comfort of their home and hospitality. In the evening we all went to the local pub, the 'Fox and Firkin', where they had a sing-song and I let myself go and sang heartily. The Sunday morning we drove to Hampstead to attend the Quaker Meeting at which Bridie's aunt and uncle, Pleasaunce and John Holtom, were the wardens. Afterwards we took Robbie and went with John for a walk on Hampstead Heath. We told John and Pleasaunce of our plans to visit the MOD the following day with Tim and Bridie, and John said he would come with us as an observer.

Back at Debbie's flat we spent the evening playing Monopoly and I wondered if it was some sort of omen that I spent most of the game in jail! As fast as I got out, I would land on the square saying, *'Go directly to jail'* or pick up a card with the same instruction.

On the morning of Monday July 1st, we rang Tim and Bridie to see if any letter had come from Michael Heseltine's office. Nothing had. They were about to leave for London and we arranged to meet them in the Embankment Gardens in the early afternoon. It was a bright, sunny day and the flower beds were a mass of colour. People were milling around and office workers were lying on the grass, eating their sandwiches. A band was playing selections from Gilbert and Sullivan. When we met Tim and Bridie, we too sat on the grass and had our lunch. We were all feeling very nervous and unsure as to what would happen. We had composed a letter saying that we intended to remain in the MOD building until we had an assurance that the Ministry would take no action against the chapel before we had seen Michael Heseltine. We made our way to Whitehall and walked all the way around the building staring up at the grey, stone walls and the vast steel doors. It is a forbidding place, and knowing that inside hundreds of men and women spend their days preparing and planning for war added to its chilling impersonality. We had hoped that some of the press might have turned up but we were disappointed. John Holtom met us and at 2:30 we all walked through the massive, metal doors.

Inside there was a lobby with couches covered with black vinyl. Glass doors lead off to corridors and lifts. But no one can get further than the lobby without a pass. Staff came in through a door with red and green lights over the top. They entered their card in a machine that resembled a cash dispenser at a bank and punched in a code, which changed the light to green and the door silently slid open, shutting close on their heels. A notice proclaimed that the building was in a state of Black Alert. I walked across the lobby and up to the glass wall behind which sat a receptionist.

Speaking to the woman I said, "We have a letter for James Calvert and I have spoken to him on the telephone so he knows that we are coming. We would like to give it to him in person."

She said, "Someone will come down and see you. Would you please take a seat?"

I went back to the others and sat down beside Ian. We were all in a row and didn't say much. The truth was that we were all scared stiff as to what might happen. All around us were men standing on guard, each with a walkie-talkie. The red and green lights flashed on and off and we were conscious of eyes scrutinising our every movement. After a few minutes a young man came down. I gave him the letter and asked him to read it. He skimmed through it and said, "I will pass on your message, thank you."

Realizing that he was about to walk away, I said, "I am sorry but I don't think you quite understand. We intend to stay here until we receive the assurances we have asked for in the letter."

We all started explaining about the many letters and petitions and said that we were representing a large body of people who were concerned about the fate of the chapel, and I finished by saying, "So that's why we want an assurance today, and we will wait here until you can give us one."

"You will have a long wait," he said.

"That's all right, we are quite prepared to wait," I said.

He looked at us, seeming to waver, then re-read the letter and said, "Will you hold on a little while?"

He went behind the glass petition and made a phone call, getting the number out of a book. We sat apprehensively wondering if at any moment the doors would fly open and the police would come in to remove us. Nothing happened; we hardly dared breathe but just smiled at each other. When all was quiet I reached down for my handbag and, to my utter confusion, there was a resounding crash, I had knocked a telephone off the table beside me on to the floor. Everyone jumped and I blushed crimson. I could hear myself apologising over and over again, feeling most uncomfortable.

Behind the glass petition we could see that our young man had returned, bringing another man with him, and they both went to the desk and used the phone. The new man spoke loudly and we could hear some of what he said. He said he had spoken to Lord Trefgarne and then we heard him say, "Yes, here," and looked over at us. We had now been in the building for over a half an hour, and although people came in and looked at us no one said a word. We watched and waited.

At just after three, out came three men through a turnstile exit guarded by two security men in dark suits. They walked towards us and standing in front of us one said, "Can I help you?"

Without thinking, I said, "I hope so!"

200

With that they began to introduce themselves and we stood up, only John remained seated as he wished to remain simply an observer. The man who had spoken was in his early forties with sandy brown hair, a friendly smile and a sharp intelligent look in his eye. He introduced himself as Richard Mottram, personal private secretary to the Secretary of State. The second man was called Andrew Ward; he was also quite young with dark, wavy hair. He was less self assured and glanced at Richard Mottram for approval when he spoke. Finally, the last man said, "My name is Malcolm Lingwood."

So this was the man who had all the letters to answer. He was older than the other two, a big man who looked ill at ease in this situation. Then it was our turn to say who we were. The introduction complete, we all sat down. As the five of us were sitting on the only available seats, they sat on the low glass tables and we began to discuss our reasons for coming.

I looked at the others and launched off, "As you know, we have sent thousands of signatures for our petition and many letters concerning the future of the Peace Chapel. All we want is some reassurance that you won't do anything to it without giving us the chance to explain our point of view to the minister in person."

The others chipped in, there were many people who had strong feelings about the chapel, it would be good to be able reassure them that the building was secure. Tim said, "We have the money to complete the construction."

Andrew Ward, who, it became clear, was responsible for surveying and planning work at Molesworth, responded. "You had no right to build on Ministry land without permission."

Tim didn't agree and he said, "The MOD knew about our plans to build Eirene before we started building. We gave the MOD police a letter and sent a copy of the plans to the Royal Air Force engineers at Bedford."

The three men looked from one to another. We tried another tack. We explained that a recent letter from the Ministry had seemed to indicate that the chapel might be endangered as a result of the successful Christian CND attempt to block the sale of George's field. Andrew Ward responded that it was true that the difficulties over gaining access to the Church land were forcing them to reconsider the layout of the entrance of the base.

"We are compelled to keep the bridleway open," he explained. "That means that we would have to divert the southern end and the exit route would lie directly across the land on which the chapel stands – we have no option. It is the only possible site for an alternative entrance if you people prevent us from purchasing the Church land."

We noted afterwards that they all referred to Eirene as 'the chapel' or 'the Peace Chapel', they did not seem to feel it was necessary to preface the phrase with 'so-called' as they had done in correspondence, neither did they seem interested in making debating points about the fact that it was not consecrated. They accepted its significance and importance to us without question. But they gave no undertaking not to demolish the chapel. I looked Andrew Ward in the eye and said, "Are you going to demolish the chapel?"

He smiled and said, "Well, I haven't got a task force of Royal Engineers ready to go and destroy the chapel tonight!" I thought, 'Yes, not tonight, but next week, or next month.'

Ian turned to Richard Mottram. "Look, all we are asking is that we should have the chance to put our case to Michael Heseltine. He's seen the RAMS people, if he believes in democracy in all fairness he should see us too. Isn't that fair?"

"I'm afraid I cannot speak for the minister, I'm simply a civil servant."

"But don't you think our request is reasonable?" Ian pressed on. "After all, we represent a lot of people, a lot of concern. I mean, what do YOU think?"

"Look, what I think is immaterial," Mottram replied. "I cannot give assurances on behalf of the minister. Only he can make the decision to see you. What I can do is to put him in the picture. He's not even in the building this afternoon. But I give you my word in good faith that tomorrow morning I will personally put all your papers in front of the minister and tell him what you have been saying."

We looked at each other with a realisation that we were not going to get any further, but at the same time unsure whether we could really let the matter drop. Had we achieved our objective? In one sense we certainly had not.

John, who had been taking no part in the conversation, decided to break the silence. "I think I'd like to say something. I really came along just to observe what went on, but I think I have something to say. I've been in the armed forces and I've also worked in large organisations, so I know the kind of constraints you folk work under. I think that you have gone about as far as it is possible for you to go." Turning to the four of us he added, "And I think that you have achieved as much as you could expect from these men."

It was good to hear John say this because none of us wanted to feel that we had been fobbed off. The atmosphere, which had always been relaxed throughout our conversation, lightened further. I said something about ringing Richard Mottram to find out what was happening and he grinned and said, "I don't mind you ringing but don't give my name and phone number to everyone. That's what CND did and every time a cruise convoy goes out I get dozens of phone calls!"

We smiled and he continued, "I promise that I'll write this week telling you the outcome of my talk with Mr. Heseltine. All right?"

We all stood up and as we left I shook hands with the three of them and Ian and the others followed suit. We said goodbye and walked out into the sunlight.

We all began to talk at once.

"I thought we were going to get arrested."

"Did you see that man Lingwood? I thought he looked really ill, must be the pressure of work, all those letters from the peace movement."

"I suppose it was quite good really, we were talking to them for half hour."

"Oh Jennifer! When you knocked the phone on the floor – it was so funny."

"What about a cup of tea?"

"Oh, yes!"

We turned to a policeman to ask him where the nearest café was and he gave us directions. Then we asked John to take our photo, standing outside the building, which looked much less sinister than it had an hour earlier. As we walked up Whitehall to Trafalgar Square, still recalling what had happened and who had said what, we decided to go to the cafeteria in the National Gallery. John treated us to tea and cakes, and I suddenly had the idea of sending the three civil servants each a copy of the card with the black and white illustration of Eirene drawn by Ian. I had three in my bag and we all wrote messages inside. While we were sitting there, we started talking about the banner that we had left in our knapsack. John had not seen it, so we produced it and with Tim and I taking corners, we displayed it much to the amusement of other people in the restaurant. Two young men at the next table wanted to know what it was all about, so we quickly gave them a potted version of what had happened. They were interested and supportive.

It was time to go our separate ways. Tim and Bridie and John left to catch an underground train and we walked back to the Ministry of Defence. Without a thought, we once more walked through the massive, steel doors and into the 'space-age' lobby. Once again, we greeted the woman receptionist, handed in the cards and left to make our way back to Blackheath.

We waited for seven days for the promised reply from Richard Mottram. It read:

July 4th, 1987

'Dear Jennifer and Ian Hartley,

'At our discussion on July 1st, I said that I would write to you about your request for a meeting with the Defence Secretary, once I had been able to consult Mr Heseltine. As I also told you, I cannot comment on the future of the building which you call the 'Peace Chapel' and the Ministry of Defence must reserve the right to demolish, without prior consultation, any unauthorised structure on its land.

'I have now been able to speak to the Defence Secretary about our conversation and have reported to him the points which you made to me, which reflected your earlier letters. Mr Heseltine is therefore aware of your views. As a Cabinet Minister responsible for a very large department, the Defence Secretary has many calls on his time. He is not, therefore, himself able to see you. He suggests that, like others who wish to put forward their views to ministers, you may wish to contact your Member of Parliament. Mr Heseltine knows that your Member of Parliament, Mr John Major, takes a close and conscientious interest in matters concerning RAF Molesworth.

'Perhaps I could look to you to pass the contents of this letter to Bridie and Timmon Wallis, who may also wish to approach their Member of Parliament.

'Yours sincerely,

'Richard Mottram,

Private Secretary.'

★★★

A lorry drove up just inside the Main Gate and a group of Public Service Agency workmen jumped out of the back. It was July 13th and once again the fence surrounding the chapel was being taken down. This time it was because of the action on Maundy Thursday where Andy Riddiford had sat in the fence. At a court case in June, Neil, our solicitor, who was also representing Andy, had proved the fence was in the wrong position. The surveyors had made a mistake when marking out the boundary and the MOD had taken a few yards of Cambridgeshire County Council land. Now they had come to move it back several feet.

Tim was very keen that we should hang our banner with the rainbow-coloured wording saying *'Save Eirene Peace Chapel Molesworth'* on the new fence when it was in place. At 4:30, Bridie, Tim, Ian and I each took hold of one corner of the pale blue sheeting and attached the banner to the wire. The words stood out boldly. The young policemen 'guarding' the chapel deliberated between themselves before two of them walked out of the black steel gate and came over to where we stood singing.

"Will you remove that banner? You know it's against the bye-laws to put anything on the fence."

"We want to draw attention to the chapel being behind fencing."

"People want to use Eirene for acts of worship."

"The building is a symbol of hope to people of all faiths."

Quietly we all explained why we wanted the banner left there.

Looking at me, one of the policemen cautioned me, saying I was under arrest. "Would you come with me, please?"

The other officer, using the same words, arrested Ian.

"What about us, we hung the banner up, too?" Tim asked.

"We only identified this couple," replied the policeman.

With a policeman holding on to my elbow, I was guided through the main gate and into a waiting transit van, followed by Ian. I looked at the policemen. The one sitting next to me, my arresting officer, was tall and slim with black hair. He looked to be in his early twenties. He had a handsome face and dark brown eyes. The one next to Ian was about the same age with a round face and fair hair. I was still holding on to the booklet that we used at the vigils.

"Let's sing," I suggested to Ian, "there's no law against singing."

"Let there be love shared amongst us, let there be love in our hearts," we sang as the van bumped its way across the rough ground to the middle of the base. It had been dubbed 'Portacabin City' by the Peace Camp and I could see why. Row upon row of these narrow structures stood side by side like a small town. We were escorted into one of them.

We kept singing, as I find it always helps in these sorts of situations! The acoustics were marvellous inside the portable building. '*Seek Ye First the Kingdom of God*' resounded around the empty room. A sergeant came in and took down our names and address. Ian was taken out to be questioned by the CID. While I was on my own, an inspector whom I knew, came in.

"I don't expect you remember me, Mrs Hartley, but I was there on the day of your wedding anniversary, and I'd like to say how much I enjoyed the service you held that day."

He then took me to an interview room where I was asked a lot of questions. I could not see the relevance of many of them, so I refused to answer. I was asked to sign a form, which said I accepted a caution. If I did, they would proceed no further. I was in a quandary whether to sign. I wondered what Ian would do. In the meantime, as I later discovered, Ian was going through the same procedure. In the end we both signed. Ian wrote in his notebook: *'I was very worried about my dirty hanky which lay on the table along with small change, keys, matches etc. I felt I had to apologise for it!*

'I felt mixed up. I was glad that I'd been arrested, deflated that we'd been let off, guilty because I suspected a) I hadn't been totally clear in my motivation and b) thought there was some element of ego in the whole affair. It's so difficult to know what to do. The strain of seeming acquiescent with so much injustice and potential horror (veiled by inactivity, politeness and humour), counterpoised with a desire to confront opposition, injustice (loss of civil liberties) and the horror of the bomb. Yet not knowing if any particular manifestation justifies the response.'

There was an interesting footnote to this. Tim repeatedly hung the banner on the fence. On several occasions he was arrested, refused to accept a caution and released. He was finally charged, appeared in court and was fined £10. More than eighteen months later, Tim was sent to prison for five days for non-payment of the fine.

Chapter Fifteen
Black Coffins

I wanted to see our cat, Lucky. We had driven to Ipswich to see Jane, Ian's brother's wife, who was expecting their second baby. The baby was overdue and there was talk of it being induced. Jane looked well and the doctor decided to let nature take its course for a little longer. We called at our home in Arthurs Terrace. Lucky, was sitting in the front garden. As soon as I called her name, she slowly got up and wandered over to me. I picked her up. She felt very light, just skin and bones. I knew that she was eating. Mike had told me that she ate more than his two cats put together. Something was obviously wrong.

"I'm afraid her kidneys have shrunk to almost nothing, I can't feel one of them at all, the other's the size of a pea." The vet had finished his examination.

"Is there anything you can do for her?" I asked.

"No, she's literally just wasting away before your eyes. I'm sorry."

I held Lucky in my arms. I loved her so much. We had her as a kitten and she was part of the family. I couldn't bear to think of her dying somewhere on her own in discomfort. I looked at Ian, then back at the vet. I knew it had to be me who made the final decision. There was no alternative. The vet took a needle and while I cuddled her, talking to her all the time, he gave the injection. I was heartbroken. I knew how much Lucky meant to the children, she had been with us fourteen years. As we were not living at home, we asked Gordon, my first husband, if she could be buried in his garden. I rang Antony and Debbie; they were very upset and I cried myself to sleep that night.

I was red-eyed the following morning when we travelled up to London by train. We were to meet a delegation from the Soviet Peace Committee that was visiting this country. The meeting was arranged by Friends and held at William Penn House. I think there were ten people from the Soviet Union, only one of whom was a woman. The British group numbered about thirty. We split into groups to discuss various topics and ask questions. Ian's group discussed human rights and the Helsinki Accord, my group talked about the Soviet peace movement. It was all rather formal and neither of us felt we had made any real contact. Lunch gave us the chance to chat with individuals. I talked to a man from Latvia. He had a daughter the same age as Debbie and we discussed the various interests they shared, showed each other photographs of our families and we exchanged postcards and badges. I kept thinking how good it would be if more people were able to converse with the so-called 'enemy'. It was a very friendly occasion.

We decided to go back to Molesworth, returning to Ipswich at the weekend. By then the baby should have arrived. As we had arranged to see the Bishop of Ely on the Saturday morning, we drove on to Ipswich afterwards. While Ian was getting some petrol, I rang his mother to see if there was any news.

"A girl," Mum said. "Born at nine o'clock this morning, Anna Louise. Jane and the baby are fine."

Jane's ward in Ipswich Hospital was light and airy. I bent over the crib and looked at our new niece, stroking her velvety, pink cheek. Anna was the second baby to be born into the family while we were away from home. Bridie had arrived at the caravan on May 1st saying, "You are an auntie again Jennifer." She had taken the telephone message giving me the news. In fact, I was a great-aunt for the second time. Christopher was a baby brother for my great-nephew, Simon.

We arranged to stop in Ipswich for a week to help look after Victoria, Anna's two-year-old sister. One evening when we were not needed to baby-sit we drove into town to see friends. Passing the end of our road we saw Mike, our tenant. He waved us down, saying he wanted to ask us something. We turned the car around and parked outside our house. It always felt funny going back there, seeing different furniture and ornaments on the shelves.

He didn't waste any time, "I'd like to buy the house, how do you feel about it?" Some time earlier we had suggested to Mike that it was possible we might sell the house at a future date, but we had not given it any real consideration. Our immediate reaction was to say, yes, we would sell it to him. He phoned the friend who was going to buy the house with him and arranged that we should all meet later in the week.

I had no time to think about selling houses as I rushed to catch a train early next morning. Cambridgeshire County Council were meeting in the Shire Hall and the stopping up of the loop (Peace Lane) was again on the agenda. The new council passed the motion so once more the fate of our caravan was in the balance. A motion for a nuclear-free Cambridgeshire was tabled, but once again it was lost, as was a motion brought by Emily Blatch to have peace protesters removed. It was nearly midnight when I arrived back at Ipswich station, and the early hours of the morning before I had related the day's events to Ian.

Sitting in our own front room, we drank a toast to the sale of the house to Mike and Andrew. I looked around thinking it was a shame we wouldn't be coming back here to live. In the immediate future, we would continue to live in the caravan and later we would look for a small house in the Molesworth vicinity. Back in Cambridgeshire we visited estate agents in Huntingdon and Thrapston in Northampton-shire. We imagined that prices of houses near the base would be very cheap. Who would choose to live near a cruise missile base? We were wrong. Prices of houses, even smaller than our own, were far more expensive than in Suffolk. The more houses we looked at, the more depressed we became. I loved our home in Ipswich, and soon realised that we'd made a terrible mistake in agreeing to sell it without first looking into the possible alternatives.

We made yet another flying visit to Ipswich to find our MOT certificate, which had been left behind in a box of important papers under the bed in Ian's parents' house. While we were there, Mike rang us to say he had arranged a mortgage. I was in a frantic state. I wanted to back out of the deal but didn't want to let Mike and Andrew down, it seemed so unfair. We drove back to Molesworth in despair. What could we do? If we didn't think fast the only home we would have would be the caravan outside the base. We hadn't realised the sense of security our house had given us.

August 1st was Ian's birthday and one he would not forget in a hurry. We set off to look at yet more houses: a one-bedroomed flat in Huntingdon with rising damp and an old terraced house in Thrapston in need of complete renovation. Both needed a lot of money spent on them, far more than we could afford.

"It's no good, I can't go through with it, we'll just have to ring Mike and tell him." I looked at Ian. "I don't know what he'll think of us, but there's nothing else we can do."

Ian dialled our phone number. He looked strained and pale. It had been a horrid birthday, even though Bridie and Tim had done their best to cheer us up by taking us for a cream tea in Oundle.

Ian put the phone down. "I told him we've changed our mind. I feel dreadful, Mike sounded very upset. Still, it's done."

I breathed a sigh of relief. We had learnt a lesson; never again would we rush into a decision before sitting down and quietly thinking about all the implications.

Now we began to think seriously about how much longer we would stay at Molesworth. We had started out with the idea of staying six months and the six months were up. As if to remind us of this, a local weekly paper, the *Trader*, sent a reporter to see us a few days later.

"I want to do a piece on the fact that it's six months since the fence went up. What I'd like are your thoughts on this past six months, what you think you've achieved, what your plans are - that sort of thing."

The article appeared under the headline, *'THE COUPLE THAT STAYED BEHIND'*. The only reference it made to the future, was a short final paragraph: *'As for the future, current moves to stop up the former highway, where their caravan is parked, may mean their days are numbered.'*

We simply had no idea how long we might be allowed to remain in Peace Lane. 'Supposing,' we thought, 'the caravan is left here for another six months, a year, could we stay that long?' The answer, we realised, was no.

One date began to emerge, becoming a certainty. In December, we were going to India. The idea of visiting India had first been planted in our mind in 1984, when we were in France. One of the delegates at the IFOR conference, Daniel, had said, "Why don't you come to see me in Bombay?" At the time, it seemed impossible, almost laughable. Later, he had written to Ian at Concord Films, asking him if he could arrange to let him have some old 16mm films for use at his new peace centre. At the end of the letter he wrote. *'The WRI Triennial is in December 1985, why don't you come?*' Ian told me about the letter, but it still seemed inconceivable that we should go. We forgot anymore about it until April, when we spotted a leaflet pinned to a notice board in the Old School. It was headed, '*RESISTANCE AND RECONSTRUCTION, War Resisters International XVIII Triennial.*' Underneath were the magic words, '*Swaraj Ashram, Vedchhi, India*'.

Inside the leaflet, it explained that the conference venue was a Gandhian community in Gujarat and gave details of the programme and dates. December 30th 1985 to January 6th 1986. The conference sounded exciting; it was to address not only the nuclear threat, but also the present dangers of war, famine, disease and pollution. Ian and I talked seriously about the possibility of going. It would only be possible if we could get some kind of travel bursary. We wondered if the War Resisters' International would feel that we had something to offer to the conference and would give assistance with the fares. It was worth writing a letter. Not surprisingly, they wrote back to say they had no funds, but they would like us to go. Indeed, they had already thought of inviting us to attend! They also listed some suggestions of possible sources for financial help. It still seemed a remote possibility. One suggestion of a trust that might give us a grant proved negative. Then, on July 5th, a cheque arrived from a Quaker Trust for £750. We could not believe our eyes. We had written to them in May telling them of our plans, and asking if they would consider sending a contribution towards our travel costs. They had sent us almost enough to pay both our air fares. The trip was on.

Now, in August, after the dilemma over the house, we recognised that the trip to India offered us the way forward. It would be the next step in the journey.

★★★

It was not only our future that concerned us, but the future of Eirene, too. We had been disappointed with the letter we received from Richard Mottram, but determined not to let up in our efforts to gain access to the Peace Chapel and to try and save it from demolition. The planning group met again and came up with a plan of action. We would reply to the MOD's letter pointing out that we were already in touch with John Major, that thousands of signatures for the 'Save Eirene' petition had been sent to the Secretary of State and that we still wanted to see Michael Heseltine in person. Jeanne agreed to produce a briefing paper for churches. Tim printed a leaflet and we agreed to try to meet the Bishops of Huntingdon and Ely to discuss our fears for the future of Eirene.

We had received a copy of a letter that the General Secretary of the British Council of Churches had written to Michael Heseltine and were pleased to see how much it echoed our own ideas:

July 19th, 1985'

'Dear Secretary of State,

'Re: Peace Chapel, Molesworth

'Mr M.G. Lingwood of Secretariat 9 (Air) wrote to my colleague, Dr Roger Williamson, on April 24th, 1985, giving the Ministry of Defence's view of the status of the chapel built at Molesworth. I think it is important to share with you the continuing concern about the future of the chapel in a large part of our constituency, by no means only those who built it and wish to use it or those opposed to British defence policy. It is recognised by many Christians as a place dedicated to prayer, dialogue and reconciliation and, for that reason, there remains considerable consternation at the thought that it may be demolished.

This is in no way to deny that the Ministry may have a technical legal right to demolish the chapel, but rather to suggest that it would be insensitive and would lead to unnecessary confrontation if use were made of that right. The technical distinction between a blessed and a consecrated building is, in this context, totally irrelevant. What is important is that human beings, some of whom belong to religions outside the Christian tradition, but most of whom are members of the British churches, recognise in this place a symbol of God's presence. We would hope that the Ministry would recognise the importance of such a symbol and would recognise that it could be reopened for prayer by all who accept the sovereignty of God, and by no means only those whose interpretation of the faith leads them to reject nuclear weapons. Why should not people of differing convictions pray together in such a place, dedicated to peace, which is also the stated objective of Her Majesty's Government in pursuing its present defence policies? If it is the wish of your Ministry to avoid confrontation, then let this place of prayer symbolise the possibility of dialogue between people of differing convictions.

'It is my experience that there is a great need for creative encounter between those who describe themselves as members of the peace movement, and members of the armed forces whose self-understanding is very similar. The destruction of this building would symbolise a breakdown in communication. Its creative use would

213

symbolise a common attempt to discover God's will and also a creative aspect of a democratic society at work.

'*As a very last resort, if the land on which the chapel stands really was needed for defence purposes and this was not merely a pretext for getting rid of the chapel, then I hope it could be dismantled and rebuilt nearby at a place to be agreed and with the help of Her Majesty's Government.*

'*Seen in that light, this small building, which in itself is not of great significance, could be an important symbol of a society that is not at war with itself. The fear that a minority might conceivably misuse the chapel is certainly not an adequate ground for its being permanently out of bounds or for its demolition.*

I should be grateful to have your views on this.

'*Yours sincerely,*

'*Rev Dr Philip Morgan,*

General Secretary of the British Council of Churches.'

Tim and Bridie suggested that we should celebrate the anniversary of the dedication of the chapel at the beginning of September. This could be an important way of creating publicity, and so we began to plan 'Eirene Day'. Someone had the idea of producing full-colour postcards of the chapel, one of which would serve as an invitation to the anniversary, luckily, several hundred pounds was in the Eirene account, to pay for them. A local printer, Kevin Cummins, had printed Ian's black and white drawing and that was a great success. The first five hundred had been sold and a second five hundred were on order.

We spent some time looking through colour transparencies and prints for suitable pictures. In the end we settled on a close-up of the chapel in the evening light, surrounded by leafy trees, for the invitation card. We chose three other designs: one showed the interior with a woman meditating, another showed a man helping with the building of Eirene and the last was a shot of Tim putting up the sign for the roof fund. All the pictures were taken before the fence went up. Mallen, who understood more about the technicalities of colour printing, arranged to get the postcards printed in Peterborough and by the beginning of August they were ready. We were delighted with the results. Now began the laborious process of writing names on the hundreds of personal invitations.

We all agreed that a specially prepared commemorative booklet would be a good idea. Earlier in the year, a book of songs had been printed at the School House for use at the vigils. Over the intervening months, most of these had been taken away by visitors. We were pleased that people had found the songs inspirational and had wanted to keep a copy, but clearly we needed a new edition. This time, it should include some background on Eirene, photographs and readings as well as songs. We had great fun deciding what should go in it. One day in early August, Tim, Bridie, Mallen, Ian and I, sat in the caravan with a pile of books on the table, sifting through possible items. We all had our favourites and, inevitably, not everything could be included.

Quotations from writers, poets, politicians and mystics included: Dietrich Bonhoeffer; Heinrich Heine; Dwight Eisenhower; Gandhi and Martin Luther King, while many more found their way in. A poem by the American artist Judy Chicago was a favourite of Ian and me. It has no title.

'And then all that has divided us will merge
And then compassion will be welded to power
And then softness will come to a world that is harsh and unkind.
And then both men and women will be gentle
And then both women and men will be strong
And then no person will be subject to another's will
And then all will be rich and free and varied
And then the greed of some will give way to the needs of many
And then all will share equally in the Earth's abundance
And then all will care for the sick and the weak and the old
And then all will nourish the young
And then all will cherish life's creatures
And then all will live in harmony with each other and the earth
And then everywhere will be called Eden once again.'

On one page, we had a quotation from the writings of the seventeenth-century social reformer, Gerard Winstanley. He was influential in a sect called the Diggers, who maintained that the land should be held in common. It ended, *'if everyone did but quietly enjoy the earth for food and raiment, there would be no wars, prisons or gallows.'*

This was followed by the words of the eighteenth-century Quaker, John Woolman, who campaigned tirelessly for the abolition of slavery. He spoke of there being a principle in the human mind that in different times and places has had different names: *'It is, however, pure and proceeds from God. It is... confined to no forms of religion, nor excluded from any, where the heart stands in perfect sincerity.'*

We followed this with a quotation from the Native American, Chief Seattle: *'This we know. The earth does not belong to people, people belong to the earth. This we know. All things are connected. Whatever befalls the earth befalls the children of the earth. People did not weave the web of life; they are merely strands in it. Whatever they do to the web, they do to themselves.'*

The next day we had to put aside the task of preparing the booklet. It was time for another, much more momentous anniversary.

★★★

It was 40 years since the bomb the Americans called 'Little Boy', was dropped on Hiroshima on August 6th, 1945. By today's standards it was a small bomb. Each cruise missile carries a warhead fifteen times as powerful. Over one hundred thousand people died that day in the city of Hiroshima and they are still dying from the effects of radiation. At Molesworth on that summer morning 40 years later, Ian and I wore black arm bands.

Steve Hope rode up on his bike looking hot and having just completed a sponsored cycle ride from his home in Durham. It had taken two weeks. He was wearing shorts and a vest and was very thirsty.

"Have you got a cold drink?"

"Is orange squash okay?" I replied.

"Great!"

He collapsed on the settee and proceeded to tell us about his journey. At that point Helen Richardson arrived. She had offered to look after the caravan at the end of the month. We had arranged to go and stay with my mother, while my sister and her husband had a holiday. Helen had come today to find out what things she needed to bring with her. Before her retirement she was in charge of a centre for disturbed adolescent girls. Now she spent her time working for the disarmament cause as an enthusiastic member of Pensioners for Peace. It was nearly eleven and time for the vigil. We all made our way over to the gate as usual to ask the police if we could hold the vigil in the chapel. As we stood beside the heavy, black metal gates, a policeman came over to say good morning.

"Hello, how are you today?" I said.

"Not so bad." He spoke with a Lancashire accent. He had red hair and a little moustache. He was wearing dark glasses. With the peak cap, his appearance reminded me of a Latin American secret policeman, but the accent spoilt the effect. We knew him quite well; he had a dry sense of humour.

"Do you know what today is?" Ian asked.

"How do you mean?"

"Did you know it's 'Hiroshima Day'?" I enquired.

"No."

"It's the fortieth anniversary of the dropping of the Hiroshima bomb."

"Oh, aye." He looked decidedly uninterested.

After a few more exchanges, we asked him if we could go into Eirene.

"I'm afraid you can't. You know the orders as well as I do."

We thanked him and moved over to the gardens. We stood by the fence, looking at the chapel. The little tree beside the fence was in full leaf. The sky was blue and the ground had dried out. Sparrows were busily flying from bush to bush, landing for a moment on the chapel wall. High overhead a lark sang. We had chosen a couple of readings. Ian read an account written by Takako Okimoto when she was fifteen, of the dropping of the atomic bomb. It comes from an anthology called *My Country is the Whole World*. I read a poem about another Japanese girl who died when she was seven.

Afterwards we all drove over to Faye Way and walked to the fence at a point near the bunkers and the firing range. Jimmy Johns, an enthusiastic exponent of direct action, and a member of Essex CND, had organised a 'Hiroshima Day' event for East Anglian CND groups. When we arrived, we could hear the sound of guns. The red flag was flying to signify that American service personnel were having rest and recreation, blasting away at targets with automatic weapons. More and more people were wending their way down the lane and past the Rabbit Catcher's caravan to the beginning of the western bridleway. The Rabbit Catcher had been around for years, we were told that the MOD employed him to shoot rabbits on the base. He was not sympathetic to the Peace Movement. He had a twelve bore and had been known to fire it over the heads of demonstrators. The irony was that people, seeing a caravan beside the fence, often assumed it belonged to a Peace Camper. They soon found out their mistake as a stream of four-letter words greeted them. That afternoon he came out to hurl abuse, but after a while he must have felt overwhelmed, because he went off in his van. His dog, tied up outside, continued to bark ferociously at anyone who passed.

The theme of the event was that the bomb had not kept the peace for 40 years. Every year since 1945 there had been wars around the world, every year thousands had died. All one could say with honesty was that there had not been a war in Europe. The 'superpowers' now fought their wars by proxy and fuelled the conflicts by selling arms, often to both sides. In order to illustrate the theme, groups came carrying a coffin. There was one for each of the past 40 years, and each black-painted coffin bore a year and the numbers of those who had died in military conflicts that year. The coffins were carried by pall bearers dressed in mourning, who slowly proceeded down the bridleway. It was an impressive sight. Later at a given signal, the hundreds present stepped up to the fence and in defiance of the by-laws, solemnly hung printed placards on the coils of razor wire. The placards read, '*A 1000 times NO to Hiroshima at Molesworth*'.

As usual we saw so many people we knew, and afterwards were left with the feeling we had not really spoken to anyone properly. Many of our friends from Ipswich had made the journey to Molesworth, including Grace Thomas, who is a stalwart campaigner. She has very bad arthritis in her hips and walking is not easy, even on flat ground. The western bridleway was overgrown and covered with huge puddles, almost ponds, requiring great ingenuity and nimbleness of foot to negotiate. Grace smiled valiantly, undeterred. She came up to me, holding a brown paper bag.

Passing it to me, she said, "It's your copy of *Christian Faith and Practice* – from the meeting. I have to welcome you into membership."

I was now officially a Quaker. The book is a collection of extracts from the writings of Quakers over the past three hundred years. If you want to know what Quakers think, *Christian Faith and Practice in the Experience of the Society of Friends* is the nearest you will get to the Quaker view. I had been an attender at meetings for many years and had considered applying for membership before. Now, having been a rather public Quaker for several months I felt the time was right to request full membership.

Helen drove us back to Peace Corner in time for the four o'clock vigil. Before she left for home, we went over the arrangements for her stay. She was planning not only to bring her dog, Gypsy, another Sheltie, but also her cat! In the evening, when everyone had gone home, we went to talk to Tim and Bridie about the arrangements for 'Eirene Day'. We arrived in time to watch the six o'clock news. Television crews from ITV and BBC had both filmed the day's event and coverage was shown on the main news that night. For once no shots of angry confrontation were shown, just the silent procession of coffins and the symbolic breaking of the by-laws. The commentary was accurate and the point we were trying to make was put across clearly. It made a change.

In the following few days we finalised the details for the production of the booklet with Pat Collins, the printer, who lived in Kimbolton. Pat had a bigger and more sophisticated litho machine than the one at the Old School and he was now producing the bulletins. Mallen prepared four-colour art work and the results looked very good. By this time, he had finished at art school and was living permanently at Molesworth. For a long time he slept in a Gore-Tex bag in Peace Garden. It was high summer and the roses were in full bloom. All the hard work that had been put into the gardens had borne fruit. As well as flowers and shrubs, herbs grew such as thyme, mint and marjoram. We hoped that it would still be looking good on 'Eirene Day'. But there were still three weeks to go, and at Molesworth a lot could happen in three days.

Chapter Sixteen
In the Hands of the Church

The woman in the wheel chair began to sing. She had a powerful voice and sang unaccompanied. The music flowed from her as she sang *Four minutes to midnight*. It was a song about the four-minute warning preceding a nuclear attack:

"Four minutes to Armageddon..." She sat hunched in her chair, her hands bent, grasping one of the songbooks. Despite the summer sun, it was cold and she had a blanket tucked around her shoulders, but the biting wind still blew over her unprotected head. Her hair was very fine and blonde, almost white. As she sang, she stared fiercely at the barbed-wire fence. Her two little girls hung on the chair, the younger creeping on to her lap to hide under the blanket.

Jan had been crippled by polio. When we arrived at Molesworth, she was living in a converted coach with a man called Convoy Jim. The weather had been very hard and she had decided not to spend all her time at Molesworth. She had a house about 40 miles away, and was living there when the eviction of Rainbow Village took place. This had caused her deep distress. Jan had been involved in the campaign at Molesworth for years, and as a member of Christian CND had regularly participated in all their activities. She had two daughters, Son and Seph, lively girls of around eight and six. Jim acted as Jan's legs, pushing her chair and driving her about in an assortment of old cars.

Jim and Jan made an unlikely pair. Jim, as his nickname suggested, had travelled with the Peace Convoy. It didn't take much to make him angry, but his dark moods were generally short-lived, and soon he would be laughing and joking about the latest 'motor' he had acquired. To start with, they were always great little runners, but gradually their

220

defects began to come to Jim's notice and he would start to search for something new. Jan was very patient with Jim, quietly accepting his changing mood.

In early summer, Jan left her house and came to live in a bus at the Peace Camp in Faye Way. She was a regular visitor at Peace Corner, coming over to join in the vigils and to discuss her plans for moving back into Peace Lane. That weekend in August, she had come over for the Sunday afternoon vigil. Sheila and Chris from Rainbow Village were with her. Sheila had come to the Old School to help Andy run a meditation workshop. It was the day before Chris was due to appear at Crown Court for the incident involving the tow-truck driver in April. We stood for a long time, with just the sound of the wind whistling through the barbed wire. Jan's strong, clear voice broke the silence. Someone spoke about the trial and prayed for the man who had been hurt, and for Chris, that he would be given strength to face the difficult days ahead. Chris looked thin, his cheeks hollow; the strain of waiting, the uncertainty of what might come, had taken its toll.

The sound of motorcycle engines disturbed the atmosphere of quiet; I looked around and saw a group of about a dozen young men parking their motor scooters at the side of the road. Most of them had skin-head haircuts and were dressed in long khaki coats and tatty jeans. I wondered if they had come to cause trouble. I left the vigil and walked over to them. One of them told me it was the first time they had seen the base and had stopped out of curiosity. I was telling them something of the history of the place when, without warning, there was a sudden downpour. As we were all beginning to get soaked I asked if they would like to shelter in the caravan. It was a bit cramped. Ian introduced himself and put the kettle on. We soon discovered they knew nothing about the base or what it was going to be used for. One by one they started firing questions at us, showing a genuine interest. Each one thanked us before leaving. I commented to Ian when they had gone, how easy it was to misjudge people purely on the way they dressed and how glad I was that I had spoken to them.

Chris's trial lasted the next three days. He was found guilty of reckless driving, given a two-month suspended sentence, fined £300 and banned from driving for a year.

August was a strange month. There was so much uncertainty about our future. What would be the effect of the road closure, due to be decided by the magistrates on September 10th? Tim and Bridie were away for two weeks and we missed their support. We had arranged to leave the caravan for a fortnight and now, just before we were due to leave, one of the people who we thought had agreed to look after Halcyon Spirit for a week, had got in a muddle over dates and had to drop out. On August 20th I wrote in my diary:

'Tuesday, cold, wet and windy...

'I feel I should write down how I am feeling. I feel disillusioned and TIRED. I cannot see how we can leave the caravan here... We don't know what Mike is going to do, so we are not sure when we can go home. We have had a tax bill for £500 and we have vet's bills unpaid. The car suspension is going and it is rusted through in a lot of places. So things are pretty worrying. Ian and I love being together and we like being in the caravan, but there is too much pressure being outside the gates with the 'public image'. I wish I knew what is 'right' and how I am supposed to feel about things and where I am supposed to go and what I should do. There are no answers any more – why? Have we done anything worthwhile or has it all been a waste of time?'

On the positive side, we had begun to establish a working relationship with the RAF. On August 9th, 'Nagasaki Day', I met Flight Lieutenant Angus McDougall. I had written a letter about the possibility of harvesting the wheat grown on the base and was wondering if I would get a reply. That day a big man wearing a carefully laundered, khaki military uniform, shiny black boots and an airforce grey peaked cap appeared in Peace Lane.

"I'm looking for a Mrs Jennifer Hartley," he said in a Scots accent.

I smiled. "Looks like you've found her."

"I just wanted to introduce myself in person. I have taken over from Wing Commander Nelson. I believe you have written us letters."

"Frequently!" I responded.

"Well, I shall be answering them for the base commander in future and I thought I would deliver this one by hand." With that he pulled himself upright, and drawing himself to attention presented me with a brown envelope. "I'm afraid it won't be the answer you wanted," he said.

"Well, I shall just have to write again, I'm very persistent when I think I'm right."

We invited him inside for a cup of tea, but he said he was in a hurry. After he had left, I opened the letter. It was a reply to one I had written to the base commander on August 2nd, which read:

'Dear Wing Commander Shaw

'I am writing to you on behalf of a group of people who were and are involved with the plight of the starving in the Third World. Last October, as you are no doubt aware, wheat was sown on a piece of land at Molesworth belonging to the Ministry of Defence, to try and show a positive alternative to the land being used for the deployment of cruise missiles. At this time the land was unfenced and a great many people believed in the morality of this action.

'The wheat that was planted has now grown and we are writing to you to ask if you would allow a few people on to the base to harvest the crop. We feel this would be a real gesture on your behalf and show that you, too, are concerned with the same injustices that we are. We await your reply,

Yours sincerely...'

The reply read:

'Dear Mrs Hartley,

'The station commander has asked me to thank you for your letter... He shares your concern for the "plight of the starving in the Third World". I am sure you will be aware of the Royal Air Force's current involvement in Ethiopia. To date, we have flown over two and a half thousand hours delivering some 20,000 tonnes of food and medical aid. We hope to be able to continue this work.

'Your request to be allowed to harvest a crop of wheat on MOD land has been carefully considered. Regrettably, the circumstances prevailing at Molesworth make it impossible for us to agree to your request.

'Signed A.D. McDougall Flt. Lt. for OC.'

We felt pleased that some thought had gone into this reply, but as many questions remained unanswered, it seemed worth writing again. I got out my typewriter and composed the following:

'Dear Flt. Lt. McDougall,

'Thank you for coming to see us the other afternoon and bringing by hand the reply to our letter. We appreciate the fact that you, too, feel personal communication is important. We would like to see meetings taking place between yourselves and members of the peace movement, as we feel that a much better understanding of differences occurs when people meet in person.

'Would you please pass this letter to the Officer Commanding, as I am sure that he makes the decisions. Of course we are aware of the very valuable work that the Royal Air Force are doing in Ethiopia and cannot speak too highly of it. This does not in any way alter the fact that there is wheat growing on the base, and that it was sown to make the very real links between the poverty in the Third World and the arms race. We are not quite sure what the phrase, "circumstances which prevail at Molesworth make it impossible for us to agree with your request", actually means, as you must realise that we are people of good faith, acting in a Christian spirit.

'We are, therefore, asking if you could harvest the crop for us as you no doubt have men available who could do it and it would only take a short amount of time. Instead of conflict this would, we feel, be a gesture of the co-operation we are trying so hard to work for.

'Please visit us again, as although we have asked, it seems we are not allowed access on to the base to speak with anyone working inside and we would welcome the chance to talk with you again.

'Yours sincerely...'

A reply came at the end of the month.

'August 30th, 1985

'Dear Mrs Hartley,

'Once again the station commander has asked me to thank you for your letter and directed me to reply. We acknowledge that any problems that might arise can be resolved by personal contact. To that end, we would be prepared to respond on an ad hoc basis to any request for meetings. We do not, however, feel that such an arrangement needs to be formalised. Contact can be made by asking the duty staff at any of the gates to pass a message to either myself or the station commander, or by calling the number on the letterhead.

'Your letter goes on to discuss the wheat sown on the base. We are unable to agree to your request to harvest the wheat on your behalf. All our men are committed to their primary tasks. We have nonetheless inspected the wheat and I am sorry to tell you, in common with other local wheat, the poor summer has seriously affected its growth. The wheat achieved only patchy germination and growth has been thin. Such wheat that has grown is heavily mixed with weeds and various grasses that would contaminate the wheat if harvested. Further, the wheat is still unripe and there is considerable mildew and other rot in the ears. It is unlikely that any useable quantity of wheat would have resulted from the harvesting.

'On a personal note may I thank you for your invitation to the service on September 1st, 1985. I regret that I am unable to attend, although I will no doubt be in church elsewhere on that day.

'Yours sincerely,

'A.D McDougall for Officer Commanding.'

★★★

Helen Richardson greeted us. We had travelled from Leigh-on-Sea to Molesworth to celebrate 'Eirene Day'. Although it was still only midday, people were arriving all the time. A box of groceries and fresh peaches had been left anonymously in the caravan. Helen made us a cup of coffee and we sat and listened while she told us about her week there. She had been delighted when an MOD policeman had given her some four-leaf clovers that he had picked on the base. Helen had mounted them on pieces of card and covered them with cellophane to give to VIPs who visited.

We were anxious to see Bridie and Tim to discuss last-minute arrangements so we drove around to the School House. The house was full of people. I recognised Lord George Macleod of Fuinary, the founder of the Iona community, sitting in an armchair, and was surprised that at 90 years old he had made the long journey from Scotland. We shook hands with him. He told us he had travelled from Edinburgh on an overnight train. The only sleeping accommodation was in First Class and he refused on principle to travel this way, so he had sat up all night! He looked remarkably fresh. Having spoken to Tim, we returned to Peace Corner.

Steve, from Stevenage, had just arrived and brought with him postcards of the rainbow photograph that Ian had taken after Easter. Stevenage CND had paid to have them printed and he handed us a thousand to sell in the caravan. Ian recalled the day he had taken the photograph. It was the Tuesday after Easter and it had been raining on and off for 48 hours. The sun suddenly emerged from a gap in the clouds and, as we watched from the caravan window, a double rainbow formed over Peace Gardens, lighting up the brightly coloured pennants left over from the demonstration. Ian dashed out with a camera and quickly took a couple of shots. Now one of them was printed as a postcard.

I had brought a bunch of flowers with me to go inside the chapel. I carried them out in a jar of water.

"Do you think you could put these inside the chapel for me?" I asked the policeman on duty.

"I don't see why not," he said, reaching over to take them through the wire.

The sergeant came over, had a word with him and then came to speak to me.

"I'm sorry Mrs Hartley, you will have to put your flowers outside the fence."

"Surely you could make an exception, as it's a special day."

"I'm afraid not," he said and started to walk away.

I ran after him prepared to have one last try. "Perhaps you could ring through to someone in the RAF to see what they say, they may not mind." I didn't hear any more. The flowers stayed outside the fence.

Tim had hired a public address system, which was being unpacked and set out in the gardens. It was powered by a small petrol generator, which was hidden away in the ditch. A group of musicians with a variety of instruments, including a trombone and several guitars, were tuning up and practising. More and more friends were appearing and coming up to say hello, including a large group from Ipswich.

It had been agreed that the service should take the form of our usual vigil. Around three hundred people had gathered and the new green booklets were handed out to everyone. We knew that George Macleod had prepared something to say and Gordon Roe, the Bishop of Huntingdon, had been asked to say the final words. After welcoming everyone, Tim explained that anyone was free to speak or sing as the spirit moved them.

Out of the silence, Jean Hutchinson spoke. She talked of the early days of the peace camp and of the first Eirene built by Architects for Peace. In a loud voice she told how the campers had gathered in the new building made of wood and polythene. Someone had said a carpet was needed and another agreed, suggesting it should be a green one. And, Jean continued, the next day a visitor arrived by car bringing a *green* carpet. She went on to say that the story of the peace witness at Molesworth was a series of seeming endings, followed by 'and then...', and who could say what may happen next? George Macleod spoke as a Christian about the obscene danger of nuclear war. We sang *Eden's Garden*, and *Walk in the Light*, accompanied by the small band. Lots of people spoke. Angela remembered Caroline, while Andy from Peterborough said he would rather be at home making biscuits with the children than at Molesworth, but until cruise missiles were scrapped he would keep coming. Alf Willetts, a retired vicar from Cheshire, wearing his stole covered in badges, quoted Socrates. Cliff Reed, the Unitarian minister from Ipswich, read some words from *Deuteronomy, Chapter 30*:

'Today I offer you the choice of life and good, or death and evil... Choose life and then you and your children will live...'

Jan sitting in her wheelchair, read Martin Luther King's vision of the lamb and the lion:

'I have the audacity to believe that peoples everywhere can have three meals a day for their bodies, education for their minds and dignity, equality and freedom for their spirits. I believe that what self-centred people have torn down, other-centred people can build up.

'I still believe that one day humanity will bow before the altars of God and be crowned triumphant over war and bloodshed and non-violent redemptive goodwill will proclaim the rule of the land. And the lion and the lamb shall lie down together and everyone shall sit under their own vine and fig tree, and none shall be afraid. I still believe that we shall overcome.'

It seemed natural after this, to break into the Negro spiritual *We Are Climbing Jacob's Ladder*. The words always filled me with hope. *'People of all faiths and nations... Holding hands we climb together... There is nothing that can stop us... Climbing towards our dreams.'*

The bishop, in his purple cassock, moved forward to the microphone. He gave the closing prayer and blessing. The sky had grown dark with threatening, grey and black rain clouds piled up in the north-west as we looked over towards the base. We stood holding hands in a vast circle that encompassed not only the gardens, but also the large open space outside the big, black gates with their sinister metal crosses. As people began to move away, the Japanese Buddhist monks, dressed in their white and saffron robes, began to beat their prayer drums, reciting an ancient mantra.

★★★

Returning to Halcyon Spirit a week after 'Eirene Day', we realised that the story of the County Council's attempt to close Peace Lane had reached another critical stage. It would only be a matter of days before our future would be decided in the magistrates' court. In June the newly elected Transportation Committee had met and reflected the new balance of power within the County Council. The new chairman, Mike Evelegh, was a member of the Alliance and the Conservatives no longer had an overall majority. By this time we had established a cordial relationship with the Alliance group. Despite this, the Committee decided to recommend that the Council should proceed with the 'stopping up', as it was technically known. It was helpful to know their reasons. Although we were now dealing with a more sympathetic County Council, the local parish councils and the District Council remained staunchly right wing. There were those who suggested that these councils were working hand in glove with the local MP and Tory whip, John Major, to get rid of all peace protesters around the base.

Chris Bradford, a member of the Alliance and now leader of the County Council, had written to explain the background to us:

June 17th, 1985.

'Dear Mr and Mrs Hartley,

'You may be somewhat concerned at the decision of the Transportation Committee to agree to stopping up the lay-by on which your caravan stands. The decision was taken by my group after a great deal of thought and I should like to explain it to you.'

After explaining that the effect of the stopping-up order would be to make the Church responsible for the land on which the caravan stands, he continued:

'The council's present difficulty is that both the Molesworth and Brington Parish Council and the Old Weston Parish Council have now made formal representations to the County Council under the Highways Act 1980 to take steps to remove the obstructions to the highway. The County Council as highway authority is then bound to take such action, and I am concerned that if the County Council retains the highway it would in law have to take action to remove you and anyone else on the lay-by. If it refused to do so, it could be ordered by a court and would have to meet the costs of such an action.

'All in all, we took the view that your security was safer in the hands of the Church than in the hands of the County Council, which is bound to take action against you...

'The real difficulty would be if the Peterborough Diocese sold their piece of adjoining land to the Ministry of Defence. I have written in a personal capacity, asking them not to do so... I think that there is every chance that you may be able to manipulate the situation to greater effect [if the Church owns the land] than if the land had remained a highway. I hope so.

'Yours sincerely,

'Chris Bradford.'

On July 23rd, the County Council met and for a second time ratified the decision to stop up Peace Lane. Once more signs were posted giving due notice that the matter would be settled at a magistrate's hearing now rescheduled for September 10th.

We went to the hearing in Huntingdon. We had decided not to contest the matter, so had not asked Neil to attend. I sat next to Emily Blatch who had obviously thought it worth her while to be there. Ian spoke to the county solicitor's representative who wanted to know if there were many objectors. Ian told him that, as far as we were aware, no one was objecting. The solicitor looked relieved and said in that case the hearing would proceed, indicating that if there had been a lot of objectors present, he would have asked for an adjournment. It was all a formality. Notices had to be served on Telecom, the electricity and water boards, the MOD and the Church of England. These were all duly read out and once it was established that all the correct procedures had been complied with, that was it; we were now on private land! That afternoon, we had a visit from two Cambridgeshire police inspectors and later a WPC and sergeant came to see us. Everyone was very curious to see what would happen next.

After September 10th, we had new neighbours. Jill Hutchinson and Jan Livesey wrote an article in the *Molesworth Bulletin*, describing the setting up of Earth Camp. Jill explained their intention: 'A small group of Christians decided to camp on Church land to challenge the C. of E. about their response to nuclear weapons and the Molesworth base in particular.' Jill had given up her job as a teacher, in order to live at Molesworth. It ran in the family. Her mother, Jean Hutchinson, along with Helen and Angela, had started the original Molesworth Peace Camp. Her brother Gus had also lived at the Peace Camp in the early days and her father,

John, a graphic artist, had vividly chronicled the people and events over the years.

We first met Jill shortly after the eviction. At that time she was still working and was agonising over whether she should give in her notice. It was inevitable, given her passionate concern, that she eventually made the decision. She moved into a caravan in Faye Way, otherwise known as Warren Lane. Jill, like us, was a Christian and as a result was intrigued by the implications of the Church owning the field next to Peace Lane. She once remarked to us that the vicious barbed wire on top of the fence around Eirene reminded her of the 'crown of thorns'.

Jan explained her involvement. *'I used to live on Peace Lane in Rainbow Village days. In some ways it feels like being home. But home is sadly changed. The light, the generators, the fence and the constant patrols...'* She went on to explain, *'We were fortunate to manage to bring in one caravan before both ends of the lane were obstructed by huge concrete blocks.'*

Two days later, on a bright and sunny September afternoon, quite a rare event for Molesworth, we were both sitting reading outside when we heard a car stop. I looked up and saw our friends Keith Ollett and Chris from Crowborough. We were very fond of Keith. He had been a frequent visitor all the time we had been living in the caravan and took some fine photographs. The day after the eviction he had arrived on a bicycle that could be used for cross-country riding over very rough ground. He had cycled over the snow-clad fields to reach us.

They backed the car up as far as they could and we called and waved as they got out.

"It's good to see you again, what a nice surprise and you've actually managed to choose a decent day for a change."

They were both grinning as they opened the car boot and began to unload some boxes.

"What on earth have you got there?" I asked, full of curiosity.

"Well, you said you wanted a Martini umbrella," Keith shouted back.

He was referring to a conversation we had had some weeks earlier. On a warm day, when the daily chores were complete, letters written and water collected, Ian and I would get out our garden chairs and put them in the lane. We often felt a bit self-conscious, but laughed it off to visitors. Sometimes we sat facing the caravan, sometimes the base that was still, thankfully, hidden by the hedgerow. It depended where the sun was. Often we would have our meals outside. Eating was among the high spots of our day and we took trouble to make the meals interesting and varied. It was on just such a day that Ian had remarked to Keith, who was visiting, "All we need now is a Martini umbrella!"

Gradually we could see what all the cardboard cartons contained. It was a complete patio set in a bright red-and-white-striped material! They carried it over to where we were sitting and proceeded to put out four garden chairs and a circular white table, onto which they fixed a large umbrella. But that was not all! Chris delved once again into the car boot and brought out an ice box and some glasses. We were invited to sit down on one of the new chairs neatly arranged around the table, while Keith and Chris opened the ice box and produced a bottle of chilled Martini, ice and lemon!

"Keith, this lot must have cost you a fortune, we can't possibly accept it as a present," I protested.

"It has been more than worth it just to see the look on your faces," he said.

We could see the Ministry of Defence police, who guarded the chapel, looking over towards us and wondering what on earth was going on. We raised our glasses to them and called out, "Cheers!"

We all found our cameras and posed for each other. This was something for the photo album. Several of our friends camping further down the lane came up to see what all the noise was about and joined us in an ice-cold drink and enjoyed the expensive joke.

As I was sitting there, I noticed two RAF men walking up the lane towards us so I got up to speak to them. One I recognised as Squadron Leader Johnson, a big, friendly man whom we often talked to. The other one, a much shorter and stockier man, I thought looked vaguely familiar, but I could not place him. I said, "Good afternoon, I don't think I have met you before, have I?"

"Yes you have," he replied. "I'm the station commander."

I had written many times to Wing Commander Shaw, but had only occasionally seen him and had forgotten what he looked like. I took the opportunity to speak to him about the cowslips that had been sprayed with weedkiller inside the wire. I also spoke about the correspondence over the harvesting of the wheat that was growing on the base. He stayed and talked for some time, and I explained about the patio set as it made me a little self-conscious. I thought he looked slightly bewildered by it all. Later in the day, we shared out the patio set with the others camping there and just kept two of the chairs for our own use.

Wing Commander Shaw became a regular visitor after that day. He used to call early in the morning, driving up to the Main Gate in his black Vauxhall Cavalier car. One morning, he arrived and stood looking at the small garden we had created on the opposite side of the lane to the caravan. It was still a matter of dispute as to who owned the land on that side of the lane, but the MOD thought they did. I went outside.

"Hello, how are you?" I asked.

"I have just come to look at MY tomatoes," he said and looked up at me with a grin.

"MY tomatoes you mean, don't you?" I replied. "I'll tell you what, you can have the first one when they ripen, how about that?"

I did indeed send the first ripe tomato in to him a few weeks later, and when he called several days afterwards he said he had eaten it but it was rather hard and didn't taste very nice! I was not altogether surprised. They had taken ages to ripen as we had very little sun that summer.

We enjoyed talking to the Wing Commander. He often came into the caravan and would stay and have a cup of tea or coffee. We would talk about all the aspects of the nuclear issue, as well as many other subjects. We were able to have long conversations without getting into arguments, although there were obvious points of disagreement. It was good when we found points on which we could agree and we appreciated his giving up his time to talk with us. We found him very fair and over the last few months we were at Molesworth we built up a good relationship with him. If ever there was anything we wanted to discuss or question, we were told to ask at the gate and someone would come out to speak to us. I wrote letters frequently and passed them through the fence. They often contained a quotation or a poem. I suspect our file must be fairly large by now, as I still write to the base although a new station commander has now taken over.

We turned our attention to the Peterborough Diocese. Now we were on their land, we felt the time was long overdue for us to get

232

better acquainted. As we explained in the next issue of the *Molesworth Bulletin*:

'When the closure of Peace Lane as a highway finally went through on September 10th at the magistrates' court in Huntingdon, we felt that contact should be made with Peterborough Diocese to find out their intentions. We had a meeting with a clergyman who is also on the Finance Board and he was prepared to talk to us on the relevant issue. He agreed to visit Molesworth to see for himself the layout and the land question. We have reason to believe that fairly soon there will be another meeting of the Diocesan Finance Board and that the issue of the field and, also, now half the lane belonging to the Diocese, will be discussed.

'We understand that around 646 letters were received by the Peterborough Diocese and that four bids have been received to purchase the land. One of these is from the Ministry of Defence, another from Christian CND and we think one may be from a local farmer. The fourth one we are not sure about.'

Paul Johns, the chairperson of Christian CND, came to supper with us. He suggested the idea of putting up a Christian symbol in the lane on Church land. We talked to Jill about it and she thought it was a good idea. Paul, a Methodist local preacher, asked us to find out what it would cost. We had it in mind to ask Jimmy from Bishops Stortford if he would make us a large cross of seven- or eight-foot high, out of hardwood. On September 24th, the Bishops Stortford CND contingent arrived for one of their frequent visits and they quoted us a price of £200 to make and erect the cross. It was a lot of money, but we knew how beautifully Jimmy had made the sign board. He told us he would use an African wood called iroko, as it was cheaper than the oak or mahogany that we had suggested. The next day, Paul Johns paid another visit and left us a cheque for £200. Christian CND was prepared to pay for the cross, which would be a gift to the Diocese of Peterborough. The date we fixed for erecting it was Sunday, October 20th. But a lot was to happen before then.

Earth Camp was also interested to find out what the attitude of the Diocese would be to their presence in Peace Lane. Another of the Earth Campers, Mark Rogers, a young ordinand, described in the bulletin how, on the last Friday in September, this small group of Christians, in an effort to pin down the Church authorities, *'took up residence at St Oswald's Chapel in the South Transept of Peterborough Cathedral. We were not sightseeing, but here to seek sanctuary as distressed people about to be evicted from our home. We were there to pray and fast for peace and unity amongst all peoples, and we intended to stay until the Church gave us an assurance that they are not selling Earth Camp's land to the MOD.'*

As Mark went on to report: *'By eight o'clock we had been given an assurance by a member of the Glebe Committee that the Church was delaying making a decision on selling the land until at least January.'*

We were away on the weekend that this 'sit-in' took place, but when we returned the following Monday morning, we found that a letter had been left for us by solicitors representing the Peterborough Diocese. We were stunned to read that: *'Our clients instruct us to request that you vacate their property within seven days of today's date. We appreciate you are not able to remove the caravan at the moment because of the presence of the concrete blocks, but arrangements can be made for the necessary blocks to be removed so that you can remove your caravan.*

Chapter Seventeen
Turning the World Upside Down

We discovered that everyone in Peace Lane had received a similar letter. The letters were not addressed to named individuals and despite the reference to 'today's date', were undated. The reference to the concrete blocks was also interesting, as the blocks had been placed at either end of the lane by the RAF. On September 10th access was still possible, as they were only on the Ministry's side of the lane, but the next day, after Earth Campers brought Peace Link caravan on to the lane, the RAF had positioned more blocks on the Church side. When we questioned the Squadron Leader supervising this work, he made it clear that he had the authority of the Church to do this.

It was difficult to find out who was issuing the orders from the Diocese, though it seemed likely that the Secretary of the Board of Finance was responsible. It was also clear that not all the Board of Finance members were kept informed or consulted about the actions taken. We were often told that, of all church committees, the Board of Finance was likely to be least sympathetic to our activities. Most members would be land owners or people with knowledge of finance and accounting; few would be radical Christians, for these people would be involved in other endeavours. However, there were a few members of the Board who had shown misgivings about the sale of the Church land to the military and it was to these we now turned, only to discover they knew nothing about the decision to issue solicitor's letters or the moving of the concrete blocks.

It became clear that we needed to open new channels of communication. We wanted to speak to the bishop, The Right Reverend William Westwood, and to the secretary of the Board of

Finance, Philip Haines. At first neither seemed willing to see us. We had written to both men on several occasions, but the only replies we received from Philip Haines were single sentence letters informing us that our letters would be placed before the committee. We never received any acknowledgement to our letters to the bishop. We decided that we must try a more positive approach. The next day we wrote the following letter:

'Dear William Westwood,

'Yesterday, a letter was handed in to someone who was kindly looking after our caravan for us. It came from solicitors acting for the Diocesan Board of Finance. It did not have our name on it, but we take it that in fact it was for us. As you know, we have lived here since January 21st this year and have been witnessing for peace as Christians since that time. We have written to you on other occasions and have never had a reply from you. This makes us sad as we should be able to communicate with each other, as we are all sisters and brothers in Christ. We would very much like to see you, to explain our position here and to listen to what your feelings are concerning this matter.

'We will be in Peterborough on Friday this week and will ring on Thursday to see if it is convenient to have a short meeting with you.'

On Thursday we rang the cathedral and someone in the Diocesan Office told us that neither the bishop nor Philip Haines would see us. A journalist from *The Sunday Times* contacted us, as she was interested in the story of the Church land. We told her our view of the situation and she seemed quite enthusiastic about writing an article, but like us, she wanted the Bishop's views and he would not speak to her, either. Through the Rural Dean, we then tried to arrange to see the Bishop of Ely, in whose Diocese we were living. We had met on several occasions the Suffragan Bishop of Huntingdon, Gordon Roe, who had special responsibility under the Ely Diocese for our area, but Bishop, the Right Reverend Peter Elien had been ill so we were unable to talk to him about our situation. Now, it appeared, he had recovered from surgery and was able to take up his pastoral duties again. He agreed to see us on Saturday. In the meantime, we went to see our friends at the Community of the Sower at Little Gidding.

Our link with Little Gidding stretched back to our first visit to Molesworth when Ian had spotted a signpost saying, 'Gt. Gidding 4 Miles'. Turning to me, as the junction flashed past, he said, "I wonder if that's anything to do with the place T.S. Eliot wrote about in the *Four*

Quartets?" We discovered in conversation with Tim and Bridie that next to the village of Great Gidding was the tiny hamlet of Little Gidding. When Eliot visited the little church, it was neglected. The community, founded by Nicholas Farrer, friend of the seventeenth-century poet and hymnist, George Herbert, had long since faded into the mists of time. But shortly after the Second World War, a Cambridge scholar, Alan Maycock, researched the origins of this small religious community. T. S. Eliot knew Maycock and he visited Little Gidding with him. Then had come Eliot's poem with its reflections on the nature of time and the pilgrimage to a place where *'prayer has been valid'*, and Little Gidding was resurrected.

One of the first people to get through police road blocks to see us after the night of February 5th had been Robert Van de Weyer, vicar and member of the Community of the Sower. A few days later, it had been another community member, Ed, who had brought me a bottle of cough linctus when he heard we were reluctant to leave the caravan and go to a chemist ourselves. Later in the year, we had taken up the invitation to join in the weekly Saturday evening communion service. We discovered that Little Gidding was growing. Old outbuildings were being converted into living accommodation for several families. The main house was simply decorated with white walls, light-coloured woodwork and beige carpeting. As well as a communal kitchen and dining room, there were other shared living rooms. In one of these rooms, the Lord's Supper was celebrated at eight o'clock each Saturday evening. We enjoyed attending these services, which were informal yet inspiring. The liturgy, like the furnishings, was simple, combining old and new. We sat in chairs or on the floor, perhaps twenty including a few children. At the point where the 'Sign of Peace' is given, we discovered, everyone moved around the room, shaking hands or kissing each person in turn. The music was provided by Chris who played a guitar and Ed who played a flute. Some of the hymns were new to us; one has remained a firm favourite, *'Turning the World Upside Down'*. A modern hymn, it talks of the radical, even revolutionary nature of being a Christian. It was the same phrase that groups like the early Friends and the Diggers used to describe the call of the Gospel. The fourth verse says:

'The world wants the wealth to live in state,
But you show us a new way to be great:
Like a servant you came,

And if we do the same,
We'll be turning the world upside down.'

That Friday in September, we were determined to explore every possible avenue to open up some kind of dialogue with the Church authorities in Peterborough and we felt we should talk it over with our friends at Little Gidding. Robert Van de Weyer's wife, Sarah, invited us to lunch. Robert was away but others were interested to hear of the latest developments. Pamela Tudor Craig, who had always shown a great interest in what we were trying to do at Molesworth, invited us back to her rooms for a cup of coffee. The more we told her, the more annoyed she became and determined to try and help.

"Look, I know the bishop; I'll give him a ring. It's just too bad, it really is!" With that Pamela walked through to the kitchen to use the telephone.

We could hear her talking, mentioning our names. When she reappeared, she told us that the bishop had been out. "But," Pamela continued, "his secretary said he had given her a message to give you. If you ring again after four o'clock the bishop will speak to you."

We were delighted; at last we were getting somewhere. We thanked Pamela and drove back to Molesworth. After the vigil, we went to Clopton to telephone the bishop. We spoke for about fifteen minutes. He listened to all we had to say, but he explained that he felt unable to comment and that he would be leaving any decisions to the appointed committee. While we appreciated that he was concerned about the way the media might distort his views, we were sad that he felt unable to see us and explore the issue in confidence. He was, after all, a frequent broadcaster and well acquainted with the media. We imagined this would have given him some ability in handling difficult publicity. Perhaps it had and perhaps that is why he remained obdurately silent.

That night, we heard that a woman had been raped in Peace Lane.

★★★

It was dark when Jill came into the caravan to tell us that a woman living at the camp had been raped. She was someone we had grown to know and like well, as she had lived at Molesworth for some months. Reading through my diary, there were many times when I wrote of her, but for the sake of her privacy we have omitted all mention of her in these pages.

It was a great shock when Jill told us what had happened to the woman. A few nights earlier, she told us several of those living in the gardens and in the lane, had gone to spend the evening in a pub nearby, one of a few that still consented to serve Peace Campers. On their return, two of the men had invited the woman into their tent. She knew both men well and saw no harm in this. First one man, then the other, had sexual intercourse with her. Later the woman herself spoke to us, telling us that what had happened was against her will. She said she had been raped. We never spoke to either of the men about the incident, they were asked to leave and not return. Neither Ian nor I have since laid eyes on them.

Looking back, I wonder what we could have done that we did not do. It is one of the saddest memories I have and it has made both Ian and me think a lot more about the subject of rape. Like many people, our idea of rape was of a hooded man, breaking into an unknown woman's bedroom and assaulting her at knife point. More and more evidence is coming to light suggesting that, far more common is the rape of women by men they know, even love, perhaps men they are married to. The violence is in the act, done against the woman's will. The pressure to comply may be emotional more than physical. Men in our society grow up much more assertive and the majority of young girls still learn subservient roles. To institute legal proceedings is very intimidating for a woman who has been raped. First she has to report to a police station and she has to do this quickly, while the pain and confusion of what has happened is still all too real. Then she has to undergo examination and questioning. The defence of rape all too often relies on discrediting the sexual morality of the injured party. Did she wear her skirts short? Did she sleep with her boyfriend? As a single woman, why did she use an oral contraceptive? Her name is dragged through the gutter. The woman at Molesworth, not surprisingly, never reported the incident.

We were not allowed to dismiss what happened as an isolated incident. The following spring, after we had left, another rape took place. It was hard to come to terms with the fact that such things could happen in the peace movement. It was as if, because of our fear for the future of our planet, we had immunity from ordinary human wickedness, or that if we believed in the possibility of a world free from greed, hunger and violence, we were ourselves without vices. Not that we believed it of ourselves, but other people did expect it of us. In a trivial comparison, I know that some people were surprised to learn that Ian smoked while he lived in the caravan and that I enjoyed a gin and tonic. It did not fit the image.

On reflection, it seems more surprising that there were not more examples of human frailty and wickedness. All of us were living in a most stressful environment. As far as expressing sexuality was concerned, Ian and I were lucky, we loved each other and despite the bright lights and generators, we had a normal sex life. Most of the others were single. We all needed a lot of emotional support, but the line between a comforting hug and an unwanted sexual advance can, in those circumstances, be hard to discern. There were those in the peace movement who felt so angry to think that such a thing could happen that they called for the camp to be closed. Neither of us could agree with this demand. In a way it seemed to us that to try to deal with what had happened in this way was to make a scapegoat of the Molesworth Peace Campers for the violence that is in us all. The Peace Camp was simply a microcosm of the society in which we live. The whole world is an unsafe place for women and the only way to change it is through creating a more loving community where men are encouraged to see women as individual people, not as objects, a world where no one seeks to dominate and exploit others.

'And then both men and women will be gentle
And then both women and men will be strong...'

(Judy Chicago)

The gap between the world we want and the world that is, remains. And in the meantime, all we could do was to get on with the tasks that presented themselves.

★★★

The following day we travelled to Ely to talk to the Bishop of Ely about the position we were in now that the caravan was on Church land. He listened carefully to us and asked lots of incisive and pertinent questions, which showed he had a good grasp of the situation, and we left feeling that if the opportunity arose he would at least be able to explain our position clearly to Bill Westwood.

We decided we must try and see Philip Haines, secretary of the Finance Board. Jill Hutchinson had managed to arrange a meeting where we could all go together, but, at the last minute, we pulled out.

We heard that a local Christian peace group in Peterborough had organised a protest outside the cathedral for the same day. We were concerned that, if we were to see him at the same time, this might prejudice his response. Our fears proved to be groundless; Jill went with a friend and was given a fair hearing. She came back with the news that he would be happy to see us at a mutually convenient time. She also gained the reassuring impression that the Board had no intention of evicting us if we refused to leave Peace Lane. But it was not until after the symbolic erection of the cross that we met Mr Haines.

The cross looked beautiful; Jimmy had done a marvellous job. It was built in layers of iroko that were pegged together so that the finished beams were some five or six inches square. The wood glowed, a deep bronze red. The cross piece was cleverly jointed into the upright and the sharp edges had been bevelled. It was simple, elegant yet rugged. Jimmy had driven over with Charles and other members of their group, and while we waited for the ceremony to begin the cross lay cushioned on the lush, green grass. In the morning, Jill, Ian and I had sung hymns out by the fence and one of the policemen had said afterwards that he was looking forward to the service in the afternoon.

We started the service near Eirene at 2:30. While we began with hymns and readings, the working party from Bishop's Stortford began digging a hole at the far end of Peace Lane. About a hundred people had arrived and after twenty minutes we walked down Peace Lane singing. Arriving at the other end, we were in time to see the cross being lowered into a deep hole and watched as cement was shovelled in. A small, square, wooden frame was placed around the base of the cross and more cement filled in to create a plinth of shuttered concrete. Guy ropes were strung from the centrepiece, holding the cross vertically until the cement set. Jimmy carefully checked it all with a spirit level and gave instructions for a few minor adjustments and it was accomplished. Robin Anstey, the vicar who had brought Christian CND's legal action, spoke. Another clergyman from Thrapston, whom Jill had got to know well, broke bread that we all shared. The few Cambridgeshire police who were standing by were happy to take bread with us. Just as it was all finishing, a minibus drew up and out came a group of middle-aged Japanese. An interpreter, travelling with them, explained to Ian that they were Hibakusha, survivors of the atomic bombs dropped on Hiroshima and Nagasaki. They were travelling through Europe in an effort to promote nuclear disarmament.

Ian clapped his hands, shouting to the dispersing crowd, "Listen, before you go, a group of Hibakusha have just arrived. They would like to talk to us about their experiences. Please, can we listen to what they have to say?"

People turned and started to walk back towards the cross and one of the Japanese, a man of 50, respectably dressed, perhaps a business man, began to speak. He spoke of his childhood 40 years ago. He talked of the bomb falling on Nagasaki, of the devastation, misery and sickness, which no one understood. How gums began to bleed, hair fell out and the vomiting. How people, became listless, unable and unwilling to fend for themselves. As he spoke the interpreter relayed his words. It was profoundly moving. Strangely, many who died in Nagasaki were Christians. The city had been the main centre of Christian mission work in Japan. The cathedral had been destroyed in the blast. And now, here we were, 40 years later, putting up a wooden cross, just outside the perimeter fence of a new nuclear base, listening to a survivor of those first terrible explosions. Ian asked us all to pray that it should never happen again.

Jill's father, John, had made a small, carved wooden cross and Paul Johns had arranged that we should take this little cross to the cathedral. After saying goodbye to the Hibakusha, Ian, Paul and I left for Peterborough. Jill travelled in her own car as she had promised to take a friend to hospital. Paul had spoken to the dean and agreed to meet him at the main door to the cathedral at five o'clock. It was nearly 4:30 when we left Peace Corner and the cathedral clock was striking the hour as we walked briskly through the cathedral grounds. Jill was nowhere in sight. I wanted to wait, but Paul felt we shouldn't keep the Dean waiting. I just hoped she would arrive at any minute. The Dean greeted us; he was joined by two canons, Canon Christie and Canon Hyam. We told them that the cross at Peace Corner was a present to the Diocese from Christian CND. We handed over the small, wooden cross to the Dean. He invited us to come into one of the side chapels, St. Oswald's Chapel, which was dedicated to peace. The cross we had brought was placed on the altar. We all knelt in quiet reflection. The Dean recited the Prayer of St. Francis: "Lord, Make me an instrument of Thy Peace." After a few minutes we exchanged 'the sign of peace'. It was all over before Jill appeared. We were sad to think she had missed this moment; she had done so much to make it possible.

★★★

242

October 24th was 'United Nations Day' and the start of the 'International Year of Peace'. In September we had been invited to a festival in the Royal Albert Hall officially to launch the year. Jeanne and Mark Steinhardt had been invited to take some friends along to share a box. It was what might be called an extravaganza, but a rather ill-conceived and hastily concocted one. Among the guests who made special appearances was Bob Geldof. When he spoke he put the whole thing in perspective. He said that ringing church bells and children singing wasn't going to bring peace, in fact he wasn't sure he believed the world was capable of living in peace, he had enough of a struggle dealing with the internal conflict within himself. But, a peaceful world was still something to struggle for, a goal at which to aim.

The Molesworth contribution to IYP was more constructive than ringing bells. The Ploughshares Campaign, 'Breaking New Ground' was a creative and positive initiative to collect and refurbish agricultural tools and send them to Eritrea. A group had been meeting, mainly at the Old School, to plan this project. The idea was that, as a first step, speakers would talk to peace and development groups about the project and encourage them to start collecting and renewing tools in their area. They would set up stalls in public places where tools could be handed in and at the same time passers-by would learn about the project. It was envisaged that by Easter, the next stage would take place, a walk to Molesworth. It would start at a place just south of London called St George's Hill.

The significance of this was that in 1649, Gerard Winstanley and a group of Diggers had ploughed the land and created a settlement there, reclaiming the common land. Their experiment was short lived, but it had not been forgotten. About ten years earlier (1975), a film had been made about the story, called Winstanley. Strangely, our Rainbow Village friend, Sid Rawles, had a star role. He was cast as the leader of a group of Ranters, who were the most anarchic of the seventeenth-century dissident groups! In 1981, contemporary songwriter, Leon Rosselson, had written a song about the Diggers. It was called, *The World Turned Upside Down.*

> *'In sixteen forty-nine, to St George's Hill,*
> *A ragged band they called the Diggers came to show the peoples will,*
> *They defied the Landlords, they defied the laws,*
> *They were the dispossessed reclaiming what was theirs.*
> *'We come in peace, they said, to dig and sow,*

We come to work the lands in common and to make the waste ground grow,
This earth divided we will make whole,
So it will be a common treasury for all.'

It was now part of the folklore of those working for social change, and the Diggers Walk to Molesworth was designed to build on that tradition.

The plan was for the marchers to stop each day to collect tools, and with a mobile workshop, repair and renovate those that needed attention. At Easter, it was intended that digging should take place, both inside and outside the fence. The handles of the tools would be marked, 'Property of the Eritrean Relief Association', once more making the connections between disarmament and development.

A week before the big CND rally in Hyde Park on October 26th, Tim and Bridie asked me if I would be willing to speak about the Tools Project. I was a bit uneasy as neither Ian nor I had taken an active part in the preparations. In the end I was persuaded that, with time so short, I was the best choice. I agreed on condition that others wrote and approved the address. Privately, I suspected that they asked me because I always talk so loudly!

It was a bright, dry day on the 26th and we travelled to London from Ipswich. We were staying in Ipswich for the weekend as it was Anna's christening on the Sunday. It was a novel experience to be behind the enormous scaffolding stage, instead of part of the 20,000-strong, seething mass that stood out front looking at the huge mural of two missiles by Gerald Scarfe. I was given a pass, permitting me into the enclosure; I managed to get one for Ian so that we could be together. Michael Foot was leaning on a walking stick, his little terrier dog beside him. They had walked the route of the march. I noticed Julie Christie sitting on the grass eating salad. Then I spotted Malcolm Harper, the director of the United Nations Association. We had met before and I went over and said hello. We were both to speak and he was immediately before me. I was surprised to find that I didn't feel nervous. When it was my turn to speak I climbed up the steps on to the stage and looked out on the sea of faces. It was an amazing sight and I felt very small. The backcloth behind me was higher than a house and on either side of the stage were enormous loudspeakers. I found reading my notes and trying to speak into the microphone, as well as looking out at the crowd, was quite difficult and in spite of the amplifiers I had to shout to make myself heard.

When I had clambered down the scaffolding steps, Ian and I raced across the park in search of the Christian CND tent. The programme was running late and we were supposed to be making a contribution to a service that was already underway. At the end of the rally we had an invitation to attend to a reception at County Hall, laid on by the GLC. A piano and string ensemble was playing as we entered. It was good to see so many familiar faces in this rather incongruous setting: Brigadier Harbottle of Generals for Peace; the Secretary of Quaker Peace and Service, Ron Huzzard; and Howard Clark, the General Secretary of War Resisters' International. We were pleased to see a small group of Japanese men and women, the Hibakusha who had been at Molesworth a few weeks earlier.

We had not seen much of Tim and Bridie that day, just a glimpse as we entered the park. They were handing out leaflets about the Ploughshares campaign. Bridie was expecting their baby any day and she looked very pregnant.

Before returning to Molesworth on Monday, we had arranged to have the second typhoid and cholera injections we needed for travel to India. The plans for our Indian trip were beginning to come together. We had been given the name of a travel agent called Terence Khushal.

North South Travel was a charitable trust whose profits from the business went to development projects in the Third World. Terence, an Indian, ran the operation from a small flat in North London. When we first contacted him by telephone, he invited us to join him for a simple lunch. "Just curried dhal and rice," he had said. The tiny room he used for an office was piled with papers and brochures. Books lined the walls; there was scarcely a square inch of free floor space. At one end was a small gas ring.

We had a long conversation; Terence was full of good advice. We hadn't realised just what would be involved. Our original plan was to travel by the Russian Aeroflot line, stopping in Moscow on the way. It was no more expensive and we hoped to visit two countries for the price of one. We had to forget that plan as we couldn't get tickets on an Aeroflot flight any time in December. Terence not only booked our tickets, but also planned our itinerary making our journey as full and varied as possible. But this was all in the future. That first meeting left our minds whirling; we hadn't even got passports and we needed them before we could apply for visas. Then there were the inoculations.

Driving back to Molesworth, we were relieved to think we only had one more injection to go, for Hepatitis, but that was not until December. As soon as we had unpacked, we drove the four miles around the base to Clopton. We wanted to talk to Bridie and Tim about Saturday. We were met at the door by Bridie's brother, Ross.

"They've had a daughter!" he announced.

"But Bridie was in London, carrying great bundles of leaflets on Saturday!"

Ian muttered something about carting boxes of leaflets inducing labour. I just couldn't believe it, I had so wanted to be nearby when the birth took place and now I had missed it all. Ross went on to tell us that it had happened very quickly in the hours around dawn. He had driven Bridie and Tim to the hospital, worried that the baby might arrive before they got there. The labour was extremely short and within five minutes of Emily's birth Ross was able to take some photographs. Twelve hours after Bridie had begun her contractions, we were all seated in the kitchen and I was nursing Emily. She was wearing a purple knitted cardigan; Tim had chosen the wool colour. Emily had round cheeks and daintily formed full lips that seemed shaped into a permanent kiss. Her arms, hands and fingers made constant graceful movements, describing artistic shapes in the air. From that moment, Ian and I were 'hooked'. During the next few weeks we found any excuse we could to go to the School House to take turns in cuddling Emily.

On November 4th we finally saw Philip Haines, secretary to the Peterborough Diocese Board of Finance. We had set the alarm for 7:30, earlier than usual, as we had to get to Peterborough by ten. The Indian summer was over. The weather had turned colder and the morning was grey and misty, as we walked through the cathedral grounds searching for the Diocesan Office. The trees were bare once more, the pavement wet and slippery underfoot. Ian looked at his watch; it was five-past-ten. Eventually we found the door through an old archway. A secretary welcomed us, asking us if we would like coffee. Mr Haines entered the room and shook hands with us. He looked different to the picture I had conjured up in my mind of someone much older, who would be very formal. Mr Haines was relaxed and friendly as we sat down to talk.

We raised the question of public opinion, and cited the many hundreds of people from all over the country who had written to the bishop, begging the diocese not to sell the land to the Ministry of Defence. Mr Haines said their views were of no great importance to the Committee, as they were only interested in the feelings of local people. He said that the opinions and feelings of the local vicar, the Reverend George North, would be given careful consideration. George North lives in Brington and we were more than aware of his views. He strongly condemned the peace presence at Molesworth and supported the building of the base. We had only met him twice, the first occasion being back in January, when we went to his church one cold Sunday and had been ignored. The second, more recent occasion, had been when we had called at his house in an effort to get to know him. He had been courteous, but avoided all our attempts to open the subject of his feelings about the base or our presence. I remember asking him if he had read our letter as we had not received a reply. He said that he didn't read all his mail; he got so many letters from cranks! After ten minutes of 'small talk' on the doorstep we thanked him for giving us his time and left.

We asked Mr Haines why Mr North's views were so important. We pointed out that his parish was not in the Peterborough Diocese, and, we argued, if his opinion carried weight, surely the views of his bishop should be sought. Mr Haines explained that the Finance Board would meet again on November 15th and he would recommend they ask for new tenders to be submitted. These would be considered by the board in January. By then, diocesan elections would have taken place and the decision would be made by the incoming board. This, Mr Haines felt, was more desirable than having a decision made by an out-going committee, the consequences of whose decision would have to be met by newcomers. We talked about the various bidders and suggested that perhaps the answer was not to sell the field at all, in view of the controversy. We argued that if the Church offers a spiritual home for people within the military and many who oppose the use of all weapons, let alone nuclear weapons, perhaps the Church has a role as reconciler. Mr Haines spoke about the need to sell off land that was of no practical use, as the capital was of more benefit than the small rent it brought in. We suggested that if the land had to be sold for these reasons, a restrictive covenant could be placed on the sale, in order to ensure its continued use as agricultural land.

The meeting had been useful, but in order to make sure that the board listened to our case, Ian suggested we write a submission for their consideration. After all, we were local people! Philip Haines agreed that the new board would look at our submission before coming to any decision. Before we had time to write this letter, another event was to change the situation.

Chapter Eighteen

Chainsaw Massacre

I looked back at my diary to see what we had done in November. Our last full month had gone so quickly. Emily frequently enticed us to the School House. An attempt was made to bring Andy's van back on to Peace Lane. In the aftermath of the rape, it would provide somewhere for women to sleep, a place exclusively for women. Andy donated his old Commer van and towed it over from Warren Lane. The van got as far as the entrance to the lane, when the police prevented it from moving past the concrete blocks. 'Mowana' was now parked in front of Halcyon Spirit and we could no longer see the chapel out of the window. On November 5th, a group from Wisbech came and held a firework party in the gardens. It was great fun watching the children, all wrapped up in thick coats and scarves, clutching their sparklers, as we stood around sipping mugs of steaming hot tomato soup.

We had begun to notice an increase in the number of lorries going in and out of the base each day, and together with Bridie and Tim, planned to walk all the way around the perimeter to see what was going on inside and how far work had progressed. We now had regular meetings with Wing Commander Shaw. He often came in for a chat. We enjoyed talking to him and appreciated his dry sense of humour. We were able to talk in depth about the nuclear issue, and as he grew to trust us he spoke more frankly. We gave a talk to a group near Cambridge, went to Little Gidding, attended a County Council liaison meeting and helped pack up the 'Ploughshares' mailing.

November 11th was 'Remembrance Sunday' and I wanted to mark the event. I thought I would make another banner to hang on the fence. On the Saturday, on an old, white double sheet, I wrote, '*NO MORE*

WARS, LET US LEARN, LOVE AND REMEMBER' and in the top left-hand corner I painted a white poppy. That same weekend, a snowball action took place. The symbolic fence-cutting actions had been happening throughout the year and each time the numbers grew. Pete Brown, a potter from Gloucestershire, was organising the Molesworth Snowball. Pete had been arrested time and time again for the snowball campaign. That evening he joined us for supper and I discussed my feelings about 'Remembrance Sunday'. I said how important it had been to us as a family when I was young. Ian recalled how at eleven o'clock, people had stopped for two minutes silence, not just in Whitehall, but up and down the country. I had mixed feelings about the ceremony now, wanting to remember the dead and respect their memory, but feeling at the same time that all the military pomp seemed to glorify war. Afterwards, I went over to the chapel and spoke to the MOD policeman on duty.

"I thought I ought to tell you that I am going to put a banner on the fence tomorrow, as it is 'Remembrance Sunday'," I told him.

"You can't do that," he said. "It is against the by-laws."

"Yes, I know, but it's very important to me, and I will remove it at the end of the day."

"You'd better have a word with my sergeant." He whistled to the policeman standing behind the main gate. He came over.

"Hello, Mrs. Hartley. How are you?"

"I'm fine, thank you. I was just telling the policeman here that I intend putting a banner on the fence tomorrow as it is 'Remembrance Sunday'. It's so important that we never forget the horrors of war."

"Right Mrs. Hartley, if you have any trouble just ask for me, all right?" So that was settled.

I had been interviewed by Chiltern Radio for the religious programme that went out on 'Remembrance Sunday'. We listened to it in bed. I typed out a statement about war and peace and handed a copy to all the police on duty. It read: *'Today we remember all the men and women, husbands and wives, sons and daughters and lovers who died in wars.*

'May we also remember the words written in Micah 4 *and* Matthew 5.

"They shall beat their swords into mattocks and their spears into pruning forks. Nation shall not lift sword against nation, nor ever again be trained for war.

"You have heard it said, you shall love your neighbour and hate your enemy, but I say to you, love your enemies and pray for those who persecute you."

'Let us who are living show to those who died our ultimate gratitude by ensuring that no more wars ever take place.

'BE AT PEACE WITH ONE ANOTHER.'

I hung the banner on the wire where it stayed all day in full view of the road. I don't know why they didn't arrest me for breaking the law.

Small groups were arriving to take part in the Snowball. At a pre-arranged time they walked up to the fence, each person carrying a piece of hacksaw blade and began sawing the welded steel wire. The wire was a quarter of an inch thick and it took a long time to cut through one strand. The police preferred to confiscate the blades and only resorted to arrest when someone came back two or three times. We couldn't help noticing that they often chose to arrest the younger ones first, especially if they looked unkempt.

That evening we went to Cambridge to listen to Terry Waite speak in Great St. Mary's Church. We identified with his kind of peacemaking, which relies on creating trust by listening without judgement, and by trying to find the words to explain why someone else feels aggrieved. It is a slow process; it requires great sincerity and tenacity. But it offers the possibility of real justice, the kind on which peace must be founded, if it is to last. I managed to give him one of our cards with the drawing of the Peace Chapel on. Inside we wrote a message, saying how much we admired his work in the Middle East. We also gave him one of the green Eirene booklets before he left.

On the 17th we went to Leigh-on-Sea. My mother had arranged to take my niece and her husband, together with Ian and me, for a belated 84th birthday celebration. She took us out to a restaurant. It was an unusual, though pleasant, contrast for us to be sitting at a table covered in a thick, white damask cloth, with gleaming cutlery, being served by deferential waiters. It was ten o'clock in the evening before we got back to Molesworth. Mallen had been looking after Robbie. He told us it had been a fairly quiet day, as a lot of people had gone to the CND Annual Conference in Sheffield for the weekend. It had been a relaxing day for us, too, but after the journey back I was feeling tired and ready for bed.

We were asleep when we heard a knock on the caravan door. It was one o'clock in the morning. Who on earth could it be at this hour?

Ian, still half asleep, slid open the door to the kitchen and shouted, "Who is it?"

A voice with a strong Northern Irish accent replied, "It's Mark! They're coming to put a fence down Peace Lane."

"Oh no!" I groaned, throwing back the bed covers.

We were up and dressed in minutes and went outside to see what was happening. About two hundred MOD policemen were standing in rows around by the gardens and the Main Gate while huge machines were driven into the lane. An MOD policeman was asking who was the owner of the Mini parked by the concrete blocks.

When I said it was ours he said, "Would you please move it off MOD property."

"The car has been on this spot since January with no problem, why do we have to move it now?"

He said he would ask the flight lieutenant to come and speak to us about it. After a few moments the familiar, rotund figure of Flight Lieutenant McDougall emerged from the gloom.

"Good evening, Mrs Hartley." He smiled and said, "If we could just step aside for a moment, I'll explain what's happening." We moved off down the lane and then he continued. "As you know, I have told you on several occasions recently that at some time a fence would be put up to mark the MOD boundary. Well, tonight is the night."

Neither Ian nor I could think of anything to say. Before long a military-style operation was in full force. I stood in a dazed and distraught state and watched as contractors drove huge diggers into the hedgerow that ran down the side of the lane. Two men with powerful chainsaws were lopping off branches in a random fashion, carelessly swinging the saws with one hand. It seemed they had only one thought, to destroy and obliterate the hedge as fast as possible. The tree that was outside the window of the caravan was rammed repeatedly with a bulldozer until it fell. The men with chainsaws were soon upon it, dismembering it, branch by branch. A policeman came and suggested to me that I dig up the cabbages and geranium plants in our small garden on the MOD side of the lane. I refused. A few minutes later, I saw a contractor digging up all the plants and putting them beside the caravan.

Suddenly I remembered the apple tree that was growing near the chapel. The tree had been planted in the Spring of 1984 when Tim and Bridie were married. It had survived when the troops put up the first fence in February and we had watched the green buds grow. We had even seen pink and white blossom later in the year. Only a few days earlier, at one of our daily vigils, Bridie's father had movingly spoken of the tree and what it symbolised. Now it was threatened, as it was obvious that the heavy machinery was going to knock into it. We found the Flight Lieutenant again and asked him if we could dig it up. That was not allowed, but a few moments later someone came over and borrowed our spade to dig up the tree, which was put behind the caravan with its roots wrapped in polythene. It survived the night and was replanted in the gardens a week later and is still there. The Eirene sign was cut down with a chainsaw and taken inside the base, though we were told that it would be handed back to us later.

I felt quite sure that the chapel was going to be demolished, but to our astonishment, they erected scaffolding around it and also around the wooden cross in Peace Lane, to protect them. It was one of those strange contradictions that we could never quite understand. This whole night-time operation deeply affected me and I spent most of the night sobbing uncontrollably. I hated seeing live trees being hacked down. I knew that the only reason for their destruction was that they stood in the way of yet another huge, metal fence that would one day protect nuclear weapons. We had lived by the hedgerow throughout all the seasons of the year and watched the bare branches become green, the wild flowers bloom and the red berries appear. At dusk the birds would come to roost on the branches. Seeing it destroyed was like watching a massacre.

There were about ten Peace Campers living at the camp at the time. They had been fast asleep when the operation began and now stood around in various states of undress, one in a dressing gown and slippers, staring in disbelief at the scenes going on around them. We watched as a vast machine slowly trundled towards us. It had an enormous circular blade designed to cut through concrete. It was making an ear-splitting din as it continued to crawl towards us. Suddenly Karl and Dominic climbed onto it. The driver, who wore sound-proof ear muffs, was completely oblivious, but a policeman had spotted them and they were soon hauled off and arrested. The huge machine was cutting a deep trench along the centre of Peace Lane and across the gardens where the new fence was going. I thought of the hours people had spent digging the garden and sowing seeds. I remembered Carol spending a whole day on her knees planting bulbs. Now it was being cut almost in half. The place where we had stood and held our daily vigils would soon be behind a fence and the chapel itself would be even more isolated than before. When the old barbed-wire fence was taken down, Mark and Andy managed to get into the chapel but they were soon removed.

Ian and I drove around to the Old School House to make phone calls. Tim and Bridie were away, but we knew they would not mind us using the phone. We rang Roger Spiller, the East Anglian regional secretary of CND, *BBC Breakfast TV*, and the Holtoms (Bridie's aunt and uncle), to get a message to Bridie and Tim, Mallen and a press agency.

When we got back to Peace Corner another consignment of MOD police was arriving to relieve those who had been on duty. It was a bitterly cold night and the shifts changed frequently. I stood by the coach as they alighted, trying to persuade them to turn back.

"You don't have to do this, you have the choice between good and evil, right and wrong. Choose life, it's more important than money!"

One or two smiled as they walked passed me, others kept their heads down averting their gaze. No one spoke. As dawn broke the full horror of what had been done could be seen. The chapel, stark and vulnerable stood alone, surrounded by a high, cold steel mesh fence, surmounted by a roll of barbed wire. It seemed a more powerful symbol than before. The ground around it was a quagmire with huge furrows where the giant machines had driven through. There was no grass, simply mud.

Another camper, Chesh, and I took chairs and put them in the middle of the old entrance. We just sat and watched as the sun slowly rose. In front of us were row upon row of policemen standing shoulder to shoulder on guard. Guarding what? Inside the base was still grassland where sheep silently grazed. It was without doubt the best-protected field in the whole of Britain. Soon the press started to arrive as local TV and newspapers all clamoured to get a story.

At 11 o'clock we held our usual service, asking the policeman at the fence, as we had done so many hundreds of times before, if we might use the Peace Chapel. Many people had arrived during the morning so there was a large group of us to stand together in silent worship. A line of scaffold poles marked out the new boundary, while the new fence stood about two feet behind this. We walked in a file between the scaffolding and the fence, as near to the chapel as we could. We had to give assurances to the MOD police that we would only be there for about twenty minutes, as we were now standing on MOD land.

The rest of that day passed in a dream. We were very tired, but did not expect to be able to sleep as the contractors were putting up the high security fence right outside the caravan and the welding tools made a loud singing noise. However we slept well, no doubt due to the emotional experience of the night before.

The next morning Flight Lieutenant McDougall brought us back the Eirene sign and tried to be friendly. It was difficult for us to respond in our usual way as the events of the night before were still too fresh in our minds.

He smiled and said, "I'm sorry that you were so upset last night. But nothing was done to the chapel, was it? You might not know, but I spent most of the night inside it seeing that no harm came to it."

"But what about the trees and the hedge?" I said.

He clasped his hands behind his back and leaned forward looking me straight in the eye. "You mustn't be too upset about that. Once all this is finished we will be landscaping the whole perimeter."

"But the trees and hedges you've destroyed had grown on that spot for around three hundred years."

He left saying that he was praying that the summit talks would be a success and that Molesworth would never need to be used. As he walked away I turned to Ian and he shrugged his shoulders. What could we say? I still had a great deal of anger in me at what had happened and felt that I had to make some sort of protest. We drove over to the Old School and I told Bridie and Tim what I wanted to do.

"I've decided to make a large banner of a tree in leaf, symbolising the one that was outside our window. Have you got anything I can make it with?"

Tim gave me paints and a piece of old sheeting and between us Ian and I made a banner. Underneath the picture of the tree I wrote '*Protect Life*'. When it was dry I hung it on the fence at the place where the tree had been. Two MOD police came over and asked me to remove it, but

I refused. Instead I showed them photos of the lane as it looked before the onslaught. I sat down beside the banner and stayed there for a long time. It was freezing cold and I had a hot water bottle pushed up inside my coat. The police decided to ignore me. I was, in fact, breaking the by-laws that prohibit anyone from hanging anything on the fence and should have been arrested. After some time, when it was clear that they were going to ignore the offence, I took the banner down and walked over to the Main Gates and hung it up on one of them. I unfolded my garden chair in front of the gate and sat down. I was again asked to move.

I politely explained, "I have put this banner on the fence as a protest at the destruction of the hedgerow last night. I'm not doing it to annoy you, I'm sitting here as a protest at the way in which the operation was carried out."

Some minutes elapsed and then Chief Superintendent Hutchinson, head of the MOD police and only recently posted to Molesworth, walked through the gate. I thought, 'Ah, now I am going to be arrested.'

But he said, "Good afternoon, Mrs Hartley, I do hope you are feeling better. You were very upset last night and I am sorry about that."

I showed him the photographs and explained why I felt I had to make a protest.

"I understand, but I have some good news for you," he said. "We are going to landscape the whole area where the trees have come down. We will be replacing them with new trees and I can assure you they will not be cheap ones either."

He looked hurt when I tried to explain that it would not make any difference, arguing that surely it would have been better to leave the trees already growing there. But we had to differ.

As he turned to leave, I said, "I thought you were going to arrest me."

He looked at me and quietly said in his lilting Irish voice, "And what good would that do, Mrs Hartley?"

After Mr Hutchinson had gone back inside the base, a van arrived at the gate. I was asked to move but refused. I thought they would have to arrest me now, but no. They managed to manoeuvre the vehicle through just one gate and left me sitting there! Bitterly cold, but a lot calmer and feeling that I had made my point, I got up and went back into the caravan for a hot cup of tea.

★★★

The RAF had done more than simply move the fence that night. Apart from putting up a twelve-foot high fence right down the centre of Peace Lane, they had re-routed the bridleway that separated the land on which the Peace Chapel stood from the main area of the base. It appeared that the Ministry had finally lost patience, and could no longer wait to see whether they would be able to buy the Church land for use as the main exit for cruise convoys leaving the base. They were taking up the other option, which the civil servants had described when we went to the MOD in July. They now planned to run their exit road out through the land around Eirene. The next time we met Wing Commander Shaw I asked him if he could give me an assurance that the chapel would not be demolished.

Smiling, he said, "Jennifer, come on, you know perfectly well I can't give you any assurance. But look," he said, pointing out of the caravan window to where Eirene stood, "you see those wooden markers? That's the route of the road. You can see it's not running directly through the chapel."

Ian and I looked out, it was true; surveyors had driven in a line of T-shaped wooden stakes across the muddy ground behind the chapel. So, that was to be the new entrance to the base.

I turned to him, "Are you saying that you have no plans to demolish the chapel?"

"I think I can safely say that when you get back from India, it'll still be standing."

The Ministry still appeared to wish to buy the field, but their action on November 18th severely weakened their argument that it was essential to the development of the base. This had been the very point, which seemed to have held greatest sway with the Finance Board of the Peterborough Diocese. It had been said that it would cost the tax payers a lot more money to build an exit route anywhere else other than through the field behind Halcyon Spirit.

As we knew we would be on the other side of the world when the Board finally decided on the fate of the field, we spent some time drafting our submission, trying to include all the arguments and hoping and praying that it might carry some weight. On November 22nd, we finally dropped the following statement into the post box: *'We have been living at Molesworth outside the proposed cruise missile base since January 1985. We are registered on the electoral roll. Our caravan is situated on a disused highway between the small piece of land belonging to the Diocese and the perimeter of RAF Molesworth.*

We are both communicant members of the Anglican Church as well as being members of the Society of Friends. During our stay here, our days have been spent talking to the MOD and civilian police, RAF personnel and local people. Each day we have held two acts of worship near the fenced-in Peace Chapel, and have been joined by many others who share our convictions about the immorality of nuclear weapons and the power of prayer.

When we came to live here to oppose the construction of yet another nuclear weapons base, we had no idea that the field next to our caravan belonged to the Church of England. We were deeply shocked when we heard that the Board of Finance was considering selling the land to the Ministry of Defence, and were greatly relieved when legal action by a clergyman from the diocese and Christian CND persuaded the diocese to reconsider its decision.

We understand from the Secretary of the Board that the question of selling the field will be raised again at a Board Meeting in January. We believe that at this meeting the Board should not sell the land to the MOD for the following reasons:

1. *The original reason the MOD gave for wishing to purchase the land no longer applies. They had intended using the area as the main exit for cruise convoys leaving Molesworth for deployment in the countryside. We understand that they have now chosen an alternative route for their entrance road.*

2. *In the light of (1) if the MOD still considers it necessary to purchase the land, it can only be because it offers some sanctuary to those like ourselves who wish to witness against the building of the base. Even though demonstrators have never used the field, they have only used the old lay-by that separates the field from MOD land. Our caravan has been on this lane since January when it was a C.C. highway. The road was stopped up in September and since then the diocese has presumed ownership. We contest that this is the case but even if we are proven wrong, we feel the diocese should allow Christians to continue their witness against cruise. The right of peaceful protest is enshrined in our liberal democratic traditions. This right is meaningless if there is no place where it can legally be carried out.*

3. *The General Synod of the Church has stated its opposition to the first use of nuclear weapons. Cruise missiles are intended to destroy Soviet missiles before they can be launched. As cruise missiles travel very slowly they would have to be launched in anticipation of a Soviet attack in a pre-emptive strike. As a Government pamphlet has described their role – they would be used at the "eleventh hour". To our mind, cruise incontrovertibly violates the 'no first strike' principle. For the diocese to sell land that would become part of a missile complex seems clearly to flout Synod policy.*

4. *We believe that the land should be retained by the diocese and left in agricultural use as a sign that the vision of the Church is of a kingdom where swords are beaten into ploughshares. If it is necessary for financial reasons to sell the land in order to release funds for clergy stipends, then it should be sold with restrictive covenants, which require the land to remain in agricultural use. We know that this solution would meet with the approval of many local people, and would be seen by the wider church and the nation as evidence that the Diocese sought reconciliation between people with opposing views.'*

We were pleased to learn, on our return to England the following February that at the January meeting, the Board had decided, after all, not to sell the land.

★★★

'*Is it possible for the weather to get any worse? Thick, wet, sticky mud, drizzle, fog, cold...*'. So often my diary entries started this way. What had happened to the summer we had so looked forward to? It was November 24th and Bridie and Tim were holding a 'Thanksgiving Day' celebration feast. That people ventured out on such days to visit Molesworth, never ceased to amaze us, but by eleven, a crowd of us gathered at the fence. Gerrie, a friend from Ipswich read *The Parable of The Sower*, which tells how the seed was scattered, some falling on stony ground, while some fell where weeds choked them and others fell on good ground. As she finished speaking she moved closer to the fence and threw handfuls of Honesty seeds on to the base.

Ian and I drove to Winwick to buy a contribution to the meal. A local family sold fresh garden vegetables and fruit. It was open all hours and very cheap. We bought some watermelon, grapes, apples, tangerines and a small pumpkin. We were not simply celebrating the traditional American festival, recalling the arrival of the Pilgrim Fathers, but also the arrival of Emily.

The School House was brimming over with people. Chairs were drawn up in a circle in the large, airy room, and a small wooden table covered with an embroidered cloth stood in the middle. In the centre of the table was a vase of flowers and beside it lay a copy of *Christian Faith and Practice* and the Bible. The chairs began to fill, eyes closed, heads bowed. Latecomers crept in on tip toe, trying not to disturb the silence. The meeting for worship lasted for an hour, ending as we shook hands.

The room was rearranged and was now filled by a long, wooden table. Emily lay in Bridie's arms, oblivious to the festivity going on around her. Alf, Bridie's brother-in-law had made Gazpacho. Jacket potatoes, flans and salads appeared and soon disappeared, followed by apples and oranges. The room was full of chatter and laughter. The door opened and a woman walked in looking tired.

"Teddy!" Bridie and Tim leapt up. It was Tim's mother, arrived from America to see her new grand-daughter. Bridie placed the sleeping Emily in her arms. The room fell silent. Teddy gazed at the bundle, lightly stroking Emily's face. She shook her head in wonder, smiling broadly. Someone pulled up a chair for her and she sat down, not taking her eyes off Emily. She had flown the Atlantic and hadn't even taken her coat off.

Tim looked at his watch. "Hey, it's nearly four o'clock, we'll have to finish this later," he said. We trooped out and into an assortment of cars, which made its way in a procession to Peace Corner. It was growing dark and a cold, damp fog hung in the air. Bridie and Tim had bought a tree to plant in the garden to mark Emily's birth. We all stood around as Tim dug a hole and Bridie guided the small tree into it.

"We've got something for you and Ian, too," Tim said.

"For us?" I exclaimed. Bridie leant over and handed Ian a polythene bag containing a rose bush, a Peace rose. "How lovely, thank you."

After we had put our bush in, Bridie and Tim replanted the apple tree that had been dug up the previous week.

Thirty of us stood in the fading light giving thanks and singing. Ian read from Eliot's poem called *Little Gidding*:

"*Midwinter spring is its own season
Sempiternal though sodden toward sundown
Suspended in time, between pole and tropic.
When the short day is brightest, with frost and fire*

The brief sun flames the ice, on pond and ditches,
In windless cold that is the heart's heat,
Reflecting in a watery mirror
A glare that is blindness in the early afternoon.
And glow more intense than blaze of branch, or brazier,
Stirs the dumb spirit: no wind, but pentecostal fire
In the dark time of the year.'"

He finished with the lines, "'...*what you had thought you came for is only a shell, a husk of meaning... there are other places which also are the world's end... but this is the nearest, in place and time, now and in England.'"*

"Who's for pumpkin pie and home-made ice cream?" Tim called out. We had heard about Tim's ice cream; it sounded very special and it was. It tasted altogether different from that bought in the shops. When the dishes had been cleared away about thirty people moved into the School Room. The carpet had been taken up and cushions lay scattered around the edge of the room. Marguerite began to play her fiddle, joined by Pete on guitar and others with instruments. They played a jig. Soon the floor was full of people whirling and twisting in time to the music. We danced until we were exhausted, then dropped on the cushions. Tim picked up his guitar. Soon the familiar chords of well-loved peace songs rang out and we all joined in.

It seemed strange to be saying goodbye. Many of the friends at the School House that day came from miles away. Next time they came we would have left Halcyon Spirit to go to India. We drove back to the caravan in high spirits; it had been such a happy day. In a week's time, on December 1st we were returning home. And in another fortnight, we had our flight booked to India. I had not given it any thought at all. I had never flown and was simply terrified at the very thought of it. Molesworth had been all-consuming and until I actually left I could not focus my thoughts on anything else.

Mallen had agreed to dog-sit for us while we went to London. We had to see Terence Khushal to finalise the plans for our four-thousand-mile train journey through India. It still seemed to me like a dream I couldn't take seriously. He welcomed us into the small room he used as an office. His suggestions for our route sounded exciting, but at the same time frightening. As soon as we left, I put it all out of my mind again. At Hampstead we once again visited Pleasaunce and John Holtom. They had visited us at Molesworth on many occasions and we valued their friendship and advice. John offered to co-ordinate the rota of people taking over the witness in the caravan. This would be a great help.

It was in October when we first discussed the future of the caravan with staff at Friends House, the main office of Quakers in London. Since then the Peace Section had organised a meeting for people who where interested in staying in Halcyon Spirit once we had left. Helen Richardson, who had looked after the caravan in August, was very keen to take part. Mallen was at the meeting and he offered his enthusiastic support. Peggie Preston, who had worked in South Africa and Vietnam, was also very interested. Peggie was to later take an active role in the organisation of the rota. Neither Ian nor I had ever conceived that the caravan would still be there more than ten months after our arrival. Now we were talking about a scheme to see that it remained and that the daily vigils continued throughout the coming year. We wondered if it was right for us to expect others to take it on, but everyone at the meeting seemed so positive that the 'Halcyon Spirit witness for peace' should continue that we were left with no doubts.

We were delighted when Mallen offered to take care of Robbie in our house in Ipswich while we were away. Once more, the pieces were all falling into place. With less than a week to go, we wanted to find a way to say goodbye to all our friends. I typed an invitation out on pieces of paper and stuck them into Eirene cards. We sent the invitations to all the people we had come to know during our stay. That included our friends in the Peace Camp, local people, the police, both civilian and MOD, and the RAF. We had no idea who would turn up.

The invitation read:

'Dear...

'On Friday Nov. 29th from 4:30 onwards, we would be pleased if you could join us in a farewell drink. We will be leaving Molesworth on Dec. 1st to attend a conference in India and expect to be away for at least eight weeks. However the witness will continue in our caravan whilst we are away. Thank you for all the support you have given us during our stay.

'THERE IS NO WAY TO PEACE, PEACE IS THE WAY.

'Love, Jennifer and Ian.'

We went to the supermarket in Huntingdon and bought two boxes of wine and some crisps and biscuits from the wholefood shop in readiness for anyone who turned up. Bruce Watkins, the first of the Halcyon Spirit rota, arrived to take over from us. That evening we had a succession of visitors: two local people from nearby villages; a couple of Cambridgeshire police inspectors; Mallen, Jill, Rob and other friends living in Peace Lane. Chief Superintendent Hutchinson of the MOD police came, but we were disappointed that there was no one from the RAF. We did receive a hand-written letter from Flight Lt. McDougall saying that he would be away in Scotland and so would be unable to call in. He wished us a safe journey to India and said he would look forward to renewing our discussions on our return. Wing Commander Shaw called to see us earlier in the week and brought a Christmas card.

The following day was Saturday and we went to Little Gidding to say goodbye and to join in their evening worship. That night as I lay in bed, I thought how strange it was that this was our last night in Halcyon Spirit. I woke at five the next morning and started to pack up our belongings. Neil, the solicitor, came with a document for us to sign, giving Tim and Bridie power of attorney while we were in India. It was eleven, time for the vigil by the chapel. Bruce was with us. We stared once more at the little half-built chapel standing isolated, without even a blade of grass around it now. It was very muddy, but for once there was no wind and it felt quite mild. Pam Norris, a friend from Ipswich, arrived in her Dormobile to help transport all our bits and pieces. We couldn't believe how much we had accumulated during our stay.

We were ending one journey and starting another. We had come to Molesworth with only one thought, which was simply to be at the place where, in our eyes, a great wrong was taking place. It was hard to say what had been achieved, but perhaps all such journeys are simply a process of discovery.

'Do not depend on the hope of results. When you are doing the sort of work you have taken on... you may have to face the fact that your work will be apparently worthless and even achieve no result at all, if not perhaps results opposite to what you expect. As you get used to this idea, you start more and more to concentrate not on the results but on the value, the rightness, the truth of the work itself. And there, too, a great deal has to be gone through. Gradually you struggle less and less for an idea and more and more for specific people. The range tends to narrow down, but it gets much more real. In the end, it is the reality of personal relationships that saves everything.'

Thomas Merton

Chapter Nineteen
And Then...

Radio Orwell news bulletin, April 14th, 1986.

'The MOD sent in workmen this morning to demolish the anti-nuclear protestors' Peace Chapel at RAF Molesworth, the Cambridgeshire cruise missile base.'

I was still in bed when Ian rushed upstairs to break the news.

"I've just seen Mrs Alderton in the garden. She says the chapel's been demolished; it was on the local news headlines on *Breakfast Time TV.*'"

"What!" I sat up in horror. "Oh, no, they can't have done." I tried to collect my thoughts, as I pulled on my clothes. "I'd better ring Tim." We were not on the phone so I ran up the road to Veronica's house.

As I reached her drive, she opened the door calling, "Quick, Tim's on the phone for you, I was just coming round to get you."

"Have you heard the news?" Tim asked.

"It's true then, I was about to ring you to check. I just can't believe it. Look, we'll come up to Molesworth, you can tell us what happened when we get there."

I rang Radio Orwell, which had been trying to contact us to get an interview. Now, as our Mini sped along the A45 towards Molesworth, we tuned in to listen to the news on the car radio.

The first story was about tension in the Middle East. There had been an alert on at Lakenheath, but the spokesman said it was just a routine training exercise. The second story was on Molesworth. Ian was straining to catch the reporter's words, while juggernauts roared passed the car.

"...workmen moved in early this morning to pull down the structure, which was fenced in more than a year ago when a new perimeter fence was built. It had been blessed by the Bishop of Huntingdon. Christian CND member, Jennifer Hartley, from Ipswich, says she's mystified why the Ministry's chosen this moment to tear it down. Mrs. Hartley, who lived in a caravan on the site for ten months with her husband Ian, is going to Molesworth today."

It felt strange hearing myself; my voice was high and I spoke rapidly, hardly pausing: *"I want to go and try not to be too sad. I want to go there and I want to witness in the way that we were doing while we were living there. I want to show that, although the actual building is gone, that what the building stood for and the spirit that was in it and around it, is what matters. And that's what we are going to continue to do, we are not going to be downhearted... That little building, although not completed, gave people some hope. I mean, on a nuclear base, to have somewhere you can pray seems to me quite a sensible thing in a Christian country. I think there should be a peace chapel at every base. Because whether you believe that nuclear weapons are keeping the peace or whether you don't, you can all pray for peace in a chapel..."*

We drew up at Peace Corner and jumped out. Tim Eiloart from St. Ives had been staying in the caravan and he greeted us. In the early hours of the morning, he had heard some noise but had not realised what was happening. By the time he looked outside, the demolition operation was almost complete. At the School House the phone kept ringing. Despite the fact that there was no national media publicity, the news had begun to filter through. I felt for Bridie and Tim. They, and others, had worked so hard to build the chapel and everything it stood for. I rang the base to ask to see the Wing Commander, Doug Shaw. I was told he would come to the caravan to see us. At four o'clock the vigil went ahead as usual, though we could no longer ask at the gate for permission to hold it inside Eirene. That evening, Bridie and Tim had arranged to be out, so we spent the evening answering the telephone and watching all the news bulletins. It wasn't mentioned. Annette, Bridie's mother, arrived back from London and told us about the protest held outside the Ministry of Defence. Several arrests had been made.

We slept fitfully on the floor in the schoolroom, waking early. The radio was on in the kitchen and Annette and Oscar were making tea. We were talking when Annette spoke.

"I wasn't really listening, but I think they've just said the Americans have bombed Libya."

We all fell silent, the radio was turned up.

'F1-11s left bases in Lakenheath in Suffolk and Upper Heyford in Oxfordshire, last night, to take part in bombing raids on Libya… there have been many civilian casualties.'

At eleven that morning we were once more at Peace Corner. Ian and I walked over to the welded-mesh fence. The sunlight reflected on the galvanised wire, making it difficult to see what lay beyond. It was a sea of churned-up mud. Here and there, a small piece of concrete rubble poked through the dark brown earth. I tried to recall where the chapel had stood. All the landmarks had been obliterated. Further off, two trees had been left standing. One was a conifer, the other a young sapling. For some reason I felt strong. I thought, 'this isn't going to beat us, you can destroy bricks and mortar, but you can't kill the spirit of Eirene.'

We began to sing…

Postscript

John Major went on to become Foreign Secretary and subsequently Prime Minister. The United States and Soviet Union agreed to remove and dismantle a range of nuclear weapons including cruise missiles. The Berlin Wall was torn down, Germany reunified and the Soviet Union fell apart signalling the end of the Cold War. But we still live with the threat of nuclear catastrophe.